PRAISE FOR *MUPPETS IN MOSCOW*

"In a sparkling memoir of the era and the enterprise, Natasha Lance Rogoff recreates the frantic and vertiginous efforts to launch *Ulitsa Sezam* against what turned out to be tremendous headwinds." — **Wall Street Journal**

"There has been no shortage of journalistic books, memoirs and political analyses written by Russians and foreigners on the country. Yet none is quite like this one." — **Financial Times**

"[H]ighly entertaining." — **Guardian**

"Natasha Lance Rogoff writes with infectiou **Supplement**

"In this thrilling debut, television producer and filmmaker Rogoff recounts her mission to bring *Sesame Street* to Russian audiences. The resulting tale is one of perseverance and creativity that illuminates how even the most disparate cultures and perspectives can find common ground." — **Publishers Weekly, Starred Review**

"The inspiring story of bringing *Sesame Street* to Russia . . . provides lessons for businesses on how to overcome cultural clashes." — **Forbes**

"Translating this [*Sesame Street*] to Russia proved tricky. . . . The difficulties make for a story that draws you in. Rogoff looks back on her time in Moscow and reflects 'how precious, anarchic and fleeting Russia's brief liberalization was.'" — **Daily Mail**

"In this hilarious, eye-opening memoir, an American TV producer recounts her adventures in bringing Bert, Ernie, Oscar, and friends, to post-Soviet Russian television in the mid-'90s." — **Philadelphia Inquirer**

"[S]killfully written and a joy to read. The tale of this collaboration between U.S. and Russian artists working toward a shared educational goal creates a very unique story that is important and timely. For all readers interested in understanding international media and film production and its role in U.S. diplomacy." — **Library Journal, Starred Review**

"A fascinating, and sometimes horrifying, look into the clash of cultures and political instability [Lance Rogoff] has to deal with as executive producer of *Ulitsa Sezam*, the Russian version of the beloved American show." — ***Daily Beast***

"Oligarchy ends up being no match for Oscar the Grouch and Rogoff's plucky team in this retelling of a unique point in U.S.-Russian relations." — ***Booklist***

"Above all, it is a story of great poignance and a love letter to the ideal of educating children through television." — ***New York Post***

"[T]he cheery ethos and bold aesthetic of *Sesame Street* ran headlong into Russia's rich, but markedly different, cultural traditions. It's a tumultuous tale lovingly chronicled in *Muppets in Moscow*." — ***Smithsonian Magazine***

"[A] gripping and intimate account . . . gives readers an unprecedented behind-the-scenes look at the core values and beliefs that shaped Russia in the 1990s and continue to play out today in the horrific struggle between Putin's Russia and the West." — **Bill Browder, bestselling author of *Red Notice* and *Freezing Order***

"Fascinating and timely and enthralling read. Loved every minute of it, and I'll never look at *Sesame Street* the same way again!" — **Ben Mezrich, *New York Times* bestselling author of *The Accidental Billionaires*, adapted into the 2009 hit film *The Social Network***

"It's a remarkable story." — **Lewis Black, comedian**

"The story of a woman with an unshakable vision along with a multinational team of people willing to give it a try. Colorful, heartfelt, self-revealing, and inspiring." — **Virginia Madsen, Academy Award-nominated actress and film producer**

"A gem of a book! A must read for anyone looking to understand Russia better!" — **Clarissa Ward, CNN Chief International Correspondent and author of *On All Fronts***

MUPPETS
IN MOSCOW

THE UNEXPECTED CRAZY TRUE STORY
OF MAKING *SESAME STREET* IN RUSSIA

NATASHA LANCE ROGOFF

ROWMAN & LITTLEFIELD
Lanham • Boulder • New York • London

Published by Rowman & Littlefield
An imprint of The Rowman & Littlefield Publishing Group, Inc.
4501 Forbes Boulevard, Suite 200, Lanham, Maryland 20706
www.rowman.com

86-90 Paul Street, London EC2A 4NE, United Kingdom

British Library Cataloguing in Publication Information Available

Library of Congress Cataloging-in-Publication Data

Names: Lance, Natasha, author.
Title: Muppets in Moscow : the unexpected crazy true story of making Sesame Street
    in Russia / Natasha Lance Rogoff.
Description: Lanham, MD : Rowman & Littlefield, [2022] | Summary: "Muppets In Moscow
    reveals how in between bombings and political chaos in 1990s Moscow a team of
    Russian and American artists, producers, educators, writers, and puppeteers overcame
    their many differences to create an unprecedented hit in a postcommunist era"—Provided
    by publisher.
Identifiers: LCCN 2022008611 (print) | LCCN 2022008612 (ebook) | ISBN 9781538161289
    (cloth) | ISBN 9781538187531 (paper) | ISBN 9781538161296 (epub)
Subjects: LCSH: Lance, Natasha. | 880-01 Ulitsa Sezam (Television program) | Sesame Street
    (Television program) | Children's television programs—Production and direction—Russia
    (Federation) | Television and politics—Russia (Federation) | Television producers and
    directors—United States—Biography.
Classification: LCC PN1992.77.U354 L36 2022 (print) | LCC PN1992.77.U354 (ebook) |
    DDC 791.45/75—dc23/eng/20220805
LC record available at https://lccn.loc.gov/2022008611
LC ebook record available at https://lccn.loc.gov/2022008612

For my mother, Charlotte Rosnick Lance

CONTENTS

PART III: BIRTHING THE BABIES

FOREWORD

As a young child raised in the 1960s, I was trained, like everyone else, to hide under desks and find neighborhood fallout shelters in case of nuclear attack. Fear of the Soviet enemy near and far dominated the evening news. Popular culture was filled with dark humor of destruction occasionally interrupted by coverage of global arms summits, which led to momentary glimpses of hope for a peaceful future.

We were taught about the "Evil Empire's" forced doctrine, which placed the collective above the individual. Freedom of expression was sacrificed. Creativity was stifled. Critical thinking was discouraged for generations of young children. Yet, we also knew of Russia's incredible historic contributions to Western Civilization in art, music, theater, filmmaking, and animation. Great writers like Tolstoy, Dostoevsky, and Chekhov spirited through our culture in profound ways.

Then, on December 25, 1991, the hammer and sickle of the Soviet flag was lowered for the final time and replaced by the three bar version of the Russian Federation we see today. It was in this context that a few of us at the Children's Television Workshop (the nonprofit company producing *Sesame Street*) saw an opportunity. *Sesame Street* was birthed out of the War on Poverty, the Great Society, and the Civil Rights movement, with an ingenious, original approach to teaching led by Joan Ganz Cooney and inspired by Jim Henson and his Muppets. Using the powerful and effective techniques of advertising for education, instead of selling sugar-sweetened cereal or soft drinks to kids, *Sesame Street* would "sell" letters and numbers and social and emotional lessons around cooperation, respect, and tolerance. *Sesame Street* took America by storm. And soon after, the Germans, the Mexicans, and the Spaniards wanted a *Sesame Street* of their own making. The idea was to take the best of American ingenuity, meshing education and media, to create indigenous versions of *Sesame Street*, which would capture local language, customs, humor, and music to engage young children and their families locally.

The collapse of the USSR set in motion a "gold rush" of sorts to the former Soviet Union, to cash in on privatization schemes and build new enterprises. However, we at Children's Television Workshop felt that there weren't a whole lot of people from the West necessarily looking out for Russia's children and families in respectful ways through partnership and positive, holistic objectives. And we wanted to change that through a Russian-language, multicultural adaptation of *Sesame Street* that would be broadcast not only in Russia, but in Ukraine, Georgia, and throughout the former Soviet empire.

Perhaps we were visionary. Perhaps naive. Or both. But we found incredible people across this once unimaginable divide to collaborate with, to unleash the impressive creative energy individual writers and artists held, and to build something quite substantial from an understandingly skeptical, challenging cadre of people on both sides of the Atlantic.

What you will see in Natasha Lance Rogoff's passionate yet steady telling of the tale some three decades later is a quite wonderful story of how wholesome aspirations ran into "realpolitik" obstacles. During multiple trips to Moscow with our *Sesame Street* colleagues, I witnessed Natasha's cultural fluency, experience, and her unrelenting focus that turned out to be the secret sauce for our success. Against overwhelming risks and challenges, in the end, the team of Americans and Russians persevered in overcoming substantial odds in creating something lasting for millions of children in Russia, Ukraine, and across the former Soviet Union. More importantly, I hope the reader will be inspired by how this team bonded together in a fragile environment to help build a foundation for a safer world with respect for human dignity. We could certainly use another infusion of similar inspiration today.

Gary E. Knell
former president and CEO of
Children's Television Workshop

AUTHOR'S NOTE

Muppets in Moscow relies on hundreds of pages of documentation, including reports detailing the *Sesame Street* production process, emails, correspondence, and meeting notes. I also kept a journal throughout the four years making Russian *Sesame Street* where I recorded events and conversations as they happened. In preparation to write this book, I also poured through video and audio tapes recorded in Moscow in the 1990s, carefully logging the footage and translating the interviews from Russian. One generous former *Sesame Street* colleague gave me access to his own journal written during the production. I also relied on a substantial archive of *Ulitsa Sezam* photographs, and I had a very rough draft of this book that I had penned in 1998. For more than thirty years, I saved these materials, moving dozens of boxes of files and video tapes from one house to another.

Then, from 2019–2011, I conducted interviews with more than fifty of my former American and Russian colleagues. All these documents, transcripts, photographs, and correspondence enabled me to reconstruct the events that became the basis for this book. That said, *Muppets in Moscow* is a memoir rather than an official account of either Sesame Workshop or the Henson Company.

Regarding literary nomenclature, where Russian language appears I have used the international system for transliteration of text from Cyrillic to the Latin alphabet. In the interest of brevity and convenience of English-language readers, I have chosen not to include Russian Cyrillic equivalents for most transliterated Russian dialogue. Additionally, I describe Russian locations according to the terminology used at the time of the story; for example, I refer to St. Petersburg as Leningrad. Where necessary, I have changed names of individuals in the book altogether to protect their identities. I refer to the company that produces *Sesame Street* today as "Sesame Workshop." Until 2000, it was called the "Children's Television Workshop." Last, but very important, when I write about my *Russian* colleagues in the 1990s, I do so to differentiate them from my *American* colleagues. However, our *Ulitsa Sezam* team in Moscow was multiethnic, including Armenian, Ukrainian, Georgian, Moldovan, Kazakh, and Uzbek artists and media professionals.

ACKNOWLEDGMENTS

Writing a book is harder than I had thought and more rewarding than I could ever have imagined. *Muppets in Moscow* gave me the opportunity to reconnect with many of my former colleagues living in Russia, Ukraine, and other parts of the former USSR. When Russia invaded Ukraine in February of 2022, nearly all of my teammates spoke out against Putin's horrific war and many living in Russia had to flee their country to avoid going to prison for expressing their views. And conversations with my Ukrainian former colleagues left me speechless and heartbroken. I am incredibly indebted to the many individuals who permitted me to tell their stories. I appreciate their magnanimity and trust in allowing me to interview them, despite the pain discussing the past and the present. Their stories encapsulate a collective passion, artistic genius, and tireless efforts over many decades to nurture a freer, more open Russia for tens of millions of children. Thank you for speaking with me: Volodya Grammatikov, Tamara Pavliuchenko, Irina Borisova, Dr. Anna Genina, Katya Komalkova, Sergei Novikov, Vika Lukina, Nana Grinstein, Masha Rybasova, Sasha Sklyar, Seryozha Zineevich, Katya Fedorovna, Elena Lenskaya, and Uliana Savilieva, and others. The Russian production and research teams included more than four hundred souls (too many to name all here). Without their remarkable dedication, faith, and efforts, there would be no story.

I am also so grateful to my former American *Sesame Street* colleagues who generously agreed to be interviewed for this book: Baxter Urist, Gary Knell, Dr. Charlotte Cole, Luis Santiero, Dr. Valeria Lovelace, Dan Victor, Steve Miller, Anna Connolly, Cooper Wright, Jeanne Taylor Hard, Mark McNease, Gregg Gettas, Brett Pierce, Ginger Knickman, Bunny Lester, David Britt, Emily Swenson, Chris Cerf, and especially the brilliant Robin Hessman, who contributed so much to the creative production of *Ulitsa Sezam* and generously opened her beautiful steel-trap mind, selflessly sharing her memories of our time in Moscow.

Thanks also to the puppetry wizards hailing from Henson Studios: Ed Christie, Marty Robinson, Kevin Clash, and Nigel Plaskett for agreeing to be interviewed and endlessly entertaining me with their incredible memories of collaborating with the Moscow team.

Ulitsa Sezam was built on the shoulders of the brilliant creators of *Sesame Street*. I felt lucky to walk in their footsteps and grateful to Sesame Workshop, the Henson Company, and all my coworkers who were instrumental in making the Russian series a success, especially the late Lisa Simon, Jon Stone, and my very dear friend Arlene Sherman.

Thanks also to the dedicated team at Rowman & Littlefield and especially, my talented editor, Christen Karniski, for her penetrating insights and guidance at every twist.

I am also immensely indebted to the brilliant individuals who provided editorial guidance helping to bring this memoir to life: Dana Isaacson, who masterfully reduced the length of my manuscript, bringing the most poignant stories more sharply in focus; Julianna Haubner, for her early suggestion to add more dialogue drawing on the extraordinary video and archival materials I had saved for more almost three decades; and Paris Spies-Gans, for her penetrating intelligence and attention to detail. Their efforts made this book eminently more readable than it would otherwise be. This book would not have come to fruition without the benevolence and thoughtful input of Marti Leimbach, a close friend and great fiction writer who literally held my hand, gently guiding me through the writing process, and also edited the final manuscript.

I am truly grateful to Gail Ross, my phenomenal literary agent, for taking a chance on me and for her wise counsel at every turn, and my smart and savvy CAA Film/TV agents: Dana Spector, Michelle Weiner, and Arielle Lever, as well as Bob Bookman, my film/TV manager who is one of the smartest most loveable men I know. Thanks also to my sparkling staff, Maislinn Helfer, Paul Coleman, and Olivia Dalfino for their tremendous creativity and organization. Without your help, I'd be drowning. Thank you also Geordie Sinclair Kenyon for help with Russian translation and Stephan Gerald Kuehler at the Harvard University Libraries for additional research. I'm also indebted to several academics for their detailed analysis of historical events in 1990s Russia, which provided essential context for understanding larger political and historical events that impacted the production of *Sesame Street*: Arkady Ostrovsky, Masha Gessen, David Hoffman, Ben Mezrich, David Remnick, Karen Dawisha, Ben Judah, Angela Stent, Owen Matthews, Anne Applebaum, Fiona Hill, Catherine Belton, and Peter Pomerantsev. Thanks also to early champions of this story: Tina Bennet, Jonathan Karp, Svetlana Katz, and Amy Lamott.

I am lucky the gifted Emily Lahey-Shoov agreed to narrate the *Muppets in Moscow* audiobook. Aided by the masterful audio engineers Jordan Rich and Ken Carberry at Chart Productions, her inspired pitch-perfect performances of the real-life Russian-accented voices make the *Muppets in Moscow* audiobook a joy to listen to.

Thanks also to Max Evry, a true friend, for his genius book cover design, and Ian Fried, a talented graphic artist who produced the final cover.

To Leonid Zagalsky, my dearest friend of more than thirty years, I am enormously indebted for his unflagging support and honesty. As my closest confidant during the filming of *Ulitsa Sezam*, I often consulted him while writing this book. I am eternally grateful for his advice, generosity, and, most importantly, great sense of humor. You can't survive in Russia without humor.

At every step of this literary journey, I was guided and encouraged by my wonderful siblings—Andy, Emily, Stephan, and Kate—and their spouses, and also many friends who patiently put up with my monomaniacal conversations about this story for two years: Beth Mendelson, Elodie Goirand, Andreas Xenophontos, Lisa Randall, Sabine Howard, Suzanne Priebatsch, Julie Wolf, Judy Warner, Max Burley, Anne McElvoy, Martin Ivens, Jim Kryzanski, Katherine Craven Kryzanski, Amy Spies, Gary Gans, Ned Temko, Annie Corbett, Sasha Borofsky, Louiza Mosendz, David Blaine, Holly Davis, David O. Russell, Nadia Zamoul, Lori Gottileb, Jean Korlitz, Cornelius Fischer, Maya Popa, Ornela March, Jessica Prato, Anna Tse, Josh Horowitz, Barbara Guggenheim, and the late Joe DeCola and Bert Fields. I also thank Pulitzer-prize winning journalist, Hedrick Smith for teaching me early on how to ask the hard questions with compassion.

My family has been my greatest source of strength throughout this long project. My children, Gabriel and Juliana, pushed me to believe that my story was "actually cool" and to this day freak out their friends with tales of their crazy mother. Their delight in my story gave me the encouragement I needed. A special thanks to my daughter for all her brilliant advice and tireless efforts at numerous stages. And finally, I am deeply grateful to my lifelong partner Ken, who has read more versions of this book than I've put pen to paper and always has been there for me; I am grateful for his love and unwavering support.

INTRODUCTION

In 1993, Sesame Workshop, the company that produces *Sesame Street*, hired me as the lead producer to adapt America's most iconic children's television show in Russia. For the next four years, I had the privilege of collaborating with a diverse team of hundreds of talented Moscow and New York artists, writers, actors, producers, and educators to bring *Ulitsa Sezam—Sesame Street* in Russian—to millions of children throughout the former USSR.

The Soviet regime dissolved on December 26, 1991, and Western leaders, euphoric over the defeat of communism, committed billions in American foreign aid to help Russia transition to a Western-style democracy. Then-Senator Joe Biden spearheaded congressional support for a Russian version of *Sesame Street*. The legislators and Sesame Workshop envisioned the Muppets as ideal ambassadors to model Western values and the benefits of an open society to children in the former Soviet Union. The new television series would be an original adaptation that would include the creation of three new Muppets and a Russian-style neighborhood, all reflecting Russian and post-Soviet values, aesthetics and culture.

But what Senator Biden and executives from Sesame Workshop's nonprofit company all misjudged was just how much resistance this children's puppet show would trigger in the post-communist nation. I too grossly underestimated the challenges the Muppets would face, despite having spent a good chunk of my still-young career in the former USSR. I quickly discovered that translating *Sesame Street's* ebullient and idealistic outlook to Mother Russia was not only incredibly difficult, but also incredibly dangerous.

As the executive producer of *Ulitsa Sezam* from 1993–1996, I was thrown into the surreal landscape of Moscow television at a time of intense political upheaval. Bombings, murders, and political unrest were near-daily events. During our production, several heads of Russian television—our close collaborators and prospective broadcast partners—were assassinated one after another, and one was nearly killed in a car bombing. The day Russian soldiers bearing AK-47s pushed into our production office and confiscated show scripts, set drawings, and equipment—and even our adored life-size mascot Elmo—most of my American friends said I should get out of Moscow while I still could.

But what made me stay, even in the face of physical violence jeopardizing our production, were the provocative and fascinating cultural battles that touched nearly every aspect of the show's development—from the scriptwriting to the set design, to the music and even the design of the Muppets themselves. I discovered that the adaptation of America's favorite children's show often pitted *Sesame Street*'s progressive values against three hundred years of Russian thought. And these clashes of divergent views about individualism, capitalism, race, education and equality resonate with the cultural discord and conflict that continues to dominate Russia's relations with the West today.

Considering that I had spent a decade working in the former Soviet Union before *Sesame Street* approached me, I ought to have been more prepared for the resistance we faced.

As a teenager, I'd fallen in love with Russian literature, even changing my legal name from Susan to Natasha. In college, I studied Russian and, at age twenty-two, moved to Leningrad as an exchange student. After six months, I became fluent in Russian and developed deep friendships with many artists and dissidents. I began publishing articles about underground Soviet culture and rock n' roll in major international magazines and newspapers, including an article titled, "Gay Life in the Soviet Union," which was one of the earliest exposés of persecution of the LGBT community in Soviet Russia, published in 1983 in the *San Francisco Chronicle*. That same year, I married my gay friend to help him escape the oppressive regime.

Later, with aspirations of becoming a diplomat, I studied Soviet foreign policy at Columbia University's School of International and Public Affairs in the mid-1980s. During the summers, I worked in Moscow as a freelance television journalist for CBS and NBC News. But my days battling for social justice caught up with me. In my second year of study, after being selected for a fellowship at the U.S. State Department that required a high-level national security clearance, I had to undergo an interview at FBI headquarters in Washington, DC. During the interview, I stepped out of the conference room to use the restroom and as I returned, hovering outside the door, I overheard the FBI agent conducting the interview say to his colleague, in a strong Southern drawl: "There's no way this gal's gonna work for the guver'ment of the U-nited States of America. She combined two things that are a no-no: Commies and queers."

My clearance was denied.

Unable to work for the U.S. government, I returned to Moscow, fortunate to find employment producing the four-hour PBS television series *Inside Gorbachev's USSR*, which received a Dupont-Columbia Journalism Award. I went on to direct and produce other documentaries, including a feature-length documentary, *Russia for Sale: The Rough Road to Capitalism*, which was broadcast to wide acclaim on PBS television in 1993 and excerpted on ABC's *Nightline with Ted Koppel*, along with my on-air commentary.

My background in film and television in Russia led Sesame Workshop to recruit me for *Ulitsa Sezam*, and I am so grateful they did. Through the Muppets, our small team of American children's TV professionals gained unprecedented access to the inner sanctum of Russian television, the epicenter of Russian state propaganda and control, then and now. And, my American *Sesame Street* colleagues and I also gained a deeper understanding of Russians perspectives about themselves, the West, and their hopes for their children and country.

And yet, few of us understood back then how much relations between Russia and the West would deteriorate after the millennium, culminating in Russia's invasion of Crimea and later Ukraine. In hindsight, we recognize we had seen firsthand the volatile shifting tides that eventually settled into Putin's repressive regime today. I took particular notice when American movies and TV shows began depicting Russians characters nearly universally as thugs, criminals, prostitutes, and corrupt oligarchs in the mid-2000s. I became increasingly uncomfortable with this caricature of all Russians, as it did not ring true to the many passionate and brilliant Russians and ordinary people I had worked with in Moscow and who had spent their lives fighting for freedom in their country.

The incredible risks my Russian creative team took and the sacrifices they were willing to make demonstrate their remarkable commitment to giving the next generation of children hope of a brighter, more open and more peaceful future.

It is my hope that sharing this story now will show that, despite the many differences between our cultures, we still have much in common.

The generations of children who grew up on Russian *Sesame Street* are now in their 30s and 40s. Many who are living in Ukraine today, are fighting for their freedom. And in Russia, the more than a million Russians who have walked out of their country because they do not support Putin's horrific war, and those who are forced into silent opposition of Putin's regime for fear of going to prison, are also part of the *Ulitsa Sezam* generation. And this is the legacy of the *Muppets in Moscow*.

PART
I

DEAD BODIES
AND DEALS

Russia has a long, rich, and revered puppet tradition dating to the sixteenth century, and we don't need your American Moppets in our children's show.

—Lida Shurova, head writer, *Ulitsa Sezam*

1

BACK IN ~~THE USSR~~ RUSSIA

Spring 1993

On the overnight flight from New York to Moscow, the atmosphere feels carnivalesque, with everyone wanting a piece of this new Russia, whether that involves money, sex, democracy, or the salvation of lost souls. And now I've joined this cabal plotting to alter Russia's future. But my alchemy is neither religion nor politics; it is a children's television show.

A passenger across the aisle from me shrieks, awakening others in the darkened cabin. Turning toward the clamor, I see a guy in his midtwenties, broad shoulders filling out a sweatshirt emblazoned with the words YALE BULLDOG, grinning to his seatmate while leaning into his glowing laptop and loudly making lewd comments. I crane my head to see they're scrolling through a photo gallery titled "Hot Russian Babes." Since the collapse of Soviet communism, Moscow has become a magnet for young men like these: cocky, new Ivy-League graduates; investors, bankers, and lawyers with dollar signs and lust in their eyes. They envision making millions overnight while bedding destitute Slavic beauties for whom the gift of a one-hundred-dollar necklace would be akin to three months' wages.

A stewardess stops at my seat, offering me a drink. I've never flown business class before, and I can't believe someone (actually, Big Bird) is paying for my seat. I take the glass of champagne and sip it. The passenger seated behind me waves away the champagne and asks for a glass of water, telling the flight attendant he's Mormon and on his way to Moscow to lead a mission. I look around and realize the plane is filled with religious representatives from many faiths—Mormons, Christians, and Orthodox rabbis—all hoping to evangelize religion and supplant atheism in postcommunist Russia, I expect.

My seatmate, now fully awake, rubs his eyes and apologizes for snoring, then reaches his hand across the armrest and introduces himself. He tells me he's an economist. "This is my sixth trip to Moscow in two months," he says, as if to explain his exhaustion.

When asked what he's doing in Moscow, he turns toward the window, staring at the clouds. "I'm part of a team of academics helping the Russians jump-start capitalism." He speaks slowly to me about Russia's new free market, as though to a small child. I'm not offended. I never bothered to study economics seriously. He continues, "We're trying to give Russians the tools they need to make a transition to private ownership." His voice trails off at the end, as though he doesn't really believe it's possible.

He continues staring out the window, seeming deep in thought, until he turns back toward me and says with some intensity, "We have to dismantle their command economy so something new can take its place. If we fail, Russia will sink back into communism, or worse."

I guess I'm supposed to think he's one of the good guys. I'm not sure he is, but I nod along, thinking he sounds rather Nostradamus-like, but for all I know his prophesy of doom could be right. I haven't set foot in Russia in two years and could only guess how it's changed.

As if realizing he's forgotten his social graces, he smiles and awkwardly plucks out the words, "So what are you doing in Moscow?"

I tell him I'm bringing *Sesame Street* to Russia. It feels surprisingly good to say this aloud. It makes it feel real and almost convinces me that it might *actually* be possible.

Chuckling in response, he says, "Oh, that's wild."

I suspect our goals are equally wild, but I don't say anything.

Three hours later, the plane touches down at Moscow's dilapidated Sheremetyevo 2 airport. As we bump along a pothole-scarred tarmac, the Beatles song "Back in the USSR" pops into my head and I silently mouth the lyrics. Through the drizzle I see the bold red lettering "MOSKVA" across the top of the familiar concrete terminal. It sends pangs of dread and exhilaration through my body.

———

I shuffle forward with the rest of the passengers exiting the plane onto a gangway that leads to a narrow corridor framed by bulletproof glass. Two stony-faced Russian border guards holding machine guns stand at each end of the corridor, staring straight ahead, serious and immobile.

Pushed by the swell of people, I'm funneled down a narrow staircase to the postage-stamp-sized area that is border control. More and more passengers arrive, and we squish together in the tight space. The odor of sweat commingles with cigarette smoke from Russian passengers lighting up after the flight, glad to be back in a country where smoking is not banned in public places. Not much has changed. Despite the country's tumultuous transition, the agents are still dressed in Soviet-era olive drab uniforms. I look up and notice the cylindrical copper ceiling lights built for the 1980 Olympics. They are still caked in dust. The only change, it seems, is that more of the bulbs have burned out.

The line inches forward to the rhythmic stamping of documents. After twenty minutes of waiting, tempers flare. When a nearly blind woman wearing thick Coke-bottle glasses pushes past other passengers, hitting a white cane against the legs of those blocking her path, several irritated people shake their heads. One Russian woman yells, "What do you think you're doing, woman?"

I'm taken aback. Who screams at an elderly disabled woman?

But a few minutes later, after passing through passport control and making my way to baggage claim, I see the woman again. She's jettisoned the cane and the glasses, and her eyesight is good enough to beeline it to the baggage conveyer belt and effortlessly lift her oversized suitcase. I chuckle. Clearly I've been away from Russia for too long—my bullshit detector needs tuning.

2

MY INTRODUCTION TO *SESAME STREET*

A Russian baggage handler, dressed in dark overalls, carelessly throws suit-cases on the rotating conveyor belt and I watch as if in a trance, thinking back to how this journey started. Six months earlier, I was in New York presenting my documentary film on Russia at a screening hosted by my alma mater, Columbia University. Three hundred people filled the auditorium, including two honored speakers: Carl Levin, Michigan's longest-serving and revered U.S. senator, and Pamela Harriman, the legendary grande dame of the Democratic Party who was doing everything in her power to put Bill Clinton in the White House. In a clipped British accent, Harriman introduced my film, extolling the Russian people:

> Many people think that the Russians are a passive people, just waiting with their hands out to receive aid and help from us, but that is not true. This film shows the determination of Russians to create a new, more open society.

After a panel discussion, I was approached by Gary Knell and Steve Miller, Sesame Workshop's senior vice president of corporate affairs, and the vice president of international television, respectively. They introduced themselves and asked if I could help them bring *Sesame Street* to Russia.

I froze. I couldn't imagine why these television executives would possibly think I could help them produce a children's comedy show, especially after just watching my film's grim account of Soviet Russia.

Bemused, I explained that I'd never worked in children's television and had even less experience with *actual* children.

Knell saw my confusion but was not easily put off. "Come on, just meet with us," he said with a twinkle in his eye. "No one can say no to Elmo, right?"

Although I felt I was an entirely wrong fit for a children's show, the offer intrigued me. I agreed to meet their team the following week at Sesame Street's headquarters (referred to by those in the know as "the workshop").

———————

"The workshop" is on West Sixty-Fourth and Broadway. When the elevator doors opened, I found myself in an alternate universe—walls painted in bold primary colors and giant framed photographs of Big Bird and Elmo staring back at me. Fresh-faced, earnest twenty-somethings sat at desks adorned with playful kiddie toys—plastic action heroes, rubber balls, and stuffed Muppets. The sight of these noble crusaders for children's enlightenment made me feel that I did not belong, as did the smartly dressed woman with perfectly coiffed hair who led me to a conference room. In my jeans, T-shirt, and hoodie, I hadn't dressed appropriately for the interview. I felt like an idiot.

But it was too late to do anything about that now; there was Knell striding into the conference room accompanied by a tall, slender man.

It was nice to see Knell again, and he introduced me to the vice president of international production, his colleague who'd be my boss if I were to take the job. Seated at a conference table, Knell explained that for some time he and his Big Bird colleagues had been trying to bring *Sesame Street* to Russia. In fact, the company president had appeared before the Senate Appropriations Subcommittee for Foreign Affairs chaired by Senator Biden in January 1992 and had testified that *Sesame Street* could help foster democratic values in Russia's postcommunist society.

I nodded along, but I still didn't get where I would fit in.

Apparently, my first role would be to find a Russian broadcast partner, someone who could coproduce an original Russian version of *Sesame Street*. Knell was complimentary and persuasive, explaining how my substantive Moscow TV connections were exactly what was needed.

I asked if they intended to dub the American show or create an original production, which would be very expensive.

Knell replied, "We're envisioning half of the Russian series would be original production filmed in Moscow and the rest would be dubbed from *Sesame Street*'s international library."

I doubted the country's new government would spend money on Muppets when they had so many other, more pressing problems. I then asked if they expected Russian State Television to pay for the production.

Knell picked up a transcript from the congressional hearing and began reading the moving testimony of Elena Lenskaya, the Russian deputy minister of education:

Our system needs new openness and integration into the global world outside. Our kids have been isolated from their peers in the world for a very long time. But in order to communicate, kids have to share something. . . . Let them share not *The Terminator* and not *Rambo*, which is now the case [on Russian television], but *Sesame Street*.

I was impressed. "That's amazing to have such an endorsement," I said.

Knell shot me a playful smile. "That's why we need you—why Russia needs you."

Suppressing a grin, I hedged, suggesting that plenty of people with experience in children's television were better suited to help *Sesame Street*. I also emphasized that I had only ever filmed with a small documentary crew and relying on others has never been my strong suit.

But Knell continued the flattery, so much so that I almost wanted to take the job on the spot just so he'd stop embarrassing me.

But then the head of international production, who had not yet uttered a word, contorted his face into a pained expression and finally spoke. He said he'd been on a trip to Russia a year before, when his Russian hosts had put him up in a disgusting hotel with a broken window and no food. Stretching his neck from side to side and grimacing, he offered, "None of the Russians I spoke with seemed to care about *Sesame Street*; all they wanted was foreign currency."

A flash of irritation crossed Knell's face as my "future boss" continued.

"I'm not convinced it's the right time to do a full-scale coproduction in Russia," he said. He then argued in favor of another approach—easing instead into Russia by doing *Open Sesame*, an international version of *Sesame Street* that requires a much smaller amount of original production.

Clearly there was some tension between the two men.

I changed the subject, asking what the expected budget would be.

Knell explained that the United States Agency for International Development (USAID), the American government's arm for foreign assistance, was on the verge of providing significant funding to Sesame Workshop to support *Sesame Street* in Russia. He disclosed that more would come later from Russian state television or private Russian investors, bringing the total production budget for *Ulitsa Sezam* to between six and ten million U.S. dollars (between

$15 and $20 million today). And this didn't even include in-kind contributions that Russian television would make, such as the studio and equipment.

I nearly fell off my chair. The entire budget for my PBS television special on Russia didn't even come close to a million. Moreover, American dollars could buy ten times the talent and staffing in Moscow than it could in the West.

At the end of our meeting, Knell reassured me that I was "the perfect person to help," and that "now *is* the right time."

———————

Over the next few days, I scoured the bookshelves at my local library, devouring everything I could find about Joan Ganz Cooney, the founder of *Sesame Street*, and Jim Henson, the legendary creator of the Muppets. I knew the *Sesame Street* Muppets generally, in the way that everyone knew of them. But I hadn't watched the popular program as a child and certainly not as an adult. Now, I binge-watched every VHS cassette I could lay my hands on, learning as much as I could about the format, messaging, songs, tone, and every Muppet on the show.

For the rest of the week, I debated the offer. The production of a television series with fifty-two half-hour episodes would be difficult anywhere, but in Moscow, especially so. Almost as soon as the Soviet Union disbanded, the country had plunged into chaos as factions battled for power. Russia seemed to be in political limbo, teetering between its communist past and an unknown future. Such an unstable environment did not seem like fertile ground for the Muppets—or a major career move.

I also had some concerns about the potential appeal of *Sesame Street* to children living in the former Soviet Union. Knowing the country as I did, I wondered if Russian children would find the Muppets' antics as amusing as kids who'd grown up in the free world. Could Elmo's and Cookie Monster's wacky, lighthearted banter even be translated for Dostoevskian, angst-ridden Russians?

Yet the prospect of the *Sesame Street* Muppets modeling important liberal values like tolerance, compassion, and cooperation stirred something within me. For nearly a century, people in the West had dreamed of Russia joining the global community of nations, sharing democratic values and objectives. Now such an awakening seemed within grasp. There was an urgency in the air, and the idea that I could be part of this momentous transformation was both seductive and intoxicating. And if the show were to become successful, having worked for a big company like Sesame Workshop might even fast-track my television career.

Money was another objective. Making a documentary had wiped out my savings, and I could barely afford rent for my tiny West Village basement studio. I'd continued to live like a student well past college, but I was thirty-two now and needed a steady job.

With only a few hours left before I had to give Knell my decision, I called my younger sister Emily, a radiologist living in North Carolina with her two kids and her husband, a vascular surgeon. Among the five siblings, Emily is the sensible middle child who can be counted upon to provide smart but conventional advice.

When I shared news of the job offer with Emily, she laughed. "You do realize this is a show for children—about which *you* know nothing?" She then continued in the same vein, arguing that working in Russia was a bad idea. "These are your prime childbearing years. Have you considered, if you take this job, you might never have kids? Or maybe you're planning to fall in love with a Russian and have little Russki babies?" she joked. I was used to my bohemian life being the butt of family humor. Truthfully, ever since my ex-fiancé had dumped me three years earlier, I hadn't given much thought to having kids. Still, her teasing stung.

I wanted to tell her that I *needed* to take this job. I wanted what Knell had said about me to be true. I wanted to believe that I was "perfect" for the Moscow production, and that—for once—my sister was wrong.

"I'm going to bring the Muppets to Moscow," I heard myself say, deciding all at once.

The next day, I called Knell and told him "Yes."

Suddenly, I feel a push as a heavyset man brushes against me and grabs his suitcase off the conveyor belt. I spot my beat-up black bag and lug it to the customs line. Getting through customs in Soviet Russia as a filmmaker was always scary. You never knew if your video tapes—years of work—would get seized, if you'd get arrested, or worse. At least this time, I'm not bringing anything incriminating with me . . . unless videos of Elmo dancing the "Jive Five" is considered contraband by this new regime.

3

RUSSIAN MEDIA ISN'T THE SAFEST PLACE RIGHT NOW

The first rule of doing business in Russia is identifying a local you can trust; for me, that person is Leonid Zagalsky. He's promised to meet me at the airport after I clear customs.

We first met in 1988 when we were both hired by NBC News as freelance television producers during the Reagan-Gorbachev Moscow summit. After Leonid's first Jewish joke of many, we bonded, realizing we hail from the same tribe and share a similar dark sense of humor.

Leonid is an award-winning journalist who in the 1980s was recognized for an investigative story about Soviet political prisoners held in psychiatric hospitals, published in the prominent newspaper *Literaturnaya Gazeta*. In 1989, Stanford University selected him as a John S. Knight Journalism fellow and he received a one-year, all-expenses-paid opportunity to bring his wife and their seven-year-old son to spend a year in California at the university.

After one month in the land of the free, Leonid applied for permanent asylum for their family. But while he was waiting for approval, his wife decided that she wanted even more freedom, filing papers to divorce Leonid and remain in California with their child. Leonid was devastated. He moved across country to my tiny studio apartment, sleeping on the floor on an air mattress for three months. Eventually, after receiving an American green card, he crawled back to Moscow. Despite my best efforts to cheer him up, the divorce crushed him, especially because he was unsure how often he'd be able to see his son. Although we spoke on the phone every six months, the last time I'd seen Leonid was more than a year ago, when he stopped in New York on his way to visit his son. I'd call him more often, but it's too expensive.

Finally, the sliding glass doors separating customs from international arrivals open and I trudge through, lugging my suitcase. I spot Leonid in the crowd, a lit cigarette hanging from his mouth. I remember his last words to me before he left America: "Natasha, there's no light in your apartment. You live underground like a rat. You need to go above ground if you want to be happy."

I race toward him.

"Natulya, cookie, you are finally here!" he yells, using the affectionate diminutive of my name. (Leonid and I speak English together, unless we are with a Russian-speaking person, and then we usually switch to Russian.) When we embrace, neither wants to be the first to let go. When he does, he flicks away the cigarette he was still holding and grabs my shoulders, looking me up and down.

"You had sworn in blood that you would never return to Russia!" he teases. The word "blood" comes out like "blaaaaahd." We laugh. I'm surprised at how great it feels to be back.

Leonid takes my suitcase, and we make our way through the terminal to the exit where Leonid has illegally parked his car. He's left his keys with a young man who, for some reason, is dressed in a sailor's navy-blue pinafore and appears to be in charge of the numerous illegally parked vehicles. Leonid slips the parking seaman a wad of rubles, while waving away the dollars I offer.

"Your American money is good everywhere except here," he teases, breaking into a snorty, infectious laugh as we race through the rain to his car. Of course, that's not true; American currency is welcome everywhere in Russia.

Leonid's car is a beat-up 1985 *Lada*. I look for the seatbelt before remembering that Russian cars don't have seatbelts. As he shifts gears, revving the engine into drive, the smell of burning benzene (Russian gasoline) makes me slightly nauseated. Leonid's maneuvering—gunning over potholes and racing like he's competing in NASCAR—doesn't help. We speed along Leningradskoye Highway, past splashy billboards with half-naked women advertising security services, Western computers, and automobiles. Leonid gestures toward the signage.

"A lot's changed since your last visit," he sighs wistfully. "There's so much *mon-ey* here now. You could just scoop it up with a shovel."

It sounds like Leonid wishes some of these changes had landed more money in his own pockets. But with his American legal resident status and a modest savings account in U.S. dollars, he can't complain; he's better off than most Russians. And his sweet disposition makes him a good catch. He boasts, matter-of-factly, "I can date any Russian women I want." I'm happy for him. In New York City after his divorce, he tried dating, but the ins and outs of American courtship confused him and he rarely got a second date. No longer; Moscow is different.

"Tell me what's happening in Russia," I demand. Leonid senses my need to shift the conversation away from the topic of dating. He smiles at me sympathetically, knowing about my relationship misfortunes.

"Moscow is not like the place you left," he replies somberly. "I'm actually worried for you, because it's a lot more violent now." Leonid explains that it's unclear who is actually running the country. The Americans are helping the Russian government implement a hare-brained idea to convert state-owned enterprises into private ones and then distribute the country's wealth in the form of vouchers, giving each citizen a little piece of what's left of Russia. He rolls his eyes. "Most Russians have no idea of the value of these vouchers, and they're selling them for a loaf of bread or a bottle of vodka." He lifts both of his hands off the steering wheel, holding them upward in a V-shape as though making an offering, and, turning toward me, yells, "This is the biggest fire sale of the century! Everything's for sale: Soviet factories, oil refineries—even our beautiful forests."

Just as I'm telling him to "Focus on the road," the car screeches to a stop. Leonid stares ahead at the frozen traffic. "F-ing gridlock is everywhere," he says. Evidently, the number of cars on the road has doubled since the government lifted the ban on imports.

Moscow's roads radiate outward from the Kremlin in concentric circles with intersecting streets, like spokes on a wheel connecting the rings. The airport lies northwest, about a forty-minute drive from the city center where Sesame Workshop booked me a hotel room. As we approach downtown, I notice how dilapidated the buildings have become, ornate prerevolutionary mansions reduced to peeling paint and cracked facades mirroring the disintegration of the state.

"I want to show you something," Leonid announces, suddenly swerving off the main road and parking—again illegally—behind the Tretyakov Gallery.

I don't want to get out of the car; leaving my suitcase in the trunk makes me nervous.

"It's okay," he reassures. "We'll only stop for a minute."

We walk to an open area behind the museum, a graveyard for monuments commemorating fallen Soviet heroes. Various granite and marble statues lay on the ground in a row, like a calcified parade. Alongside Lenin, a bronze Stalin lays face down in the mud and his outstretched arm points to the ground.

Leonid laughs. "Stalin is showing the true path to communism."

Seeing these broken effigies to Soviet power lying in a mudhole makes me feel the full force of the end of an era. Even though I had wanted to see the

Soviet Union fall apart, I feel sad now that it has. Somehow I hadn't expected to feel its loss so deeply. We walk in silence back to the car.

As we drive toward the hotel, Leonid returns to the changes that have come to Moscow and explains that a few of his friends—"all Jews," he says—"have been profiting handsomely from the recent changes in the country."

I ask him if he thinks any of them might consider investing in Russian *Sesame Street*.

Leonid's optimism surprises me. "I think I know one or two who might." Glancing sideways, he laughs. "You don't waste any time. You're still a pathetic workaholic."

I share with him that Sesame Workshop has tasked me to find a Russian coproduction partner and broadcaster who can commit to a budget of several million to produce Russian *Sesame Street* and airtime.

"We can do that." Leonid's eyes gleam at the idea of our working together again.

I add that I'm supposed to arrange meetings for the two top executives from Sesame Workshop, who are arriving in Moscow in two days. They expect me to set up appointments for them with the heads of Russian television and key figures from American Fortune 500 companies who could possibly sponsor the TV series.

He's smiling. Like me, he loves a good challenge.

"So will you help," I ask, "and raise money for the series? Can I hire you?"

Leonid nods. He seems to like the idea.

"There's only one caveat," I tell him. "If you want to get paid, we have to convince some of your rich friends to finance the show."

"That sounds like the kind of deal a Russian would make!" That snorty laugh again.

God, I've missed him.

Leonid parks in front of the Palace Hotel, a steel and glass structure that is one of Moscow's first Western-style hotels. A security guard at the entrance asks for my passport. Leonid explains this is common practice now, to keep out riffraff and ensure guests' safety. Compared to the musty-smelling old Soviet hotels, the Palace looks like the Ritz with its shiny white marble floors, expensive chandeliers, and quite good reproductions of Gustav Klimt's paintings in heavy gold frames. The lobby is designed to resemble turn-of-the-century Vienna.

After I check in, the jet lag hits. But Leonid informs me that I cannot go to sleep yet. He's arranged for Vladislav Listyev (who goes by *Vlad*)—among the most respected television personalities in the country—to meet us at the hotel bar.

Vlad and Leonid graduated from Moscow's prestigious School of Journalism. At thirty-six, Vlad has already made a name for himself as a popular television host on *Ostankino*, Russia's largest TV network. He started out hosting *Vzglad* (Glance), an investigative news show that shook up the Soviet establishment. He proved himself a charismatic entertainer, hosting a hugely successful Russian *Wheel of Fortune* knockoff. He is now hosting *Chas Pik* (Rush Hour), a hard-hitting TV talk show similar to *Larry King Live*. Leonid relates that millions of viewers watch Vlad's programs. They have friends in common, which is why Vlad agreed to meet us.

Leonid suggests Vlad can connect us to key people in the industry who can help us produce our TV series. Even better, he says if we play our cards right, Vlad might introduce us to Boris Berezovsky, the powerful oligarch who is a part owner of Ostankino TV, the network that airs Vlad's talk show. Leonid says we have to be careful about *how* we ask to meet Berezovsky because Vlad and the oligarch have a complicated relationship.

As we wait in the bar for Vlad to arrive, we order cocktails from a waitress dressed in a ridiculously tight-fitting Viennese maid outfit with a lowcut white ruffled lace bustier and matching bonnet. Three businessmen talk loudly, trying to hear themselves over the Muzak being played on a loop on the white grand player piano in the adjacent restaurant. I recognize the prerecorded tune from the Cold War thriller *The Third Man*.

Vlad is late. One drink becomes several cocktails.

Forty minutes later, Vlad walks in, with mussed-up sand-colored hair and a bushy handlebar mustache. He wears a brown leather jacket and apologizes for being late. I instantly like him.

Our time is short, so Leonid snaps to focus, switching to Russian and explaining why we need his help.

Vlad's face lights up when we begin talking about *Sesame Street*. Surprisingly, he's familiar with the Muppets and agrees that Russian children today need to learn new values and skills.

"Our biggest challenge," he says, "is to teach our children how to express themselves freely and embrace self-initiative."

He concedes that *Sesame Street* could help.

Leonid and I are thrilled. And I am stunned at how fast everything is moving, having just arrived this morning. In Russian, I ask Vlad which station he thinks would be best to broadcast our show.

He replies, "Unlike in America where you have many independent TV networks and cable stations, we have only two that matter: Ostankino, which is partially owned by the state, and RTR, which is fully state-owned. There are a few new, smaller private TV channels, but their footprint is too small for airing *Sesame Street*."

Before the meeting, Leonid had warned me that in the TV world Vlad has both powerful friends *and* powerful enemies. On his TV show, he fearlessly invites controversy by challenging government officials and championing justice and transparency. So when I ask Vlad what challenges we can expect, I'm not surprised his face grows solemn.

"Russian media is not the safest place right now," Vlad says. "Foreign corporations are buying up commercial airtime without any regard to cost, to sell their Western products in the Russian market.

"It's one of the reasons my show is still on the air; Ostankino's making too much money off it to cancel it." He laughs, then becomes serious again.

"It's really a problem because the heads of TV departments can now sell their airtime for a lot of money, and they don't need to produce anything."

I mention that the chief director of Ostankino's Children's Studio had expressed to my *Sesame Street* colleagues his interest in partnering with us to produce Russian *Sesame Street*.

Vlad wrinkles his brow and mutters, "It's unlikely the Children's Studio has enough money to pay for a production like *Sesame Street*." He forces a smile. "You're talking to the wrong people."

Still struggling to understand what next steps we *should* take, I tell Vlad that I'd heard rumors from my friends who work at the TV station that Boris Berezovsky is the one calling all the shots at Ostankino. "Is this true?" I ask.

Leonid kicks my foot—a sign I'm overstepping boundaries of his relationship with his esteemed colleague.

Vlad then looks up and answers my question, "That's not exactly the case."

Leonid and I both know that Berezovsky could solve all our problems. He has so much power, he could offer *Sesame Street* a broadcast and advertising deal in a day.

Hesitantly I inquire, "Do you think we should talk to Berezvosky about broadcasting our show on Russian television?"

Leonid looks displeased. Vlad says nothing, staring at the bar top.

Steeling myself with a deep breath, I ask Vlad, "You must have dealings with Berezovsky, right?"

"Yes, of course," he answers.

Leonid is glaring at me, but I know this is our one shot to get to Berezovsky.

"Is there any chance, Vlad, that you could introduce us to Berezovsky?"

It's obvious Leonid doesn't feel comfortable asking for a favor, but as a foreign visitor I can.

Vlad's reply is quick. "I can try, but I don't know what the result will be."

Vlad seems impatient to leave, but I must ask one last question: does he think Berezovsky is more likely to be swayed to broadcast *Ulitsa Sezam* if the project is presented as a business opportunity or as a big philanthropic gesture?

Vlad raises his eyebrows, looking at me like I'm a babe in the Russian woods.

He reiterates that American conglomerates like Coca-Cola and Mars are paying millions to advertise fizzy sweet drinks, candy, and toothpaste to Russians. Berezovsky doesn't need *Sesame Street* to sell ads. Vlad reaches for his briefcase as if preparing to leave.

"The way things are right now, Natasha, nobody's going to let you put your American show on Russian television without—" He rubs his thumb and index finger together. "And getting involved in advertising right now in Moscow, as I said, is not as simple or as safe as it is in America." Slapping the bar twice, he smiles. "It's important that you understand that."

Leonid vigorously nods his head.

Vlad shifts his body off the barstool, pauses for a moment, and then looks me in the eye. "I don't mean to be discouraging. We have a big challenge: to teach our children about a normal society. I hope we succeed—that you succeed too. *Sesame Street* could be a tremendous contribution to our country. I only wish I could help more, but I will try to make that introduction."

After Vlad departs, I sip my drink still mulling over how much the TV industry has changed. "He's very brave," I say in a hushed tone.

Leonid pushes his glasses onto the bridge of his nose and nods. "Yes, he is."

I haven't even been in the country twenty-four hours, and I get the sense that getting past the gatekeepers might be more difficult than I'd thought.

Leonid and I stay at the bar past midnight—long enough for Leonid to chew me out and then forgive me. When I finally get up, I can barely move my legs. My dear friend wants to have another drink but I beg off, too tired to even mumble good night.

After a delicious sleep on the hotel's marshmallow-like luxury mattress (nothing like my lumpy futon at home), I'm completely refreshed. Room service knocks on the door and, miraculously, a waiter stands, holding a white plastic pitcher of coffee and carafe of warm milk on a tray. "Mor-ning koffee" he says in English, grinning awkwardly, as if his lips had only recently learned how to smile. In Soviet times I don't think I ever once saw a hotel employee look happy. To me, this is startling evidence of a nation shifting to a consumer-service-oriented culture. When I tip him with dollars because I don't yet have any rubles, I see a genuine grin.

I dress and hurry down to get breakfast before the restaurant closes. The buffet is an excess of delicacies: baskets of pastries, blini with caviar, and exotic fruits. Leonid lives in an apartment nearby. He bounds into the restaurant telling me, "I have gr-aate news for us!" He's arranged our next meeting with Igor Malashenko, a top television executive who is developing *NTV*, a new private, Western-style television network focusing on news and politics. Grinning, Leonid promises that we will learn a lot about what's going on in Russian television and about Berezovsky just from talking to Malashenko. He explains that until a few years ago, Malashenko was a Communist Party member and the deputy chair of Ostankino TV. "Now he's an entrepreneur," Leonid says.

Leonid heads to the buffet, returning with a plate piled with two servings of eggs Benedict, bacon, and sausage. Leonid loves all kinds of food, but especially food where someone else is picking up the tab—in this case, *Sesame Street*.

We spend the day working at a table by the window in the restaurant, developing a game plan for my *Sesame Street* colleagues who are on their way to Moscow. It's unsettling, debating how we can best finance and produce a television series in a country with no reliable banking system, no established rule of law, and an unstable currency. One of our biggest obstacles is that although the U.S. Congress has appropriated funds to pay for an adaptation of *Sesame Street*, USAID (the agency in charge of foreign aid) will only release the funds *after* a Russian partner and broadcaster have been identified. The U.S. government wants Russia to have skin in the game. Another problem is that we have limited time before the appropriation runs out. If we fail to find a partner, Sesame Workshop will not get a cent.

Leonid is confident. "We'll find *Sesame Street* a partner," he says. After the previous night's discouraging conversation with Vlad, his certainty surprises me. But maybe it shouldn't. Leonid has his own brand of positive thinking.

That night, we take Leonid's car to meet Malashenko at his friend's apartment on the outskirts of Moscow. It's already dark; the day flew by. Leonid circumvents Red Square by darting beneath the Kremlin's ancient brick ramparts. As we cross *Bolshoi Kamenniy Most* (Big Stone Bridge), we see the Kremlin Tower rise in the darkness, illuminated by floodlights. The shimmering red and green tower lights reflect onto the river's surface, dancing like liquid fireworks. I'd forgotten how romantic Moscow is at night.

We arrive at an apartment complex reserved for party members. Leonid parks his car at the entrance and punches in the code that Malashenko had given him. It takes several attempts because it's too dark to see the numbers on the pad. Once inside, we scrunch our bodies into a narrow open-shaft elevator—an iron lattice birdcage that slowly creaks and bumps up to the ninth floor.

Malashenko himself opens the apartment door, inviting us inside. He explains his friend had to go out. He's thin, prematurely graying, and speaks excellent English. He looks more like a college professor than a former Communist Party bureaucrat. About the same age as Leonid, he's impeccably dressed in a Western-made suit. He serves us tea, along with slices of cheese and black bread in a wicker basket.

Leonid soon gets to the subject at hand, telling Malashenko about *Ulitsa Sezam* and asking him about Berezovsky.

"No need to explain further," he interrupts, "because I *love* the dolls!"—referring to the American Muppets. Evidently, Malashenko had become enamored of *Sesame Street* while spending a chunk of his career in America as a Soviet political attaché. I am dumbfounded by the number of Russian TV executives who share a deep affection for *Sesame Street*. This makes me very happy.

Malashenko leans into the back of the couch as he talks about the Muppets. He seems keener to discuss Cookie Monster than Berezovsky. But we press him for more on the oligarch.

"Berezovsky is, as you know, very ambitious," he begins coolly. "In Soviet times, he made a decent living as a mathematician, but when the Russian market liberalized, he was one of the first to understand there was money to be made."

"He sells Ladas," Leonid interrupts, his mouth full of food. "I have one."

Malashenko half smiles. "Yes, he bought Russia's biggest automobile dealership and it's hugely successful."

As Malashenko sips his tea, he seems to be weighing his words. "Berezovsky's obsessed with television. He understands whoever controls Ostankino controls public opinion and therefore the country."

Impatient to keep the meeting focused on our goals, I interject, "Do you think there's any chance that Berezovsky would consider broadcasting *Ulitsa Sezam*?"

"There's a chance," he says. Then grinning, "But only because it's the Muppets." Malashenko is a busy man, and we soon sense it's time for us to take our leave. As he walks us to the door, he tells us, "You have to be careful doing broadcast deals nowadays because everything is changing constantly. Even signing a deal doesn't guarantee anything, and some of the people in Russian television are not particularly trustworthy."

As we rattle back downstairs in the elevator, I ask Leonid if he thinks Malashenko was hinting that Berezovsky is connected to the Russian Mafia.

He scoffs as if I should know better and says with a crooked smile, "Natasha, *all* Russian business is Mafia business. There's no other kind. Besides, only someone like Berezovsky, with his shady connections, could possibly bankroll a big production like ours."

Leonid drops me off at my hotel. I tumble into my bed and immediately fall asleep dreaming of Berezovsky the puppet master—pulling the strings of a bunch of weird-looking Russian Muppet-style marionettes.

4

THE OLIGARCHS AND THE MUPPETS

Moscow is sunny and warm—perfect for the arrival of Sesame Workshop's senior executives, Gary Knell and Baxter Urist, group president of products and international TV. I haven't spent much time with either of them and I'm worried they've come expecting more than I can deliver, including me arranging meetings with high-level Russian television executives. I've told them that I've been working with my friend Leonid, and I hope they'll agree to hire him as a full-time consultant, if they are satisfied with the progress we make by the week's end.

Leonid and I greet them in the Palace Hotel lobby as they're checking in. With blond hair, surfer-boy looks, and a perpetual grin, Baxter is not your typical buttoned-up corporate executive. He finds humor in everything. Even after a ten-hour flight, he appears to be in great spirits, describing how he'd met two American businessmen on his flight who were "stupid enough" to travel all the way to Moscow to sell swimming pool equipment. "What communists own private swimming pools?" he asks, cracking up.

Leonid laughs harder than the rest, and within minutes, he and Baxter are falling over each other adoringly. I'm relieved they seem to be hitting it off.

Even though it's getting late and the executives have dinner plans, Leonid proposes quickly going over the key players my superiors will be meeting during the next few days. We retire to the hotel restaurant, where Leonid takes out a piece of paper and begins sketching the byzantine relationships between the heads of Russian TV channels, government officials in charge of media, and Russia's new advertising moguls.

Knell leans forward, studying Leonid's drawing. With the arrows, lines, and intersecting circles, it looks like a diagram for a Rube Goldberg machine.

"Leonid, we are not trying to solve the Kennedy assassination; we're just making a children's show," he dryly quips. Knell shoots me a soft smile.

For the first time on this trip, I realize I'm having fun.

The week's agenda will entail our *Sesame Street* armada splitting into two groups. Baxter and Leonid will attend a whirlwind of meetings exploring potential sponsorship from corporations such as Proctor & Gamble, McDonald's, American Express, and PepsiCo. At the same time, Knell and I will visit the Ostankino TV network and introduce the *Sesame Street* project to Russian television executives. Later, Baxter, Leonid, and I will make a trip to Mosfilm, Moscow's largest film studio, to evaluate whether we could film the Russian *Sesame Street* series there.

Before leaving for their evening plans, Baxter walks Leonid through the standard process of getting a *Sesame Street* international coproduction off the ground. "It's like a tripod with three legs," Baxter says. He explains that the first leg involves talking to key stakeholders in the country—government officials, educators, and television executives—to see if there's interest and capacity to produce the children's show; the second leg involves identifying a viable production partner, a broadcaster, and funding; and the third leg is producing the TV series.

Leonid nods and I force a smile, trying to hide what I really think: getting even one leg of this tripod to stand will be immensely difficult.

In the morning, Knell and I meet in the hotel lobby and take a car to the headquarters of Ostankino. On a good day, the drive from the hotel is forty minutes, but the traffic is so bad we're in the sedan for more than an hour. As we approach the TV station, Knell points to its giant television tower, a bulbous rocket-like structure rising almost two thousand feet.

"Even though it looks like a prop from a 1960s sci-fi film, it's a real feat of Soviet engineering," I say, almost proudly, adding, "The tower still transmits the TV signal across the former Soviet Union's eleven time zones."

The driver lets us out in front of the broadcast complex, a mammoth cement bunker the size of five football fields with red, white, yellow, and blue corrugated metal panels decorating its exterior. It feels weird to be back at the same TV station where I had filmed interviews three years earlier for my PBS documentary.

A production assistant from the Children's Studio greets us in the entryway. He hands us TV station passes: tiny pieces of paper with our handwritten names and multiple official ink stamps. After we flash our passes, a soldier opens a gate and the PA leads us down a narrow corridor, stopping in front of a wide door. He pushes it open, and we find ourselves on the studio floor of

Spokoiny Nochi Maloshi (Good Night, Little Ones), Russia's longest-running children's television show.

The set looks as though it hasn't been updated in more than twenty years. Knell and I stand to the side, observing the videotaping of the show. There are two stars. The first is *Krusha*, a sad, worn, felt sock puppet that's supposed to look like a piglet. The other is a creepy-looking older white man who wears a colorful cap traditionally worn by Muslims from the former Soviet republics. His outfit seems terribly culturally inappropriate, especially considering that one-third of the national population is Muslim. The host and Krusha read a bedtime story and sing a lullaby.

After the director loudly calls, "Stop!" we're approached by the show's producers, two women, including one with orange-dyed hair. I ask if they have a VHS player in the studio so we can show them a video clip from the American *Sesame Street* show. They lead us to an adjacent room with shockingly outdated video editing consoles.

Knell and I exchange worried glances.

After watching the video, showcasing the American program's high production values, the producer with orange hair looks at us with wide eyes and enthusiastically exclaims, "You can include Krusha-the-pig in Russian *Sezam Street!*"

Her colleague seems less sure of how Krusha-the-pig would fare in a show as sophisticated as *Sesame Street*. She offers a small, embarrassed smile, then says, "Our little Krusha is crude but lovable."

Knell struggles to keep a straight face.

Before we leave, I let the women know how much we admire their work and commitment to educating children despite having to deal with massive cuts to state television. Once back in the car, my insides are churning. I confide in Knell that I have real concerns about partnering with the Children's Studio to produce fifty-two episodes. *Sesame Street* is technically elaborate and extremely design intensive, and it doesn't look as though the team we just met would be up to the challenge.

Unfazed, Knell turns to face me. "If anyone can do it, you can, Natasha." His confidence only makes me more anxious.

Back at the hotel restaurant that evening, we gather to share our findings. Leonid's and Baxter's meetings were equally depressing. Not one of the Western conglomerates was willing to underwrite our children's program.

Baxter shakes his head. "They all said the same thing: Russia's TV industry is too unstable to make any investment right now."

Leonid quotes one executive who'd said, "It's impossible to negotiate any deals with Russian television executives today, because one year from now any of the people in charge could be fired, in prison, or worse—dead." Knell chuckles, perhaps imagining the statement is an exaggeration, but I'm not so sure.

Leonid laughs off the comment, telling Baxter that the American corporate expats were surely exaggerating. Again, I am not so sure.

Suddenly Baxter jumps up, scurrying from the restaurant to the lobby to meet a group of men he appears to recognize. A few minutes later, he returns to our table, laughing. "It's incredible! Those are the swimming pool guys I met on the flight over. They sold the shit out of those pools to Soviet sports and fitness facilities that just got privatized." Turns out the pool guys won big while our efforts have been a complete bust.

Leonid affectionately pats Baxter on the back.

My American colleagues leave Moscow that night, and I have the sinking feeling Leonid and I have not lived up to their expectations.

A week later, I return to New York while Leonid stays in Moscow, continuing the search for a Russian partner. At least my colleagues liked Leonid enough to hire him as a consultant. I will follow up on leads from this trip and begin drafting an estimated timeline and budget for the production. Hopefully, with a bit of duct tape and luck, soon we'll have one leg of the tripod set up. Maybe.

Four months pass and the Russian series proceeds at a glacial pace, so slow that that my boss, the head of international production, assigns me to work for the next six months on *Plaza Sesamo* in Mexico. At first I am annoyed, thinking this probably means *Ulitsa Sezam* is never going to happen. But then I realize that working on the Spanish-language coproduction of *Sesame Street*, now in its twentieth year of broadcast, is the best way for me to gain on-the-ground experience with *Sesame Street* for the Russian show, if it ever happens.

It's in the Mexican sunshine in February of 1994 where my induction into the magical *Sesame Street* fraternity begins and my tutor is none other than Jon Stone, the ingenious original director of the American show, who is credited as the creative force and heart and soul of *Sesame Street*. At the *Televisa* studio in Tijuana where *Plaza Sesamo* is filmed, Jon leads a week-long workshop for the Mexican directors. I observe as he instructs the directors on how to block the actors, and puppeteers, while nurturing them to elicit their most natural and engaging performances.

At first, I'm embarrassed by my inexperience filming in a sound stage. I've only directed real-life characters in natural settings. But Jon, a large man with a bushy white beard and the kindest eyes, puts me at ease, patiently answering my many questions without any condescension. The Mexican directors adore Jon and appreciate that he's a man of big appetites. On our last night in Tijuana, we enjoy Mojitos with the directors as Jon regales us with stories of his early days with Jim Henson creating *Sesame Street*.

Later that night, we all head back to the TV studio. Jon and I take a walk through the outdoor soundstages, surprised at the number of people still working late, as is the custom in Mexico. We come across an electric donkey and Jon mounts it, awkwardly shifting his body into the saddle. "Come on up, what are you waiting for?" he calls to me, while waving a sombrero taken from the props room. Seeing Jon on top of the donkey, giving no thought to how he appears to anyone, makes me understand how this adorable man had created the most successful children's television program in the world. He extends his hand, inviting me to take a seat behind him. Until I met Jon, I hadn't truly felt at home at Sesame Workshop, but sitting on the donkey with my arms around Jon's waist, I feel like I'm part of the family.

And so begins 1994, a year I spend shuttling between New York and Mexico, supervising production of *Plaza Sesamo* and reacquainting myself with a little of my old New York life.

It feels nice spending so much time in New York. And before long, I hear from my good friend, Lisa Cleff, an actress and personal fitness trainer. She chides me for working too hard and traveling too much.

"Thank Gahd, you're still in town," she gushes in a typical New York accent. "I found you your future husband! You have to meet him."

I tell her I'm not interested. Dating is far down on my priority list.

Lisa ignores me, excitedly telling me the man in question, Ken Rogoff, is a friend of her fitness client and "very eligible." He's a forty-one-year-old divorced Princeton University economics professor, who is also an International Chess Grandmaster. "And he speaks Russian!" she yells into the receiver. "And he's Jew-ish!"

She promised her client that I'd go on a blind date with Ken.

Again, I say, "No."

Lisa pleads with me, "Come on, it's just *one* date. When's the last time you were on a date?"

Over a year ago. But that's too embarrassing to admit.

"I can't remember," I say.

Lisa is indomitable. There's no point arguing with her.

"Fine," I say, giving in just to end the discussion. But I tell her that I'll be leaving for Mexico again soon anyway.

"But you're going to dinner first with Ken," she corrects, before hanging up.

I sigh. It's true, bouncing between continents has made me lonely. Maybe going on a date won't be so bad.

A few days later, at the workshop, I'm surprised when Baxter knocks on my office door, grinning, and says, "Looks like we're going back to Moscow."

I'm taken aback because I had assumed Sesame Workshop's C-suite had put Russia on a back burner. Baxter takes a seat across from my desk and explains there's been sea change in Washington, DC. Apparently, legislators have renewed their interest in Russian *Sesame Street*. Communist forces had unsuccessfully attempted to overthrow Russia's newly democratic government in a coup in Moscow in October 1993—five months after my last trip. In fact, tanks had fired at the Russian parliament and hardline factions from the Russian army temporarily seized the Ostankino TV station.

"No one in Washington, DC, wants to see Russia revert to communism," Baxter says.

Relief and excitement wash over me. As much as I am enjoying producing in Mexico, my ambition to create *Ulitsa Sezam* has never waned. It's so great—I feel I could almost choke on it.

A day before I'm scheduled to return to Moscow, the chess grandmaster calls. He's polite, but I sense he's as hesitant about dating me as I am about dating him. "Sorry I didn't call earlier. I couldn't afford any distractions because I had to finish a draft of my book," he explains.

I gather that I'm the *distraction*, which irritates me.

"I'm busy too," I say. It's true. I'm actually packing my suitcase, in fact.

But we chat and I can't help but notice he's super smart, if somewhat awkward—or it at least sounds that way on the phone. He says he's leaving to attend some conferences in Europe, so we agree to connect when we both get back from our travels.

In Moscow, Leonid picks me up at the airport. The spring cottonwood trees have blossomed and white balls of fluff—called *poof*—blanket the streets, car windshields, and sidewalks like snow. The pollen makes my eyes itch, but I'm so happy to be back. Leonid excitedly tells me that he's arranged for us to meet Boris Berezovsky.

"Looks like the big fish we were trying to catch is becoming a whale," Leonid says with a twisted smile.

In the past months, the oligarch has become even more powerful, having convinced the Russian president, Boris Yeltsin, to give him greater control over Ostankino TV station in exchange for promising to deliver favorable political coverage.

Leonid's car is in the shop on the day we meet Berezovsky, so we take a taxi. Moving slowly through traffic, dodging municipal crews repairing roads damaged by the winter, I look out the window, wondering how we'll ever persuade Berezovsky to work with us and finance Russian *Sesame Street*.

Partnering with a man many believe is Russia's own Don Corleone might not be such a good idea for *Ulitsa Sezam*, but we have little choice. It's been more than a year since we began this venture, and we need this deal. When the taxi lets us off at Sakura, the restaurant where we agreed to meet, I take a deep breath and tell myself to focus.

Berezovsky is already seated at a table, and he rises to greet us. Elegantly dressed in a suit, red paisley tie, and matching pocket handkerchief, he looks nothing like a mobster. He's shorter than expected—a squirrely-looking man with a thinning black comb-over and an intense gaze. His handshake is firm, and he doesn't smile.

I notice two brawny bodyguards seated nearby. A security entourage is common for men of Berezovsky's stature, but these men are very large. They don't seem as though they'd be satisfied eating a few pieces of raw fish for dinner.

Sakura is the first Japanese restaurant to open in Moscow. The décor is overdone and confusing with a mishmash of Japanese and Chinese decorations. I wouldn't hesitate to venture that the designer had probably never set foot in Japan,

After we are all seated, Berezovsky picks up the menu and studies it with intense concentration, his face silhouetted by crimson light from red rice paper lanterns hanging over the table. I watch him decide what to eat, wondering what he'll decide about us.

I try to catch Leonid's attention, but he's also staring at the menu. His eyes are wide—probably shocked at the exorbitant prices. Sushi is almost thirty dollars apiece here. I pray we won't have to pick up the tab, although I'm less worried about money than having to order, translating "maguro tuna" into Russian. Fortunately, there's no need. Both the waiter and Berezovsky speak excellent English.

Soon, Leonid begins explaining, partly in Russian and partly in English, about "Bik Burd," an "i-cone" of American culture, "as famous as *Elvis Pray-esly*," launching into an impression of the Mississippi crooner. Leonid sucks in his cheeks, puckers his lips, and strums an air guitar for emphasis.

I stare hard at him, willing him to stop, but he pays me no attention.

Berezovsky barely acknowledges Leonid's impersonation of the King of Rock 'n' Roll.

Leonid wipes the sweat off his forehead with the back of his hand and abruptly stops his nervous laughter. In Russia, there's a proverb: "Laughing for no reason is a sign of stupidity," which perfectly describes how he looks right now. I want to hide under the table.

Maybe I can save this. I start talking about all the *new content* that will be created for the Russian coproduction. Beaming, I say, "Sixty percent of the show will be filmed in Moscow and the Russian show will have its own new Russian-themed Muppets who will appear in 'street scenes' with Moscow actors. And we'll shoot several hours of original live-action and animated films." Hoping to convey confidence and enthusiasm, I add, "We'll also construct a giant new set based on what a Russian neighborhood looks like."

Berezovsky leans forward, resting his elbows on the table. "Go on."

Unsure if he's really interested or just being polite, I describe the company's success in creating more than twenty foreign-language coproductions around the world. He looks at his watch, which makes me nervous. I'm convinced every second he's spending with us he's calculating the opportunity cost of his time. When he opens his mouth, I'm expecting him to say he's got another appointment and that we need to bring the meeting to a close.

Instead, he asks, "So we won't have Big-a-Bird in our show?"

Hearing this oligarch utter "Big Bird" gives me the boost I need, pleased that he's really been listening.

"Mr. Berezovsky," I say hesitantly, "the Russian series will include many but not *all* of *Sesame Street*'s Muppet characters in the American show."

"So, no Big Bird?" he repeats, looking disappointed.

"No." I say, apologetically, sharing that Big Bird does not appear in international adaptations of *Sesame Street*. I explain that three new Muppets will be designed and developed for *Ulitsa Sezam* by the Henson Company, in collaboration with Russia's very talented artists. My hope is to appeal to Berezovsky's patriotic side.

Berezovsky enjoys his sushi and nods as though considering this. "Okay."

I've been too nervous to eat anything, worrying that soy sauce running down my face would not be the best way to sell *Sesame Street* and I continue to ignore the food. We're not nearly there yet.

I explain that *Ulitsa Sezam*'s first season will consist of fifty-two half-hour episodes that will be broadcast over a two-year period. Each episode airs multiple times, as is the custom for all Sesame international coproductions. "We've found kids enjoy rewatching episodes because they like to see familiar scenes and characters," I state, affecting a slightly academic tone.

Berezovsky takes the last piece of sea urchin with a gulp of sake while I outline a plan for America to train hundreds of Russian media personnel and airlift needed technical equipment, adding, "We cannot get by on the outdated television equipment available at Ostankino."

At the mention of intensive training and technical booty, Berezovsky lifts his arching eyebrows and voices a question with little emotion: "American media experts will come to Moscow and provide training and equipment?"

"Yes," I reply, adding, "Our goal is to help develop an infrastructure for independent television production, crucial to Russia becoming a viable democratic society."

We have his attention.

"This is good," Berezovsky asserts. "Ostankino will be increasing its television production, and our producers need American know-how and technology so they can develop more advanced media skills."

Encouraged, Leonid elaborates on the project's financial upside. "Boris, we only have one children's show, *Good Night, Little Ones*, and we both know it is very old and tired. But parents across Russia continue to watch the show because there's no alternative. *Sesame Street* has much higher production standards, and *Ulitsa Sezam* will become a huge hit."

Continuing, Leonid emphasizes the potential advertising revenues from placing commercials before and after the show—which could be worth millions, "especially if Western companies underwrite the TV series." I can tell that Leonid is uncomfortable talking about money with a man who has more in common with Warren Buffet than with him, but my friend's enthusiasm outweighs his unease.

When he's done, I clarify that the American portion of the budget for equipment and training of Russian personnel in Moscow would be paid in

U.S. dollars, while the Russian portion of the production budget would be paid in rubles.

I notice a change in Berezovsky's expression, the wheels turning in his head. Maybe he's realizing Russian *Sesame Street* would give him access to more U.S. dollars. Or considering how this investment might offer credibility and integrity that his billions cannot buy. In other words, his interest in the American show may not be philanthropic at all; perhaps just a good business opportunity.

Leonid and I exchange hopeful glances.

Berezovsky begins spewing out words in a staccato style as fast as a bullet train. "So the first fifty-two episodes would be repeated for two years and half the budget will come from the Americans, in dollars, and the other half in rubles from our side. We'll have at least six advertising spots at the front and back end of every show, and we can sell these slots to foreign companies."

He pauses, doing calculations in his head as we watch, and then stops.

He looks at us, smiling. Apparently, the numbers add up.

I clear my throat and add, "And of course, Russian children will fall in love with Cookie Monster and the other American Muppets who will appear alongside the new Russian Muppets in *Ulitsa Sezam*."

A grin spreads across Leonid's face. "You will be Saint Boris," he nearly shouts, "bringing joy and laughter to Russia's children in these difficult times."

Berezovsky holds up his hand as though to put an end to such a thought. "Enough, enough," he says flatly, and then adds, "Of course, Ostankino is the best place to air *Ulitsa Sezam* because it has the largest footprint, reaching over two hundred million people. And airing the show on the state TV network will be perceived as a gift from the government to the country and to all the children in the former Soviet republics where Russian is still the dominant language in elementary schools."

Leonid and I nod. Berezovsky leans back in his chair and lights a cigarette. Everything is going so well, I don't dare believe it.

Berezovsky lifts his sake glass. "A toast to our children!" He downs the shot, then places his glass on the table and abruptly stands, holding out his hand for us to shake. The meeting is over.

We leave the restaurant together, trailed by the bodyguards. Berezovsky's chauffeur has already brought the oligarch's shiny black Mercedes 600 to the entrance, and a second car, his security detail, also drives up.

We're hesitant to hail a cab in front of Berezovsky so we stand awkwardly on the sidewalk. Then he asks if we need a ride.

Leonid mumbles something, and Berezovsky gestures toward one of his cars. "If you like, my driver can take you where you need to go." With that, his satellite phone rings. He answers and before taking the call, instructs his driver to give us a lift, then tells Leonid to visit his office the following week, where his legal team will draw up the paperwork. Leonid nods, reminding Berezovsky that Sesame Workshop will need a letter confirming his investment. He explains that the release of American government money is tied to the Russian financial commitment.

Berezovsky nods distractedly, "I'll get you what you need," he says, then returns to his phone call.

Leonid and I jump into the luxury car, sinking into the plush seats that smell of new leather. Berezovsky's driver asks where we want to go. Playing on the car's speakers is the Donna Summer's song "She Works Hard for the Money." We ask the driver to crank up the music and sing along, laughing at the irony of the lyrics. We feel like gamblers who hit the jackpot on our first try—even though we've been at this for months already.

I can't wait to share the good news with my team in New York.

5

NO GANGSTERS ON *SEZAM STREET*

Back in my apartment, after being away for three weeks, I listen to the messages on my answering machine. Two are from Ken. I like the sound of his voice and am surprised by how curious I feel to meet him. I must call him back, but right now I have to go to the workshop—to Baxter's office.

When I arrive, the door to Baxter's office is open and he's on the phone, so I wait outside until he gestures for me to enter. His office looks like Andy's closet in the movie *Toy Story*, with stuffed Muppet dolls crammed onto the shelves, alongside Big Bird backpacks, Cookie Monster lunchboxes, and Sesame 1-2-3 picture books. The only place to sit is an armchair with boxes stacked on the seat. I move one of the cartons, and they all crash to the floor.

Baxter abruptly ends his phone call and rushes over to help me pick up the boxes.

I haven't seen Baxter for more than a month. While I was in Moscow, he was in Asia, working with Chinese toy manufacturers. Now he picks up one of the cartons lying on the floor and excitedly pulls out a plush orange-colored Muppet doll that I don't recognize. "It's Zoe," he says.

She's cute with tiny pink and red bows in her hair. Baxter holds up Zoe in the air, gazing at her while rotating her furry body right and left, as though he'd given birth to the Muppet himself. "The Workshop envisions Zoe as a female version of Elmo," he explains. Elmo dolls are selling like hotcakes, but they are being purchased more for boys than girls, and the workshop hopes Zoe will change that.

"Do you like the color?" he asks, touching the doll's soft orange hair. "Isn't it a *great* color!" he exclaims, as he hands me the doll.

All I can think is, this crazy dude is in charge. He's passionate about everything he works on, and his enthusiasm is contagious. He's going to love my news.

I place the doll on the chair and launch into a blow-by-blow account of our multimillion-dollar deal with Berezovsky. Baxter recognizes the oligarch's name from coverage in the Western press.

"That's fantastic! Unbelievable!" Baxter shouts, opening his arms wide and giving me a hug. Baxter's a hugger, and I happily return the gesture. Leonid and I are fortunate to have him in our corner. His trust gives us the rope we need to get things done in Russia.

Over the next few weeks, word of our success spreads, eventually reaching my American colleagues at *Sesame Street*'s studio in Queens, New York, where the filming of the American show takes place. I ask Baxter if I can visit the studio—it would be good for me to get to know the American puppeteers and producers who'd later be training our Russian team—and the following week I take a twenty-minute subway ride to Kaufman Astoria, one of the oldest movie studios in New York, home to the Marx Brothers in the 1930s.

Kaufman Astoria Studios encompass a gray cement industrial-looking building that takes up a city block. Inside, a guard checks my name against a list and directs me down a hallway lined with black-and-white photographs of actors who've worked there—Frank Sinatra, Ginger Rogers, and George Burns. I arrive at the sound stage where *Sesame Street* is filmed and wait until the light above the door turns from red to green, the signal that taping is over.

At once, I am transported to the famous New York City street with its familiar brownstone stoop, Hooper's store, and the green-and-white street sign. Stepping carefully over the electrical cables taped to the floor and steering clear of the grips scurrying about, I cross the studio to get a closer look at Big Bird, dressed only in his striped red and pink legs and giant orange feet—absent the upper part of his costume. Seeing the original *Sesame Street* Muppets in real life is more exciting than I'd anticipated.

Arlene Sherman, the show's supervising producer and a fifteen-year veteran of *Sesame Street*, walks up to me and introduces herself. She's incredibly warm and welcoming, despite her stylishly austere appearance, dressed in all black: skinny jeans, T-shirt, and combat boots. Even her hair is jet black, cut sharply at her chin with bangs across her forehead. She invites me to join her in the control room adjacent to the studio, a small space with multiple screens on the wall. I can't believe she's paying any attention to lowly me.

I stay at the studio all day, spending most of my time with Arlene. Incredibly, in addition to working in the studio, she produces the show's short films and animations. She's nonchalant about all the famous actors and musicians she's worked with: Lou Reed, Morgan Freeman, David Bowie, and will.i.am. Hands down, Arlene is the hippest person I've ever met, precisely because she doesn't realize how cool she is.

In the control room, Lisa Simon, the show's director, uses an intercom system to direct the puppeteers on set who are doing a bit with Mike Myers, the famous actor from the cult film *Wayne's World*. It's amazing to see all these kick-ass women running the show. She yells, "Action!" and Myers spoofs his former long-haired, bong-toking character. It's hilarious. I hardly imagined children's television could be this much fun. I'm also stunned by how much the puppeteers improvise.

Still, my utter delight at seeing all this is tempered by an overwhelming imposter syndrome. Compared to these celebrated, multiple Emmy Award–winning entertainers, I feel that I don't belong and that I just might break out in hives.

What was I thinking? Can I even *do* this? I'd been so busy working on the business side and logistics of jump-starting *Ulitsa Sezam* that I'd given no thought to the creative side of the production or how I expect to produce a sophisticated show like *Sesame Street*. What if our Russian show is mediocre? Or worse?

———

I barely make it back to my apartment in time for my first date with Ken. If I hadn't had such an all-consuming day at the studio, I'd probably be a lot more nervous about meeting him. But there's no time for nerves, only enough time for a quick shower and throwing on clothes before he's ringing my bell.

He's exactly on time and shakes my hand stiffly. "It's nice to finally meet you," he says. His hand is sweaty, and I'm not sure if that's because he's nervous or because he's wearing a wool tweed blazer in the 102-degree summer heat.

I catch myself dismissing him as too much of an oddball, even though he's only just walked through the door. Taking a breath, I ask, "Would you like something to drink? Water?" I move into the galley kitchen. Peering over my shoulder, I glance at him as he walks to my bookcase and reads the spines.

"I guess it's a little weird to be set up on a 'double blind date'—you know, since you've never met my friend and I've never met yours," he remarks shyly.

I'm glad he brought this up right away and tell him, "I don't usually go on blind dates, but made an exception for Lisa." A tiny lie; as I said, lately I'd not gone on any dates at all. Intending to break the awkward silence that follows, I venture, "It's cooler along the river where there's a breeze. Maybe we could go for a walk?"

We cross the West Side Highway to the asphalt path along the Hudson River. Breaking another uncomfortable silence, I cheerily offer, "This is why I love living downtown," extending my arm toward the river. "What an incredible view."

Ken is staring at the trash and hypodermic needles strewn on the ground. He kicks one away and tells me that as a teenager in the 1970s, he'd spent a lot of time in New York City, playing competitive chess. "It was pretty desperate then, kind of like what it looks like here now."

I press my lips together, not sure if this is his way of telling me he's not enjoying our river walk.

We saunter toward Battery Park City, exchanging stories of our past. We'd both left home as teenagers. At age sixteen, I'd moved to Venezuela, where I learned to speak Spanish, and then to Luxembourg on a high school exchange program for a year, where I studied French and German. Ken describes how he'd barely attended high school, living in Europe, playing competitive chess, and supporting himself with his winnings. "I alternated between staying in five-star hotels and sleeping on park benches," he says dryly. We also share a similar heritage; his grandfather sold goat's milk outside of Kyiv before emigrating to America and my grandfather sold kosher meat in Belorussia.

In the days before our date, Lisa had told me that Ken had played simultaneous blindfolded chess against twenty-six other players at once, so I figured he was being overly modest about his skills on our walk.

There's something oddly beguiling about Ken. He's different from the creative types I dated in the past: musicians, actors, and film directors who overshared to the point of suffocating narcissism. Ken seems humble, and he doesn't wear his emotions on his sleeve for everyone to see. And I appreciate his candor and snappy sarcastic wit.

Between meeting Ken, locking a deal with Berezovsky, and making cool new friends at the *Sesame Street* studio, for the first time in a long time it seems that my personal life and career are both on an upswing. It's a rare moment that doesn't last long.

After a glorious early-morning yoga class and stopping to get a coffee, I arrive back at my apartment just as the phone is ringing. It's Leonid. The date is June 10, 1994. "I have some bad news, Natasha," Leonid sighs into the phone. "Berezovsky's car got blown up," he says.

"What? What?" I yell into the receiver. I drop my yoga bag and pull the phone with its long cord to the couch so I can sit down.

"No one knows if he's alive or dead," he says, taking a deep breath.

I'm speechless.

We listen to each other's breathing over the crackling transcontinental connection until Leonid begins describing what happened. Evidently, after a few weeks of trying to get Berezovsky's lawyers to draft a letter of guarantee, Leonid finally received a call to pick up the signed letter confirming the oligarch's commitment of three million dollars to *Sesame Street*.

Leonid sounds so agitated that he can barely get the words out.

"When I got to Logovaz [Berezovsky's corporate office in Moscow], it was surrounded by police, and no one would let me inside. That's when I heard Boris might be hurt or dead."

I can't believe this is happening. My body tenses, remembering Berezovsky inquiring about "Bik Burd," whom he liked so much.

I hear Leonid lighting a match for his cigarette in our silence.

"None of Berezovsky's people are returning my calls," says Leonid. "Russian news reports are saying Boris was in the backseat of his Mercedes when it blew up and his chauffer and bodyguard were in the front."

"You mean the same car we were in?" I ask, horrified.

"Yes." he says, taking a drag.

"So is Berezovsky dead?" I ask.

"I don't know. I already told you—no one knows." Leonid sounds exasperated. "They say Boris suffered severe burns and his chauffeur was decapitated."

I feel sick, shivering as I remember Berezovsky's chauffer bobbing his head as Leonid and I sang along to the Donna Summer song on the car stereo. I shudder, imagining Berezovsky stumbling from his car, his body engulfed in flames and his driver's head rolling down the blood-stained street.

"This is insane." I hear my voice cracking.

Leonid stammers, as though all of the life force had been punched out of him, "Natasha, he's probably dead. Everyone gets killed here. It's hopeless. There's no way to do business."

I feel crushed, but I want to fully understand the situation, so I have to ask, "Leonid, if he's gone, does this mean the money for the show is also gone?"

Silence.

He exhales. "Even if he is alive, the last thing he's going to put his money into now is a kid's puppet show." I can hear his voice trembling from the emotion of it all. "So yes, it's gone."

For the next two days, Leonid tries to find out where Berezovsky is. Eventually, we discover that he survived the blast, which is a huge relief. But he then fled to Europe. Leonid repeatedly tries to contact Berezovsky's lawyers to try to resuscitate our deal, but no one will talk to him.

On the phone, I tell Leonid that I am scared to tell Baxter about the car bombing and our now-aborted deal. "Surely now, I think, the company might have to question if it's a good time to do the Russian production. It might be too dangerous," I say.

"I dunno," Leonid says.

I feel shattered.

I schedule the appointment with Baxter.

Baxter is late for our meeting, so I curl up in the oversized chair in his office and wait. Usually, the menagerie of smiling *Sesame Street* Muppets, all propped up on his bookshelves, cheers me up, but today their big Ping-Pong-ball eyes regard me with contempt. I've failed them.

When Baxter finally arrives, I don't need to tell him about Berezovsky. He's already heard. He picks up a soft Ernie bath squirter, starts fidgeting with it and then puts it down. "Well, thankfully, we didn't get in bed with Berezovsky," he sighs. "I can just see the media covering this story: 'Big Bird's Russian partner gets blown up in car bombing—yellow feathers flying everywhere.'" He waves his fingers in the air as though they're the falling feathers.

His face then turns serious. "Natasha, this would not have been good for *branding*," making air quotes with his fingers. I bow my head in embarrassment. I should have known better.

Baxter doesn't know how to stay mad at anyone for very long. He puts his hand on my shoulder. "Everything's going to be OK," he says and walks me to the door.

I'm relieved the fiasco with Berezovsky did not get me fired, but I have no idea how, or if, the project is going to move forward.

I leave the office early and walk downtown as if in a trance, putting one foot in front of the other. After a broiling heatwave, a cool breeze from the Hudson River infuses the city with new energy. At a Mexican restaurant with orange umbrellas, I stop and watch a group of young women at a bachelorette party, wearing matching pink T-shirts with the words, "Mandy's Getting Hitched." They laugh loudly, toasting the bride-to-be.

Going back to Russia was a foolish mistake. *Ulitsa Sezam* will never happen, and I'm making too many tradeoffs—I should be enjoying a normal life, spending time with friends, and maybe even having a boyfriend. I hate myself for buying into a fantasy that I could somehow help Russia, and I feel lonely.

Then I remember Ken. Why hadn't he called me and asked me out again? Did I scare him off?

At a phone booth on the street, I stop and dig through my bag for Ken's Princeton University business card. I remember him writing his home number on the back in blue ink. I drop a few coins into the phone, willing myself not to hang up, even if he calls me a distraction again.

Ken answers on the fourth ring. After a day like today, his voice is soothing.

"Could you come into the city and meet me for dinner tonight?" My own voice sounds different than usual, more vulnerable maybe.

To my surprise, he agrees.

———

Late that night, back at my apartment, I call Leonid and tell him about my surprisingly successful second date with Ken. He spent half the dinner talking about his chess idol, Bobby Fischer and why Fischer was such an unbeatable chess player. I'm baffled at how well Ken and I get along. Leonid peppers me with questions about the new man and teases me. "This smart fucker's way too smart for you. He'll always see twenty moves ahead of you." I chuckle.

Leonid then turns serious. "Natasha, you don't want a long-term relationship. How could you possibly have a boyfriend when you're traveling all the time?"

I don't let on, but his words feel like a kick in the stomach. And besides, who am I more likely to have a successful relationship with—Russia or Ken? Right now, nothing about my future is clear.

———

The rest of the summer is sweeter than expected. Ken and I see each other regularly, or as much as time permits, between Ken's overseas travel and mine. I feel something in me shifting as I open up to this wonderful person who is so different from myself. I take a chance and invite Ken to join a group of my friends, including Leonid, renting a house together in Martha's Vineyard, Massachusetts. I don't expect Ken to say yes, but he surprises me.

Ken doesn't like the heat, much less the sun, and wears long pants and a long-sleeved shirt while hiding under an umbrella on the shore. But he's good-natured, listening as my friends tell embarrassing stories about me over wine and platters of buttery lobster during our first island dinner together. I watch his face with amusement and a feeling of tenderness sweeps over me. I'm not surprised my friends fall in love with Ken. Like me, they're intrigued by his intelligence and sense of humor. But having a serious relationship right now seems impossible.

Toward the last days of the two-week vacation, Leonid and I take a walk on the beach at night. It's so clear, the sky is filled with stars. The island feels a universe away from Moscow. Leonid talks about his son, who he will travel to see in California before returning to Russia. I tell him how much I will miss Ken once we are both back in Moscow. Suddenly he gets solemn. "Natasha, Ken is perfect for you. He's the one: smart enough to tell you when you're full of boolshit." I have the same feeling, but it scares me, so I just laugh.

———————

By summer's close, to my great surprise, it looks like I'll be heading back to Russia sooner than I'd expected. The company's approach has once again changed. This is due in part to a major grant for the Russian project from the Soros Foundation. And, apparently, *now* USAID has decided to allow Sesame Workshop to use some of the grant funds for training the Russians at Sesame headquarters in New York. Baxter asks me to fly to Moscow to immediately begin assembling a Russian production team. This is excellent news.

Two days later, I have to leave Ken behind and return to Moskva.

6

WE DON'T WANT YOUR MOPPETS

Moscow's crisp fall is already giving way to bitter cold temperatures as winter looms. The Palace Hotel security guard knows me by name and greets me with a nod, taking my bags.

Our first stop will be Ostankino TV. Leonid has arranged for us to speak with Midhat Shilov, the director of cultural programming and one of Leonid's oldest, dearest friends, whom I have met many times.

At the station entrance, the glass doors that had been shattered during the coup have been repaired, but you can still see bullet holes in the concrete exterior. I shudder, thankful I wasn't in Moscow when it happened.

After collecting our security passes at the front kiosk, we take an elevator to the eleventh floor, the network's nerve center. Midhat is waiting for us, standing on the threshold to his office with his hands on his hips, grinning from ear to ear at us as we approach.

Midhat's life story could be a film. He was born in Yalta in 1941 to a Muslim father who was the first secretary of the Yalta Communist Party Committee of Crimea. After the war, Stalin declared Crimean Tartars traitors and began deporting hundreds of thousands overnight. When Midhat was four years old, the Soviet secret police showed up in his home; they shot and killed his father. His mother died shortly thereafter, and Midhat was sent to an orphanage in Siberia. None of his relatives knew where he had gone.

For four years, his maternal grandmother, a Moscow resident, searched for him. When she finally found him, she arranged to have Midhat secretly transported to Moscow. Without any legal status to reside in the big city, Midhat had to hide under his grandmother's kitchen table whenever anyone came to visit her apartment. Eventually, when Midhat turned eight, a close friend of his grandmother's agreed to adopt him, giving him a Russian last name and the legal status to allow Midhat to attend school in Moscow.

It was only in the early 1990s, after President Yeltsin had rehabilitated the Crimean Tartars, that Midhat felt safe enough to share his secret with me.

Although he'd witnessed some of the most violent times in Soviet history, he emerged with his body, integrity, and sense of humor intact.

As director of Ostankino's cultural programming, he is still fighting battles. Leonid explained that the only reason we had not asked Midhat for help earlier is that his good friend was embroiled in a political fight for his survival at the TV station. But Midhat cannot be easily pushed aside. Everyone refers to him as "the General" because he can marshal people from Moscow to Novosibirsk at a moment's notice. And while his division doesn't produce children's programming, he might be able to help us build a team of producers who could travel to America for training.

Midhat, fifty-three years old and five feet tall with thinning grey hair and a barrel belly, leads us inside his office, respecting the old Russian superstition that it's bad luck to greet guests in the doorway. He kisses me three times and then Leonid. His corner office is enormous but modestly decorated with standard government-issue furniture. I notice the floor-to-ceiling windows on two sides are caked with dirt and grime, obstructing the view of the lovely Moscow River. I tease him, "When's the last time you had the windows cleaned?"

He shrugs, and with a sardonic smile says, "No money. Not for window washing and not for programming."

Leonid brings him up to date on the latest developments with Russian *Sesame Street*. Midhat, in turn, says it will be difficult to finance any production because the Russian government has not paid Ostankino's television employees, including him, in three months. "The state either pays wages late or not at all," he says.

"It's disgraceful," he grunts, adding, "Even the Russian army isn't getting paid on time." But enough of that; Midhat says he wants to show us his new toy.

He stands back from his desk, gesturing for Leonid to open the top drawer. Inside is a gun and a cardboard box of bullets. Midhat pulls out the pistol and then, smiling, slowly loads the cartridges into the chambers. He starts waving around the gun, ranting about how the Russian government and criminals are looting the TV station. "They should be paying our salaries, not packing their pockets!" he shouts.

A young assistant, a woman, enters the office carrying some folders. Midhat playfully points the barrel of the gun at the girl. "Should I shoot the messenger?" he asks, looking at us.

My heart skips and I look urgently at Leonid, who takes a moment to realize the danger of the situation. He half laughs, then says more seriously, "Put down the gun. Come on, Midhat."

Meanwhile, the assistant pays no attention, pushing the barrel of the gun to the side with a casual gesture. She then places the folders on his desk without a word, turns on her heel, and exits, as though a gun at her head is just another Tuesday.

Midhat lays the gun on the table and stares at it as if the weapon belongs to someone else. He tells us that he bought the gun because life in Moscow is becoming too dangerous. "You know honestly, I feel threatened, even here, at the station. Too many people are getting killed. They're just walking home and—*pop!*—they're dead."

I volunteer, "I read an article in the *New York Times* saying that the crime rate in Moscow is ten times higher than in New York City."

Midhat picks up the gun, slams it back down on the desk, and loudly declares, "I am going to learn how to use this gun, and I'm going to carry it with me all the time."

Leonid moves closer to Midhat, putting his arm around his friend's shoulders. "No one's going to hurt you."

It takes a moment for Midhat to relax and sit down again at his desk. Leonid and I take a seat, sinking into the couch with springs so far gone that it's impossible to sit comfortably. We ask for advice on finding television producers to work with us.

Midhat leans back in his chair and looks up at the ceiling as if the answer is up there. Finally, he puts forward a plan. "Why don't we tell my staff that the Americans promise to pay their monthly salaries or even a portion of their salaries at some future date in exchange for working on *Ulitsa Sezam*?" he suggests, proposing formally assigning his internal staff to work with the Americans. "They would still be entitled to their regular salary from the Russian government—if it ever gets paid—but they would also receive a promise of future payments from the Americans once *Sesame Street* has money to pay them."

This plan doesn't require the Americans to put down any money up-front. And while it seems incredible that the Russian staff would work without being paid immediately, it appears that this is pretty much the way things are at the television station right now.

"Your staff would really do that?" I ask, surprised.

Midhat crosses his arms over his belly, clearly pleased by his scheme. "Almost certainly they will trust the Americans over the Kremlin to pay them," he laughs. "Eventually."

This is ingenious because while I don't have any money to hire people, I do have money from the Soros Foundation to pay to send a group of Russians to America so they can learn how to produce *Sesame Street*.

Midhat winks, says he'll be right back, and leaves the office for a moment. He returns ten minutes later, carrying a banged-up wooden chair, followed by three unsmiling producers—each carrying their own banged-up chair— goose-stepping forward.

Midhat presents Lida Shurova, a television writer, and two TV directors: Piotr Sidorenko and Sergei Novikov. We shake hands, then they sit on the chairs they've brought.

Lida wears leopard-print leggings, black ankle boots, and a sheer cream- colored blouse, through which I can see her lacy black bra. Sitting close to her is Piotr, in jeans and a button-down shirt. Later I learn they are married. Sergei, who dresses more conservatively than the others in gray wool slacks and a striped shirt, doesn't say much and observes the scene with a look of bemused detachment.

Midhat explains that his producers have worked in film and television for about ten to twenty years, and all have extensive experience in multiple genres of television, except children's television. But he doesn't think this will be a problem.

He explains to Lida, Piotr, and Sergei why I am visiting Moscow, then asks them to turn their attention to the TV screen inside a worn and scratched wooden credenza. I slip the video I brought into the VCR player and press Play.

The segment begins with a chorus of Muppet monsters singing a parody of the famous Rolling Stones song, "(I Can't Get No) Satisfaction." The melody stays the same, but the lyrics (subtitled on the video in Russian) are: "I can't get no . . . cooperation."

Leonid and Midhat burst out laughing as the Muppets gyrate and genu- flect better than Mick Jagger himself. Midhat's colleagues sit wordlessly in their chairs, stone-faced.

"It's the Rolling Stoooones!" Leonid says emphatically.

Still no response from the three chairs. I didn't expect this.

I show another video clip, this one with Grover as a waiter serving a tiny hamburger to a client in a restaurant as a way of teaching the difference be- tween big and little.

When the clip ends, Lida makes a sour face. "We don't eat hamburgers in Russia."

"What about you?" I ask Piotr in Russian. "What do you think?"

He slowly shakes his head. "The *Sezam Street*–style Monsters are not Russian, and they are too strange looking for Russia," he says.

Before I can respond, Lida adds, with a look of disdain, "Russia has a long, rich, and revered puppet tradition dating to the sixteenth century. We don't need your American *Moppets* in our children's show."

I start to feel short of breath. I thought selling the Russians on the lovable Muppets would be the easy part of making this television series. But these television professionals don't even *like* the American puppets. I don't know whether to laugh or cry.

Leonid tries to reason with the group, but they remain steadfastly Team "Anti-Muppet."

I reach for my only other carrot. "If you join our production team, we'll pay for you to travel to New York City, where you will go through intensive training with *Sesame Street*'s experienced producers, directors, and writers."

Lida coughs. Everyone turns toward her. "What makes you think, Natasha, that your American writers could teach anything to our writers?"

I'm stunned. I didn't mean to offend her or Russia's writers. I notice her boot, tapping the floor ever more forcefully.

She continues, "If I am *Ulitsa Sezam*'s head writer—" (the position we've proposed), "—then I will only accept script submissions from members of the Union of Writers, and they do not need training from *Amerkians*," she sneers, crossing her hands in front of her chest.

The Union of Writers was established in the 1930s, and typically, most of its members had to conform to Communist Party doctrine. Obviously, many brilliant Russian writers were excluded from the union. I look desperately at Midhat, who calls for a break.

Leonid and Midhat step into the hall and light cigarettes, while the others remain seated. While they smoke, I pace the hall, unsure what to do next. I join the smokers huddling outside the room and ask Leonid in English, "How can we possibly work with these producers who seem to lack any affection for the American show?" Midhat speaks only Russian.

Leonid drags on his cigarette. "You know, Natasha, I see their point: the Russians gave birth to Pushkin and Tolstoy. We're not like you American babies with no history."

I stare hard at him.

I need to take a moment and get my emotions under control. I get that for television writers like Lida, the ground has shifted dramatically since the collapse of communism. As a state television employee, she'd earned a steady salary under communism while churning out programs that both entertained and indoctrinated TV audiences. But the recent partial privatization of television has decimated state television subsidies, along with job security, social status, and incomes.

Many of the television professionals remaining at Ostankino are relics of the Soviet era, terrified to take risks or explore opportunities in Russia's new independent media industry. I imagine they feel betrayed, having lost not only their steady salary but also their sense of purpose. Of course, they don't take kindly to an American showing up proposing a totally new angle on children's television.

"I don't think this is going to work out with your staff," I tell Midhat.

Leonid tells me to calm down and be more open-minded.

Midhat takes my hand in his. "Natasha, my dear, compromise is the mother of communist invention." He explains that this could be a temporary solution to help us get to the next phase of production. Later, if I'm dissatisfied, I can hire a whole new team.

It's a crazy way to do business. I resent that I've been put in this situation where I'm supposed to assemble a production team without any money to pay for salaries in Moscow. Baxter had called it "a chicken and egg problem," but I call it bird-brained. And I resent having to work with people who don't appreciate the genius of *Sesame Street*.

But when we return to the room, I'm prepared to hold my tongue. Leonid and I need to send a team to America, even a makeshift one. To get visas in time, we have to quickly choose the individuals who will be traveling on this trip.

Sergei, the serious young man with the oddly expressionless face, raises his hand. "How much time would we have to produce the children's TV series?" he asks.

"We have about eighteen months left on the U.S. government contract to deliver fifty-two half-hour episodes ready for broadcast on Russian television." I notice my voice sounds more like a drill sergeant than I'd intended. Sergei raises one eyebrow and, without moving any other muscle in his face, conveys his doubt about producing so much original content in such a short time. Ever the charmer, Midhat winks at the group and says, "Everything's possible with American dollars."

In a fatherly tone, Midhat reminds his staff, "We are not producing anything in our department right now. We have no budget. So what do you have to lose by working with the Americans? And you can go to America for training," he excitedly exclaims, holding his arms open like a Russian Santa Claus.

The producers talk among themselves and agree to meet again the next day when they'll give me their decision. As Midhat's colleagues file from the office, carrying out their chairs, I worry this unlikely union between *Sesame Street*'s freewheeling and progressive creative team and these conservative, risk-averse state television employees will come to a bad end.

But we have no choice and we're out of time.

The following day, without Leonid, I head back to Ostankino to find out what the Russian producers have decided about the American show. When I arrive at Midhat's office, I discover the group is still debating the issues among themselves. Meanwhile, they've invited Kolya Komov, a celebrated Russian puppet designer and performer, to meet me.

Komov is a short man with brown, stringy, shoulder-length hair and intense eyes. At the prompting of his coconspirators, he argues that if *Sezam Street* wants to be successful in Russia, then the show should use *his* puppets instead of the Muppets.

"*Your* puppets," I say.

He nods, then digs furiously into the overstuffed sack in front of him, finally pulling out two sock puppets and a wooden stick. He slides his hand inside the sleeve of Petrushka, a traditional Russian folk puppet who has a big nose and is dressed in a long red peasant-style dress shirt and sleeping cap. To me, the smile painted on the puppet's wooden face looks cruel and disturbing.

Petrushka grabs the tiny stick with his puppet hand and begins beating the female sock puppet in Komov's other hand. Petrushka is shouting in Russian, "I'm going to kill you!" Komov vocalizes the shrill sound effects of the stick hitting the puppet while I watch wide-eyed, imagining the shock of *Sesame Street*'s educational experts should they ever witness this puppet-on-puppet violence.

Meanwhile, everyone else in the room is laughing.

Komov finishes his performance. "You see? Everyone loves my puppets. The *Moppets* cannot bring anything new or valuable to what Russia's children already know and love."

Nodding her head, Lida confirms the truth of Komov's words: "We have our own traditions and our own aesthetic; any show we create will reflect those traditions, not yours."

Sergei gently intercedes, sharing his perspective. "I'm opposed to the 'Monsters' too. Because in my childhood, forty years ago, we didn't have puppets that look like your Muppet monsters. Our puppets weren't naked; they had clothes and shoes, like normal humans."

I don't know what to say. I can't agree with them that Komov's crude and violent sock puppet is funny or appropriate for children. But also, I can't disrespect their traditions. I can only tell them what I know, which is that children throughout the world adore the Muppets. I talk about *Sesame Street*'s other successful coproductions, such as *Plaza Sesamo*, which has been running for twenty years in Mexico. I tell them how every country's Muppets resonate with distinct national characteristics. For example, in *Rechov Sum Sum*, the Israeli show, the Muppet "Kippy Ben-Kipod" is a hedgehog, prickly on the outside and sweet on the inside—as the Israelis describe themselves.

Piotr scowls. "You can't compare Russia, a superpower, to Mexico or Israel."

Meanwhile, Sergei provides what he considers a scientific rationale. His view is that Russian children are naturally more rigid and will instinctively reject the unfamiliar American puppets that are made of foam, not wood, and are too strange looking.

"Our children will not appreciate your Monster-style Muppets because they are not realistic. They are neither recognizable animals that exist in the real world nor humanoid."

As we continue to debate the imperfections of the Muppets and the superiority of Komov's puppets, teacups pile up on the coffee table alongside stale biscuits and empty Coke bottles. Several hours later, after the sky has grown dark, we remain at a deadlock. Becoming ever more disheartened, I mumble something about how *Sesame Street* is not *Sesame Street* without the Muppets.

Finally, Lida stands up, stamping the heel of her boot. "In this time of great change, Russian children need comfort and recognizable characters from *our own* culture. They have more than enough going on in their lives that is terrifyingly new and different. Unless *Ulitsa Sezam* includes familiar puppet characters from Russian folklore, the show will never be truly Russian."

Then, as I'm losing all hope, Lida claps her hands and pronounces, "We must include Baba Yaga in our *Sesame Street* TV series."

I close my eyes and take a deep breath. Baba Yaga is a nasty witch who eats children. We have moved from Petrushka, who beats people, to a cannibal witch. Of course, *Sesame Street* will accept neither.

We don't have any time to find other producers, let alone ones who will work for free. I'll just have to hope the Russian producers eventually accept the Muppets. If they don't, there will be no show. And without them coming to America, there will also be no show.

Two days later, I again meet Lida, Sergei, and Piotr at Midhat's office. With some reservation, they agree to become *Ulitsa Sezam*'s head writer, live-action director, and creative director, respectively. Immediately, I make photocopies of their passports, and we begin making plans for their travel to America.

Midhat will serve as the show's executive producer until we can find someone else. He offers us the temporary use of a small office next to his that is currently empty. Using a portion of the funding for development from the Soros Foundation, I purchase three computers, two fax machines, and a printer for the new space. Midhat throws in two phone lines for local calls.

I'm grateful to have a way to contact my new Moscow colleagues; none of us on the production team have satellite phones. Very few people have them. But it occurs to me that these Russians may not know how to use computers. In these early days of Unix and AOL, I wouldn't be surprised if they'd never used email or the Web. In fact, I'd only started using email in the past year and our written communication with Moscow is still, for the most part, via fax and telex.

In any case, the computers make it look official. We're here. We're working. We have a production team of sorts and a new office. However, I can't seem to stop the panicky voice in my head from asking what will happen when my patriotic Russian producers arrive in America to be "educated" about the Muppets they clearly dislike.

A few days later Leonid stops by the Ostankino office, bringing news of another possible investor. He is Vladimir Slutskyer, an oil tycoon who also happens to own Moscow's first elite sports club—and is one of Leonid's oldest friends. He says Slutskyer might be interested in financing *Ulitsa Sezam*. I want to be as excited as Leonid is, but I haven't forgotten what happened to Berezovsky. "Don't be so pessimistic," Leonid says, telling me that he's already arranged for us to meet Slutskyer and several of his business associates the following week.

I ask where we're meeting, and Leonid explains that the location has to be kept a secret because too many people would like to see Slutskyer and all his colleagues dead. According to Slutskyer, the group never meets in the same place twice.

This is disconcerting, but I guess it's a good sign they're taking precautions. Maybe one of them will live long enough to become our partner.

A week later, I'm standing in front of my hotel closet for fifteen minutes, trying to decide what combination of clothing will seal the deal. Am I dressing to meet a group of executives or a bunch of criminals? If criminals, then what's the right outfit? A blouse showing a lot of cleavage or a proper business pantsuit?

Business culture is still quite sexist in Russia. Women are expected to dress to appeal to men, even in business settings. Deciding that pants could imperil our deal, I wear a skirt and a blouse covering my decolletage.

Leonid and I wait in front of our hotel. At 11:00 a.m. sharp, Slutskyer pulls up in a black, newly detailed Ford Explorer, trailed by two security cars, and yells to us, "Get in!"

As we roll through the city passing buildings in various states of disrepair and construction, I think about how Moscow is a city of façades, where illusion and reality intersect in the unlikeliest places. It's not easy to tell what's real. This breakneck pace of change makes it impossible to judge the legitimacy of individuals or organizations. Overnight, people go from rags to riches without anyone understanding where their wealth came from. It's like living in a giant candy store where the owner left the door open and whoever walks in first gets to steal all the sweets.

I look at Slutskyer, smoking while ignoring the fallen cigarette ash accumulating on his substantial paunch, and I wonder if he can produce the results we need. One thing I've learned in Russia is that personal relationships are essential in any business deal. It's Leonid's long-term relationship with Slutskyer that makes this meeting more promising than the one with Berezovsky.

A half hour later, we arrive at our destination, a nondescript cement warehouse surrounded by a barbed-wire fence. Twelve-foot-high steel gates rattle open, and we drive into the compound, where four security guards holding assault rifles wave us through a metal detector and inside the building. I grab Leonid's arm and give him a wide-eyed look. What kind of legit business needs a commando force like this?

We walk into the room and see ten executives spread out, comfortably seated in armchairs and couches, talking energetically, while working through the pickles and bread with black caviar on a shiny black glass coffee table. Throughout my years working in Moscow, appetizers have always played a unique function in culture and business. Filling your guests' stomachs and getting them drunk before any serious conversation is a known strategy. The din dips for a moment, and I feel their eyes on me—on my breasts and on my legs. I'm used to this in Russian business meetings. The vodka is already flowing, although it's only eleven thirty in the morning.

Two more men enter the room, drawing loud cheers of "Hoopa!" from the others. The men rise to greet one another with three cheek kisses. They make kissing look masculine, like wrestlers hugging before a fight. As the men mingle, Leonid and I stand awkwardly, clinging to Slutskyer's side, waiting to be introduced. But the men are all more interested in one another, ecstatically exchanging stories of their collective good fortune to be born during the greatest transfer of wealth from public to private hands in Russian history. I overhear bits and pieces of conversation—mainly about expensive furniture being imported to their new offices and problems with government tax collectors asking for too much money. The back-slapping and deep voices are almost too much for me. You could cut the thick, masculine competitive energy in the room with a knife.

Slutskyer raises his voice, trying to get the group's attention. Once they've settled back into their seats, Slutskyer introduces us. We meet the chair of the Russian Sports Association, whom Slutskyer explains has the exclusive right to sell imported cigarettes in Russia without paying value-added tax.

Leonid leans toward me, whispering, "The only other entity excluded from paying VAT is the Russian Orthodox Church." Apparently, the sports chair owns and operates every cigarette and newsstand in Moscow, perhaps making him more omnipotent than the church itself. Not all Russians worship, but nearly every Russian smokes.

Seated next to him is Russia's "Sausage King." He jokes, "I produce enough hot dogs each month to line them up end-to-end from Moscow to St. Petersburg." In the next seat is the CEO of one of Russia's largest commercial banks. As Slutskyer goes down the line, I realize some faces are familiar to me. I've seen them in the press. Their dress code runs the gamut from polyester tracksuits, to expensive jeans with a polo shirt, to custom-tailored suits.

As Slutskyer is talking about us, I scan the room, feeling increasingly anxious and questioning whether we should even be here asking *these* men for money. But since we're here, I try to figure out what is the best approach to convince them that investing in *Sesame Street* is worthwhile.

Leonid begins, explaining the financial upside of selling advertising on our show. "As I am sure you all are aware, the cost-per-minute price of commercial advertising on Russian television has increased tenfold in the last three months. We have spoken with many foreign companies operating in Moscow, and they are all eager to buy advertising time surrounding Russian *Sesame Street*."

I know this is entirely untrue. Baxter's earlier meetings with the Fortune 500 Moscow representatives yielded nothing of the kind, but Leonid continues. He sweetens the pitch by talking about the potential sales of show merchandise like toys and stuffed Muppets, including the new Russian plush that could be licensed for distribution in the Russian market.

The men listen attentively, although I have doubts any of them have even heard of *Sesame Street*.

I follow up with the philanthropic spiel, beginning with a crowd-pleaser: "*Ulitsa Sezam* will give the next generation of Russian children the skills and readiness to become as successful as all of you in this room."

When I finish speaking, one of the men, dressed in a red, blue, and white tracksuit—the colors of the Russian flag—stands, and raising his glass, makes a toast: "To our children!"

Hot liquid burns my throat as I down the shot. Drinking to the bottom of the shot glass is mandatory in Russia if you expect anyone to take you seriously.

While my appeal to the group's humanitarian and patriotic instincts elicits a boisterous response, it's pretty clear from the questions that follow that the men are more interested in making money.

The Sausage King asks, "If we give you the money for *Ulitsa Sezam*, can you guaran-tee that the show will be produced and aired?"

The word "guarantee," even in normal circumstances, frightens me. And these Russians already don't play by Western rules. What will they do if we fail? Looking at the Sausage King, I imagine him putting us in his grinder if we can't deliver.

Leonid jumps in to answer the question, "Natasha and I are sure we can produce the series, and we promise—100 percent—that you will get a profitable return on your investment."

I glare at Leonid. Did he just say that?

We finish the presentation and Slutskyer calls for a break so that the men can discuss our proposal among themselves. I move to the side, pretending to busy myself with paperwork while Leonid plants himself on the couch next to the Sausage King. He appears to be enjoying himself over there, bonding with the businessmen. His jokes become raunchier, his tone unlike the Leonid I know. I don't like it, but maybe he's putting on an act. If so, it's working. From what I can see, the businessmen are warming to the idea of financing *Sesame Street* and investing in us.

Slutskyer claps his hands, calling the meeting back to order. He summarizes the details of the deal itself on behalf of his associates. Slutskyer explains— mostly to me—that this "gang of twelve," as he calls the group, has unlimited access to capital from the Russian government. "You don't need to worry about how we get the money. Our cash-strapped government would fail without us."

I look at Leonid, confused. I don't understand how these men have the money to invest in a children's show or why the government would be indebted to them. Leonid merely widens his eyes at me—a signal for me to drop it.

I let Leonid take over. I'm feeling unsettled. I try to reassure myself that we're doing what we're supposed to: finding Russian financing and partnerships. These men seem to be offering both. But is this just another shady deal?

Perhaps sensing my discomfort, Slutskyer assumes a conciliatory tone that also sounds a bit condescending. "Let me explain. It's elementary, Natasha." He turns to face me. "The government loans us money at low-interest rates. We then invest the money in all kinds of activities in Soviet manufacturing, such as food—" he gestures to the sausage maker "—and commodities like copper, aluminum, and oil." He places his forefinger on his chest. "When our enterprises make money, and they are making a lot of money right now, we pay back the loan and give the government additional revenue to keep the country afloat."

The Sausage King yells out, "Without us, Yeltsin wouldn't be president." The room erupts in laughter.

I ask, "How can you be sure that Yeltsin will continue to offer the same interest rate on loans?"

The guy from the sports federation leans far back in his chair. "Yeltsin will dance like a bear to any tune we sing." This elicits more raucous laughter.

Bobbing his head enthusiastically and sounding like an adolescent desperately wanting entree into the big boy club, Leonid barks, "This is a greaaate idea."

The men hash out further details, with Slutskyer summing it up, "Our group of investors will provide the money up-front to produce *Sesame Street*," he begins. "In exchange, we retain a significant percentage of the future revenue from advertising around the show. And this group will also be offered the rights to license *Sesame Street* products in the Russian market."

The businessmen propose an investment in rubles, valued at $12 million, which they can provide immediately for the *Sesame Street* project. Leonid accepts the offer in principle but notes that he will have to get approval from *Sesame Street* in New York.

The meeting is over.

Slutskyer's security detail drives us back to the hotel. I'm drained as if I'd run around Moscow's sixty-seven-mile Ring Road and grateful the driver isn't blasting the music. Everything moved so fast in the meeting. We don't even know who these men are or if they're credible investors for a children's show. I fear this deal, like the one with Berezovsky, will fall apart. Also, I worry Baxter won't like it. But Leonid looks ecstatic.

A week later, Leonid and I fly to New York to meet Baxter at *Sesame Street* headquarters. Baxter hugs us each in turn, and then introduces us to Dan Victor, a slight man with wire-rimmed glasses whom I don't recognize. He's the new general counsel of Sesame Workshop. Baxter and Dan listen as Leonid describes the meeting with Slutskyer and his associates.

I had hoped our lucrative deal would get an enthusiastic response, but the new lawyer gives us a look like we've just proposed robbing a bank. He adjusts his glasses and then elaborates his concerns about the trustworthiness of these Russians and whether they are legit businessmen or criminals.

Baxter says nothing. I wonder if a lawyer's presence is making Baxter more quiet than usual.

Focusing his gaze on Dan, Leonid says, "These are twelve of the richest and most successful businessmen in Russia. They have no reason to lie to us." His voice rises as he adds, "Besides, who *else* are you going to get to fund your puppet show?"

I shrink in my chair, sensing the meeting going south.

I look at Leonid. I know he's tired and frustrated. We've been trying to find money for *Sesame Street* for almost two years without success. But his confrontational tone is inappropriate. We're all on the same team here.

Baxter says that he and Dan will consult with the CEO and CFO about the proposal and get back to us in a few days.

As we walk back to my office, I am sure Baxter and the lawyer have decided that Leonid and I may not have enough experience navigating big international television deals or an understanding of corporate ethics. They may be correct; rules and ethics governing corporate America are as foreign to us as Russian business practices are to Baxter and his colleagues. Even so, it confounds me that Sesame Workshop wants to succeed in Russia but is unwilling to bridge the unavoidable gap between American ethics and Russian lawlessness. Leonid and I feel cheated somehow. We had worked so hard—and I'm afraid of what might happen next.

I close the door to my office and Leonid apologizes. "I just wanted to make the deal happen," he mumbles before heading off to the hotel where he's staying.

We both need a break from each other.

That night in my apartment, I binge on a pint of chocolate chip ice cream for dinner. The conversation with Baxter and the lawyer makes me question the very point of bringing *Sesame Street* to Russia. Why teach values like justice, ethics, and the rule of law if the first thing we do is partner with Russians who violate these same principles? I vow to try harder to find investors committed not just to making money but also to *Sesame Street*'s social justice goals.

Three days later, Baxter summons Leonid and me back to his office. He sits on the front edge of his desk, arms folded across his chest as he delivers the bad news. "The workshop nixed your deal."

He looks unhappy. "Your Russian businessmen seem like they're making money from speculating with government money, and it doesn't sound like good business practice."

I feel my face turn red in embarrassment. Leonid bows his head.

Baxter sighs, then begins lecturing us as though we are irresponsible adolescents. "*Sesame Street* is a legitimate institution that conducts business with reputable governments and operates according to international laws. What you're proposing is a Ponzi scheme—cooked up by a bunch of corrupt businessmen."

My heart sinks, imagining how Baxter probably got chewed out for giving us too long a leash in Moscow.

With his eyebrows raised and a slightly gentler tone, he suggests *Sesame Street* could have ended up in an international scandal.

I know he's right, but I also think the workshop should have understood the risks inherent in trying to find Russian money.

Somewhat hesitantly, I ask, "So, what Russian businesses do you know, Baxter, that operate according to international laws?"

Leonid shoots me a wary, warning look, but I keep going. "Russia has no rule of law yet, and so what do legitimate institutions actually mean in this context? I just want to understand so we can move forward."

I feel Leonid's fingers pressing into my shoulder.

Baxter looks like a cornered animal, wanting to be anywhere but dealing with us. He presses his lips together, deep in thought. And then, slowly, a faint smile forms in the corner of his mouth. "You know, I think these Russian businessmen hoodwinked you two into believing their song and dance." Then cracking a bigger smile, he says, "It's like you were taken captive and are now suffering from Stockholm Syndrome."

It's a relief to see him laughing. I know Baxter well enough to recognize that this is not a "You're fired" exchange but a pep talk. His head is likely churning with ideas as to how to convince his superiors to forgive our blunder. Baxter pats my shoulder as he walks us toward the door. "I'll see what I can do," he says.

Leonid and I leave his office, feeling like we've just dodged a bullet. Laughing nervously, Leonid admits, "I thought it was game over."

Even though we are not fired—at least not today—we still have no money, and now we aren't even sure who we are allowed to approach for funds. Either way, to celebrate our continued employment, Leonid proposes having dinner at our favorite Italian restaurant with the best penne arrabiata in the city.

At the restaurant, two bottles of Montepulciano later, our bruised egos are numbed enough to discuss the future. Leonid worries what the Sausage King might do to us once Slutskyer tells him about the busted deal.

"I dunno what we are going to do," I groan. "We may have a production team, but we're no closer to finding investors or a broadcaster than we were two years ago." I feel terrible for having drawn my good friend—my best friend—into this impossible situation.

Reaching across the table, Leonid tenderly takes my hand in his. "If you want to quit, Natasha, I'll quit."

I don't know how to respond.

Still holding my hand, he continues, "Honestly, I don't feel good about how things have gone. I mean, look at me: I'm divorced, and I don't even get to see my son because I'm always in Russia. But we've already put so much into this: all our energies, all of our connections. Just think if we could make this work, how amazing it would be for millions of children in Russia." He pauses for a moment. "But I will do whatever you want to do," he says. "Our friendship is more important than any job."

Leonid is sweet. He senses I'm reaching the end of my rope.

I confide to him that I think I might really be falling for Ken and wonder if I should be giving the relationship more of my time.

Leonid thinks for a moment, looking serious. "You know, I like Ken a lot. He's good for you. But Tasha, you're not ready to settle down yet."

I assure Leonid that this time, I may surprise him.

He pours more wine, and staring into the glass says, "You know, I'm beginning to realize maybe I should stop dating twenty-year-olds who think JFK is a fashion brand." We both laugh.

I'm glad to hear it. The women Leonid dates seem ridiculous to me. We both need soulmates, but neither of us is ready to quit *Sesame Street*. Leonid heads back to Moscow. I won't see him until after the New Year, which I will spend with Ken.

7

IRINA, THE GOLDEN GOOSE

On January 14, the last day Russians celebrate the Orthodox New Year, the phone rings in my New York apartment. On the other end of the line, Leonid shouts, "Natasha, I think we've hit the *jack-poht!*" Leonid has found a new investor who he says is the real deal. "She's loaded, really loaded," he says. "And you'll *luf* her!" His excitement grows as he tells me about Irina Borisova, the owner of Video Art, one of Russia's top ten media firms. Leonid notes with admiration that her advertising firm is known for hugely successful and innovative campaigns, adding, perhaps for me, that it's incredible for a *woman* to be running such a big company in Russia. He sounds far more fired up about Irina than any other investor we'd encountered so far. "She's a rare goose!" he yells, urging me to return to Moscow ASAP.

Moscow in February is bleak, with endless gray skies and sidewalks coated in slippery black ice—so dangerous that you imperil your life every time you step outside. But I return to the Russian capital, prepared to take my chances to meet Irina Borisova. Leonid has arranged an introduction to Irina in Midhat's office at Ostankino. It was Midhat who recommended Video Art and its owner to Leonid, and he's excited for us to learn all about her.

"Come in, sit down," Midhat encourages, getting up from his desk when he sees us and appearing pleased to be the catalyst for our gathering. Irina is already a half hour late, so Midhat brings out a bottle of vodka and three glasses. We drink while he tells us about how Irina was a leader in the Komsomol, the Communist Youth Organization. After communism collapsed, she landed a plum job organizing international cultural programs for the Russian foreign ministry.

Forty minutes later, Irina finally waltzes in atop six-inch Christian Louboutin heels and wearing a chic red cashmere coat with an oversized burgundy fox collar draped off her shoulders. The outfit is as glamorous as any celebrity's, and she has the attitude to match. She seems about my age, with perfectly coiffed, shoulder-length black hair that makes my unkempt lob look downright frumpy. She removes her dark Jackie-O sunglasses, revealing penetrating eyes, quickly trying to size me up. Midhat stands up, taking her coat and pulling out a chair for her to sit down. Leonid and I sit opposite on the couch.

"*Dusha Moya*, darling, I am so sorry for keeping you waiting," she apologizes in Russian. Her flirtatious tone is disarming. "I have heard soooo many wonderful things about you, Natasha," she gushes, taking my hand. She's an odd combination: tough as nails yet coquettish. Her instant affection takes me aback; many Russians are typically more reserved when meeting a foreigner for the first time. But Irina exudes warmth and laughs easily.

But Leonid is annoyed. He has no tolerance for lateness, and it invariably sparks a temper tantrum.

"So, do you speak English?" he asks rudely, pretending to be more Americanized than he is.

"I do," she now answers in English.

"Are you still interested in the project?" he persists, continuing to speak English.

I'm not sure what's going on here. It feels like a competition, like hissing cats circling each other.

"I am," she repeats with a playful smirk dancing on her lips. "I'm sorry for being—"

Leonid interrupts, still brewing, "Are you serious about putting two million dollars into *Ulitsa Sezam*?"

"In principle," she answers, using a common Russian expression.

Leonid explodes, "Look, if I'm going to work with you, I don't want to hear you ever use the words 'in principle.' It has to be yes or no!"

Perhaps Leonid is angling for an advantage, but his behavior is downright rude. In any case, I don't like it. Moreover, doesn't he realize that we have no alternative to Irina? The other candidates don't live up to Western ethical standards or have fled the country. I stare at him, furrowing my brow. Irina seems equally taken aback.

Irina demurely assures Leonid that she understands, and he backs off. I exhale, hoping his tirade is over.

Irina turns to me, as if Leonid's invective had never happened and says, "You have such beautiful eyes." When Irina's attention focuses on you, everything else falls away. I point to her high heels, clucking, "How stylish."

Leonid tries to interject with poignant statements about Russian *Sesame Street*'s incredible revenue potential.

Irina waves him off, making it clear she has no desire to speak with him and that she expects the men—Midhat and Leonid—to sit quietly while we women talk about more important subjects: skin treatments, weight loss, and her children—and only after that, business.

She tells me about her company's meteoric rise as though its success was totally unexpected. "I had no background in television or advertising when the Soviet Union ended. In fact, I graduated from the Moscow Aviation Institute with a degree in systems programming and earned a second degree from the State Institute of Theater Arts." Irina laughs, then goes on to explain how in the Soviet Union there was no advertising industry like in the West: "Russian television only had propaganda. And instead of selling kitchen appliances, it was socialism that was for sale." She titters, and then continues. "I quickly understood no one had any more marketing experience than I did—and I had none."

Her confidence and ambition impress me.

Irina shows us a demo reel of her company's advertising spots, and I see right away what's unique about her work. Her creative aesthetic is fresh, playful, and feminine, integrating pastel colors like powder blue, cotton candy pink, and chartreuse. Her television ads distinguish themselves from typical bold Soviet graphic designs using jagged geometric shapes and black and red block letters—colors associated with the Revolution.

Irina informs me that her company works with Video International, the second-largest advertising brokerage firm in Russia. I tell her that a few months earlier *Sesame Street*'s executives met Yuri Zapol, Video International's president, a dashing executive who'd offered to broker the broadcast of *Ulitsa Sezam*. In exchange, he'd demanded a ridiculously high fee that we couldn't afford, and then asserted that "doing business in Moscow is just like doing business with the American Mafia in Chicago, but with onion domes." I laugh, but Irina's face remains stoic; maybe the joke was too close to the truth.

Irina nods, then explains the inner workings of Russian TV advertising. Evidently, her company is one of only a few designated by Video International to broker media spots at deeply discounted rates in return for identifying new clients for Zapol's company. "As Video International's fortunes rise, so do mine," she claims. Irina seems a born entrepreneur.

Suddenly serious, she leans toward me as though sharing a secret. "Natasha, I'm not doing this for the money. I can easily sell advertising in many other ways. But I have an eight-year-old daughter, Anastasia, and I am doing this for her. Today, every self-respecting individual understands that it's time to do something for Russian children, but unfortunately, very little gets done—except talk." I nod in agreement. "Russia is changing so quickly," she continues. "It's still very violent, and a show like *Sesame Street* could model for our people how to live in a peaceful society."

Her words are music to my ears. I really like her, though I'm not convinced she has the money she claims. Nothing in Russia is ever as it seems, but for the first time in a long time, I feel hopeful that this might work.

Irina reaches for my hand. "This is so exciting to be talking to another woman about business, especially when the men are just watching." She chuckles, glancing at Leonid, who looks annoyed to be excluded from our conversation.

Midhat leans forward, placing his palm over our joined hands. Like a priest, he gives a benediction. "This could be a perfect union," he utters, shifting his warm gaze from me to Irina and back again.

When Irina rises to leave, I admire a diamond brooch on her coat lapel. "That is a stunning piece," I observe.

"Oh, that," she replies. "I bought it in London after my company made its first million."

Irina promises to be in touch. "We will see each other soon." She kisses me three times on the cheek before marching down the hallway, heels clicking, red coat flying behind.

As soon as Irina is out of sight, Leonid turns to me, nearly hyperventilating. "You didn't pay any attention to me," he whines. "And you also blew it—talking about hair and skin treatments."

This is ridiculous and I tell him so. "*Me?* Your attitude nearly ruined our chances before I even said a word."

He accuses me of not taking him or Irina seriously, which I agree is at least partially true since I have no idea if Irina Borisova is legit, and there's no way for us to find out. It would be several years before internet searches become widely accessible. For all I know, that diamond brooch is a fake.

But the next day, Video Art's finance chief calls Leonid and says, "Irina loved meeting Natasha, and the money is yours."

Video Art agrees to invest several billion rubles—matching the multimillions the U.S. government will contribute toward *Ulitsa Sezam* as soon as contracts are signed by Video Art and *Sesame Street*.

When Leonid phones me at my hotel with this news, I feel like jumping up and down on the bed. He's already contacted Baxter, setting in motion *Sesame*

Street's lawyers beginning to draft a license agreement with Video Art. More than anything, I want to believe this development is good, but only time will tell if Leonid's golden goose will lay a golden egg.

———————

The next hurdle is finding a broadcaster. And it appears we might be in luck as Leonid discovers from his journalist friends that Berezovsky is back in Moscow, seven months after the car bombing. We hadn't expected to cross paths with him again, but it turns out that he's now advising President Yeltsin, and it's rumored that the president's approved the further privatization of Ostankino TV (now renamed ORT), giving Berezovsky and his associates near monopoly control over the Russian network.

Moreover, Berezovsky's created a new advertising conglomerate called "Reclama Holding Company," which overnight united the two largest Russian advertising firms, Zapol's Video International and Sergei Lisovsky's Premier SV, giving Berezovsky an effective monopoly over television advertising on ORT and RTR, Russia's two largest television networks.

Although we expect Berezovsky's ambitions have surpassed our little puppet show, we are pleased to discover that the man Berezovsky appointed as ORT's new executive director in charge of the television network is none other than Vlad Listyev, Leonid's former journalism colleague whom we'd met at the Palace Hotel bar nearly two years before. This is an unusual appointment for the righteous thirty-eight-year-old, whom many consider above the fray of corrupt behind-the-scenes machinations of Russian television. For us, Vlad's appointment seems fortuitous, and Leonid and I hope he'll agree to broadcast *Ulitsa Sezam* on ORT.

Vlad agrees to meet Leonid and me at the reorganized ORT TV network, where he's taken over a fancy executive office on the tenth floor with an anterior room just for his secretary. When we enter, Vlad is seated behind a massive Soviet-era mahogany desk, speaking on one of the five rotary phones. He looks up and waves us in and gestures for us to sit down. He ends his call and comes around his desk, greeting us warmly. Nodding toward the ringing phones, he apologizes that he doesn't have much time.

A few days earlier, Vlad made an unexpected announcement to the press that in two months' time, on April 1, all advertising on ORT would be banned—a decision that could cause many influential people at the TV station to lose billions, including (we suspect), Berezovsky. Why Listyev would ban advertising seems puzzling, and why Berezovsky would allow it, even more so.

When Leonid congratulates Vlad on his new position, Vlad thanks him but doesn't seem especially sanguine about it. The charismatic man I'd encountered two years earlier now appears fatigued. Aware of time constraints, Leonid gets down to business—inquiring about airing our children's program.

Vlad talks quickly, "You must know that everything is now in flux at ORT." He repeats his support for *Sesame Street* but admits he's not able to commit any funds to new programs until the TV network's reorganization is complete.

I purse my lips. This seems hopeless.

Leonid asks about the advertising ban.

Vlad pauses, explaining that he has to stem the corruption at ORT, which is leaving the network without enough funds for production.

Leonid shakes his head. To me, this seems like a very dangerous game Vlad is playing with the country's advertising moguls.

Vlad stands and puts his hands on his hips as if signaling it's time for us to leave. As we gather our bags, Vlad watches us with a paradoxical expression and jokes, "I'm not sure who wants me dead more—the oligarchs or the apparatchiks."

Vlad's secretary pokes her head into the office, announcing an urgent call.

Vlad shrugs. "Look, I'll do whatever I can to help broadcast the TV series on ORT when the time comes," he promises, returning to his phones. I press my hand into Leonid's shoulder as a sign for us to go. I feel guilty bothering Vlad about airing our show at a time like this.

As we exit the office, I whisper to Leonid, "He's even braver than I first imagined."

Back again at my hotel that night, Ken calls in the middle of the night and sheepishly asks, "Did you find the surprise I put in your suitcase?"

I get out of bed and rummage through my clothes, still unpacked after a week. Sure enough, a cream-colored, rumpled envelope falls from a folded blouse and then two more. I tell Ken I'll read them after our call. We talk for another thirty minutes. As I put the receiver into its cradle, I reach for one envelope and read the first lines about his love for me and how we belong together. I ache for him. It dawns on me that I've been given one last glimmering chance at love and found someone who feels the same way, but living so far apart is straining our relationship. I finally fall asleep, comforted somewhat by the cards stacked neatly on my bedside table.

The next morning, of course, I'm back to work. So much has happened during these last two years and I cannot believe that we are finally ready to embark on actual production of the show and bring the Russians to America. I had almost resigned myself to believing that creating anything in Russia is impossible. But here we are. We have a coproduction partner. We will soon have money and I can now begin approaching independent animators and production companies from Moscow's creative community to expand *Ulitsa Sezam*'s skeleton team.

I expect our production team will chiefly rely on hundreds of Russian freelance creators rather than on employees of the state broadcaster who are steeped in antiquated methods and years of state-imposed propaganda. While I appreciate the state-TV professionals Midhat assigned to us, I'm sure to find the most innovative and creative people outside ORT. To find these independent artists, I will have to race around the city this week, visiting animation studios and independent production houses, clocking sixteen-hour days to evaluate which of these companies and individuals have the capacity, creativity, and equipment needed to make *Ulitsa Sezam* a show with high production values. It's not clear to me that such enterprising people would even be willing to work with our more conventional team at ORT. I'll have to be persuasive.

The first studio I visit is SoyuzMultfilm, located inside a dilapidated, mustard yellow, fourteenth-century Russian Orthodox church not far from ORT. Inside the nave, dozens of artists are hunched over rickety wooden tables, illuminated by dim yellow bulbs hanging on wires from the ceiling. It's like a sweatshop for animators. The director greets me, and we walk between the tables where artists are drawing forest animals, fairies, and sprites on strips of celluloid, each plastic cel representing a single frame of a film's twenty-four frames per second. The artists are so absorbed in their work that they take no notice of us.

As I move from table to table, I observe how the cartoon drawings look distinctly different from Komov's coarse puppets with their grossly exaggerated and sharp features. The Russian animators' drawings show the characters' expressive faces as soft and round, radiating tenderness and passion. The quality of the work takes my breath away. Knowing the achievements of Soviet animation, I should have expected to find such excellence, but I'd assumed without Russian government support of the animation industry, the skills would have disappeared. It's fantastic to discover I'm wrong.

I enjoy talking to the animators about their work and lives. The familiar ease I feel with these like-minded artists makes me realize how much I was missing the creative side of the production and *my* people. Since joining *Sesame Street*, I'd felt alienated from my creative roots, having spent the majority of my time talking business with media executives, oligarchs, and a few too many thugs. Now, at last thinking about working with these unbelievably talented artists from all regions of the former Soviet Union, I get goosebumps.

After decades of communist cultural domination and repression, they seem to have an unquenchable thirst for self-expression. And the quality of the designs before me is outstanding, convincing me that by uniting these independent artists with our state TV creators at ORT, I can build a first-class team. The talent is here.

That afternoon, Leonid swings by the hotel in his beat-up Lada and we head to a studio called Pilot, run by the world-famous animator Alexander Tatarsky. He's disheveled looking, with a mop of wild black curls framing his face and an intimidating intensity. He takes us on a tour of his "school," a slick operation producing Russian television commercials for many high-profile Western firms. He sees himself as a benefactor, and his animators are some of the best in the country.

"Without me," he boasts, "our traditions would be lost. I am creating opportunities for our world-class animators."

I whisper to Leonid, "I hope he's paying his animators a fraction of what he's making here."

He may have overheard me, or at least imagined what I was thinking, because he says, "With capitalism replacing communism, our artists now face the same dilemma artists face in the West: choosing to pursue one's art or make money—the eternal existential question."

I supposed that's true enough.

We tell him about our project, and he agrees to produce about ten hours of original animation for *Ulitsa Sezam*. Tatarsky's scope of work exceeds that of SoyuzMultfilm, which will produce two hours of animation for *Ulitsa Sezam*.

That evening, Irina calls me at my hotel and asks me to come to Video Art's office first thing the next day to meet Mikhail Davydov, the man she's hired to be *Ulitsa Sezam*'s co-executive producer. According to Irina, Midhat does not have time to play this role anymore and she needs her own person representing Video Art's interests in managing *Ulitsa Sezam*'s day-to-day production and finances. I don't have a problem with this. We continue talking and I tell her about the meeting Leonid and I had with Vlad Listyev at ORT. It turns out she and Vlad were former colleagues and had offices on the same floor of ORT at VID, the media company where they both worked.

The following day at Video Art, Irina introduces me to Mikhail (Misha), a large, six-foot-three man in rumpled khaki pants and a flannel shirt, who looks oversized on Irina's dainty white leather sofa.

"Misha is from Perm"—a city in Siberia—"where he used to be a prosecutor," Irina says cheerily. I'm confused; why would someone who has probably sent criminals into Soviet labor camps make a good TV producer? "He was also a racecar driver," Irina chirps.

"Auto racing in Perm is not as competitive as your American NASCAR." Misha says, cracking a grin; then he adds, "You win if your car starts."

A prosecutor? A race-car driver? I wonder what television skills he has.

When I ask, he replies tersely, "I'm like a cat. I'm only forty, but I've already lived eight lives."

Does that mean his skills are versatile and too numerous to be summarized?

Irina calls Mikhail "Misha the Bear" because he's not someone to push around. "He's perfect for the *Ulitsa Sezam* job," she beams, placing her hands on his broad shoulders. She must be referring to his imposing presence since it can't be his television experience. Despite his size, Misha seems like a pussycat.

"Misha will handle payroll, petty cash, and any *unanticipated expenses*." She declares the last two words with an odd lilt, which makes me wonder if she's talking about bribes—often a necessary part of doing business in Russia. If Irina likes him and thinks we need him, I'm okay with that. Anyway, it's good to have an executive producer who will actually supervise the ORT team at our office. Misha will start work right away.

Before leaving Moscow for a three-week trip back to New York, I stop by Midhat's office. His face lights up as I walk through his door, and we sit together on the couch. I ask his advice about managing such a large production when I can't be in Moscow all the time. I want to know if he can recommend a trustworthy senior-level Russian TV producer to be my right hand.

Midhat is quiet for several seconds, then regards me with a serious expression. "Natasha, you need to hire an American to be your eyes and ears when you are not in Moscow." Squinting, he jokingly suggests, "Every successful Russian enterprise needs a good spy. Unless someone is watching us, we Russians do not work. We've lived in a police state for seventy years and are creatures of habit."

It seems a bit of a harsh judgment on an entire country of people, but I don't argue. I carry Midhat's advice with me back to New York and set about finding a resident associate producer.

It feels good to be back in the city—walking outside, instead of being stuck inside the ORT TV station all day. Before leaving Moscow, I'd placed an advertisement in the *Moscow Times*, a popular English-language newspaper read mostly by expats, and already my voicemail is full of messages from people who want the job. One pleasant-voiced woman, Mrs. Hessman, left three messages on behalf of her daughter, Robin. She urged me to contact her daughter, who lives in Moscow and saw the advertisement in the *Moscow Times* but cannot apply herself because she has no phone in her dorm room. It's great that Robin is already in Moscow, but I think twenty-two years old is just too young for this position.

I sift through a stack of résumés and VHS cassette tapes of the candidates' portfolios, then more as they come in. Several more messages arrive from Mrs. Hessman, and it dawns on me that this determined mother advocating for her daughter reminds me of my own. My mom died of cancer in her fifties when I was twenty-seven. She would have left similar messages about me if she'd had the chance.

And so I watch the video of Robin's documentary film, *Portrait of a Boy with Dog*. The film's narrative about a Russian orphan is astoundingly accomplished for someone so young, winning an Academy Award for Best Student film. Robin's résumé is also impressive; she graduated from Brown University with a dual degree in Russian and Film, and then moved to Moscow to attend the prestigious VGIK Institute of Cinematography. She's now in her second-to-last year of study.

I call Mrs. Hessman, trying to reach Robin. It turns out that Robin happens to be in New York City, visiting family, so I invite her to *Sesame Street* headquarters for an interview.

A few days later, standing in the conference room, Robin looks even younger than I'd imagined. In a flowing black skirt down to her ankles, oversize turtleneck sweater, and black laced, mid-calf combat boots, she's got a distinctly boho look. Born in 1972, she's young enough to be a child of *Sesame Street*.

"I grew up watching the show, and I loooove *Sesame Street* and the Muppets," she gushes. Robin then launches into a tale about how she and her brother made Muppets out of paper bags and performed the different characters.

She's remarkably self-confident and comfortable with herself, so much so that five minutes into the interview, she scoots her butt on the top of the conference table and begins swinging her legs over the side. She laughs easily, her long, straight brown hair falling naturally in front of her face, and she has the warmest eyes. Not only am I impressed with her energy, curiosity, and sharp intellect; I like her at once. The fact that she's fluent in Russian is icing on the cake.

I tell Robin about my incredibly supportive mother, who reminds me of hers, and, surprising myself, I share with her that my mother died young. Robin's face morphs into the most sympathetic gaze, and I feel myself opening up to this person I've only just met. She seems wise beyond her years in ways that perhaps even *she* does not understand.

I tell her that I'd love to offer her the job right now, but *Sesame Street* will not approve the hiring of any American personnel until an agreement with a Russian coproduction partner is signed, which is expected to happen soon. I hope this precarious situation doesn't frighten Robin away. Her lilting, carefree laughter fills the room as she tells me this is her dream job.

The next morning, I approach my boss, the head of international production, and ask him to approve hiring Robin, even if part time.

He looks at her résumé. "Absolutely not. She's too young and doesn't have any experience producing *Sesame Street*, or even any television experience." I argue that a unique skill set is needed for this project, and she has it in spades.

Pressing further I say, "Robin speaks Russian fluently, she won a student Oscar, and she knows the lyrics to every *Sesame Street* song."

Not at all swayed, my boss believes the ideal person to work with me—to counter *my inexperience*—is a seasoned children's television producer. I propose that Robin is the first candidate I've met who shares overlapping skills with me and a similar aesthetic sensibility.

He says, "The Russians would eat her for lunch."

Over the next few days, I continue to spar with my boss over the candidates, with me always championing for Robin. Finally, when I push again to get my way, he calls me out for being "too strong-willed." My boss tells me I am disrespecting him and the company's chain of command. The gender politics of this comment aside, I feel misunderstood and confused. How am I supposed to run a production when I can't even hire the people I feel will be able to do the job?

———————

On the weekend, I meet up with Ken and ask his advice—hoping he can help me figure out how to navigate the delicate situation. He recommends I speak with Baxter, my boss's boss—which I do.

After bruising a few egos (not mine), Sesame Workshop allows me to hire Robin as a temporary consultant.

I feel like doing a jig. Robin and I are kindred souls, and my hope is that eventually, Robin will be hired full time as the show's resident associate producer.

But I worry about the fallout from having challenged my boss's authority.

Leonid Zagalsky, *Sesame Street*'s representative for *Ulitsa Sezam* in Moscow. *Author's collection*

Baxter Urist, *Sesame Street* Group president of products and international TV, visits the recording studio at Mosfilm in Moscow. *Author's collection*

Irina Borisova, president of Video Art, and Leonid Zagalsky, *Sesame Street*'s representative in Moscow, in the executive suite of Midhat Shilov, director of cultural programming at Ostankino TV. *Author's collection*

Alexander F. Sklyar (Sasha), lead singer of the Russian band Va-Bank, performing at a Moscow concert. *Author's collection*

PART

II

CREATING THE SHOW

People have been listening to Bach, Beethoven, and Tchaikovsky for over a century. Who do you think will be playing *Sesame Street*'s songs in a hundred years?

—Katya Komalkova, *Ulitsa Sezam* music director

8

IS *R* FOR RACHMANINOFF OR ROCK 'N' ROLL?

Three weeks after getting approval to bring Robin on board, in late February 1995, I make my way once again to Moscow to continue building our team. At ORT, Piotr Sidorenko, our creative director, wants to introduce me to Katya Komalkova, a classically trained composer he thinks would be perfect as the show's music director.

We find Katya sitting primly on the couch in Midhat's office, her hands clasped in her lap. Dressed in a long tan velvet tunic with a lace collar, she reminds me of a timid character from a Chekhov play.

Midhat kisses me, and Piotr and I greet Katya, who has a wide face with pale skin. We both plop down on the couch, forgetting the broken springs. Piotr praises Katya, telling me that she graduated from Moscow's prestigious music conservatory and has established a name for herself composing and performing. That's impressive, but I am concerned that Katya has no experience supervising music for a multi-episode TV series like *Sesame Street*. Nevertheless, I begin my pitch.

By now, I've figured out that the best approach to introducing *Sesame Street* to prospective collaborators involves showing a short, subtitled video of the American show. So, I get up and hit play on Midhat's VHS player. Johnny Cash appears, singing a song with Oscar the Grouch called "Nasty Dan." Katya reacts with a brief forced smile. I fast-forward to a few other songs with Elton John and explain that *Sesame Street* is in its twenty-seventh year of production and this season's American show focuses on the role music can play in teaching math and language skills.

When the tape is over, I turn to Katya and explain that *Ulitsa Sezam*'s music director would be responsible for developing original songs and instrumental music for all of *Ulitsa Sezam*'s new Russian segments. I sit back on the couch (more carefully this time) and wait for a response.

We sit in awkward silence, until Katya finally clears her throat and says, "I am sure you know that the classical music tradition in our country is world renowned," making clear her preference for classical music for *Ulitsa Sezam*.

"Of course," I say; then I ask, "But you'd consider adding in other musical influences for *Ulitsa Sezam*, right?"

Katya looks away, then toward me again. "This is a difficult question that always arises when societies are changing. Even our great poets disagreed over the oft-repeated expression, 'Let us throw Pushkin, Dostoevsky, Tolstoy . . . overboard from the ship of Modernity.'" She smiles ever so slightly, adding "I prefer art that has passed the test of time."

I look to Midhat for support. He's got an impish smile on his face and seems to be enjoying our exchange but will not interfere.

Pressing on, I talk about how *Sesame Street*'s strength is foremost its music—introducing children to diverse and innovative artists like Tom Waits, Marvin Gaye, and John Cage, *in addition* to classical composers.

Katya stares blankly at me, as though these Western artists are unfamiliar to her.

I try to conceal my frustration, asking, "So, you feel that Russia's *Sesame Street* show should feature *no* contemporary music?"

Katya questions what will remain of *Sesame Street*'s music in a hundred years.

Katya's disapproval extends not only to rock music but to *all* contemporary beats: jazz, hip-hop, rap, punk, and heavy metal, all of which I imagine she considers corrupting sounds capable of spoiling Russian children's appreciation of classical melodies.

Piotr nods, as though in agreement with Katya, and says, "So, it's good? Katya can work with us?"

We desperately need a music director to travel to America for training in six weeks, and until there's a signed coproduction contract between *Sesame Street* and Video Art, we don't have money to pay salaries in Moscow. If Katya, like the others, is willing to volunteer her time working on *Ulitsa Sezam* in exchange for deferred compensation and a trip to the United States, then we are in no position to turn her down.

"Ye-e-es," I say, shaking Katya's hand. Piotr says he'll arrange for her to become a formal member of our team, whatever that means.

A few days later, Piotr introduces me to Vika Lukina, a talented animator who runs her own firm. She becomes our new director of animation, agreeing to the same terms as the others.

Over the next week, at our ORT office, I badger Katya, sliding my Walkman headset over her ears so she can listen to my favorite Russian rock artists— always hoping to persuade her to include modern music in *Ulitsa Sezam*'s repertoire.

She's polite, but after the third time, daintily lifts the headset from her ears. "This music is not pleasant," she says, holding the plastic device in front of her at arm's length, as though it might contaminate her musical sensibilities. "And anyway, people shouldn't listen to music on these things," she adds with disapproval.

I try explaining that it's not that I think contemporary music is superior to classical music; I just want *Ulitsa Sezam*'s music to be as groundbreaking and entertaining as the music is in the American show.

She considers this. "Of course," she says. But will she listen to even one more song I suggest? No, she will not.

That night, I get a drink at the hotel bar, feeling bad about how things are going with Katya. I wonder if maybe I am pressuring her to hire contemporary Russian music artists out of some feeling of obligation to living creators. When I first came to Russia in the early 1980s as a student at Leningrad State University, I fell in with a crowd of underground rock musicians, doing what twenty-two-year-olds do: drinking, smoking pot, and going to concerts.

But in Soviet Russia, rock concerts were illegal.

Since the days of the Beatles, the Rolling Stones, and Jim Morrison, the Soviet Ministry of Culture had outlawed rock music as "decadent, bourgeois, and incompatible with the aims of socialism." Essentially, the state wanted to crush Russian artists whose music aesthetic did not conform to communist cultural ideals. My Leningrad friends were barred from performing in public or recording their music in state-run studios. Unable to support themselves from selling their music on vinyl or CDs, they made audio cassettes in secret and sold them on the black market.

Sometimes, they'd organize illegal concerts, which the KGB routinely broke up, forcibly dispersing the crowds.

Katya's views are in alignment with Soviet state views that rock music is somehow "polluting." She seems oblivious to the obstacles many contemporary musicians faced in Soviet times. I care about these music artists. In some respects, my entire career up to today could be linked to my relationships with these musicians, which had moved me to tell their stories in a short film about underground Russian rock 'n' roll. *Rock Around the Kremlin* aired in 1985 on ABC's popular *20/20* show. Maybe this is why, in part, I am resisting Katya's wholesale rejection of them.

The following day, I seek out my friend Sasha Sklyar, a now-famous Moscow music artist and the lead singer of the band Va-Bank, asking him to have lunch. Sasha traded in a cushy career as a Soviet diplomat in North Korea to pursue his life's rock 'n' roll dream. I have known him since my mid-twenties. While I was working in Moscow as an intern at the CBS News bureau, I'd often attend his concerts. They were electrifying. He would feverishly smoke three packs of *papirosi*—high-tar, acrid-smelling Soviet cigarettes—to make his voice sound gravelly like his idol, Tom Waits, and sing about love, political freedom, and Russia's past. He offered young people cultural catharsis and a fresh, original sound, blending Russian folk ballads and military hymns with Western rock influences and themes. He had a lot of adoring fans, including me.

Full disclosure: I once had an enormous crush on him.

Back then, after his concerts, Sasha would often walk me home, even though fraternization with foreigners was not allowed at the time. Arriving at the complex for foreign residents where I lived, he'd hand his passport to the KGB officer standing out front and wait as his information was recorded into a notebook. I was concerned that something terrible might happen to Sasha as a result, but he was unafraid.

"The KGB is only trying to intimidate people," he'd say. "It's all *bool-shit*." We'd stay awake throughout the night, talking about music, books, and God. We had no idea that with Glasnost in the 1980s and greater artistic freedom, Sasha's band would become a heavy metal sensation, selling out concerts with fifty thousand followers. I am determined to attract contemporary Russian musical talent to our children's show. And despite how Katya feels, Sasha is the perfect person to ask for help.

I arrange to meet Sasha at the Penta Hotel, a garish glass monstrosity known for its sumptuous lunch buffet. We haven't seen each other for three years, but he looks exactly the same. His rocker lifestyle may have weathered his face a bit, but his body is youthful and taut. Again, I swoon.

After a hug, we start teasing each other, just like old times. I ask if turning thirty has possibly made him reconsider his wardrobe. He laughs because he's sporting a black leather motorcycle jacket and black leather pants painted onto his muscular thighs—the same look as when we'd first met.

Sasha smokes three cigarettes and drinks two cups of coffee, ignoring my entreaties to take something—my treat—from the hotel's lunch buffet.

We catch up, and then I describe my project and my problems with Katya.

"It's not right that she's excluding contemporary musicians from our show," I venture. Not giving him a chance to answer, I emphasize, "They should be given a shot at creating songs for *Ulitsa Sezam*."

I expect him to jump in and agree with me. But Sasha is oddly quiet.

"You know, Tasha, you are kind of being unfair to Katya," he says somewhat coolly. I press my lips together. Sasha can always be counted on for no boolshit. "You have to consider where people are coming from." He pauses, then adds, "Someone like Katya with a privileged classical music background hates a lot of the changes happening in Russia today—especially all the scary people like me with my guitar and an earring." He flicks his bejeweled earlobe with his finger while faux-growling.

I laugh weakly, though grateful for Sasha's honesty.

"Do you expect Katya to throw out everything she holds near and dear?" he continues gently. "She's doesn't want change, and it sounds like you're trying to force her."

I think "force" is a bit harsh, but I will myself to listen and say nothing.

"Russia is internationally celebrated for its classical music," he goes on. "I'm sure Katya wants *Ulitsa Sezam* to showcase our country's musical strengths."

He's right of course, and so damned wise.

"We've entered a new era in Russia," he says. "Everything is being reinvented, including music. All we had during the Soviet era was political music—mostly propaganda, and *Estrada* (pop music). Now we have an opportunity to create something exciting and new. That scares a lot of people."

I don't want to ask, but I have to. Sasha reads my mind and offers to speak privately with Katya.

At the ORT office the next day, I'm sitting beside Robin, who is working part-time with the production group while continuing her studies at VGIK. The ORT production team embraced her right off the bat as a kindred spirit, not only because she's attending Moscow's most prestigious film school but also because of her Student Oscar award. Robin also tries to make progress with Katya. I overhear her telling Katya, "*Ulitsa Sezam* must appeal to both Russian parents in their twenties *and* preschool-age children." She implores, "The parents are the age of my friends and me, who grew up loving the Beatles and underground Russian rock music. Their tastes in music are not the same as yours, and we want our show to be popular with them and their kids."

Katya respects Robin but remains firm in her beliefs, refusing to invite any contemporary Russian composers to join our team. Robin signals me with her eyes, and we head to the women's bathroom—a fifteen-minute walk from our office—for a private chat.

Robin says, "I really like Katya but she's the oldest thirty-something I've ever met."

At my hotel, I receive a fax from the Jim Henson Company, reminding me that we are running out of time to design the Russian-style Muppets. "Their design will take at least four to six months, minimum," reads the fax. "You must bring the Russian team's sketched concepts to New York ASAP."

That afternoon, I again broach the subject of the Muppets with my creative colleagues. Gathering the four producers at Midhat's office—this time without Kolya Komov and his angry Petrushka puppet—I try a new tactic. I speak of the challenges *Sesame Street* faced when the show first premiered in 1969.

"American viewers were slow to accept the Henson-style soft, furry menagerie because they didn't resemble or move like most American puppets," I explain. "But over time American audiences grew to love the characters and *Sesame Street* became the most successful children's television program in America *because* of the Muppets."

My plea does little to mollify these puppet purists, especially Lida. She stands up and turns her back. Addressing her colleagues, she says, "We don't need the Americans to produce this show. Let's do it ourselves, with our own puppets."

The others look uncomfortable. I suggest that we table the discussion for now, which seems to satisfy everyone—even Lida.

A few weeks earlier while in New York, I'd hired Anna Connolly as an associate producer along with a Russian translator to support the Moscow production from New York. They had prepared and faxed sample Excel budgets to Moscow for the Russians to use as templates to formulate their own budgets and schedules for *Ulitsa Sezam*—the first step in creating any TV show. In my absence from Moscow, I'd expected the Russian team to create spreadsheets using the computers and software already set up in the office at ORT.

But this afternoon, I discover my team has been using the backsides of Anna's faxes as scrap paper because of the paper shortage in Moscow. Even worse, they failed to prepare a single budget or schedule for me to review.

Sergei, the live-action director, looks at me with a bored expression. "Natasha, it's foolish to make a plan for any production in Russia. There's no point because anything can happen." Sadly, he's right: a camera could break, the actors could arrive drunk. There could be a coup.

Increasingly exasperated with me, Lida adds, "Natasha, it's ridiculous to predict how long a production will take in Russia." And Piotr says, "It's best to avoid delays by never writing anything down; that way you'll never know if there are delays or not."

They may have a point, but this group is scheduled to arrive in New York City for training at *Sesame Street* headquarters, where my American colleagues are expecting to review their production schedules and provide useful feedback, I explain, with a pinched expression.

Misha confirms what I fear most: no one knows how to use Excel, and almost all of these seasoned television producers are using computers for the first time.

I'm annoyed that I'm only learning this now. I'd put the computers in the office weeks ago. But I assure the group we can quickly remedy the problem with training.

But when I use the Russian word *trenerovanie* (training), I can tell from their responses that this is not the correct Russian word for what I have in mind. *Isledovanie* relates chiefly to medical training and *trenerovanie* to sports training, but, oddly enough, there's no word in the Russian lexicon for employee training, and the concept is alien to most Russians.

Lida accuses me of treating them like seals.

"We are not animals in a zoo," she says defiantly.

"Of course not," I sigh.

I try to help them understand that the adaptation of *Sesame Street* is vastly more complicated than anything they have ever produced in Moscow. Even in Soviet times, the most extensive multi-episode television series consisted of only twelve episodes. That production, "Seventeen Moments of Spring," took four years to produce! I explain that as a team, all of us will need training. We're producing the first mixed-medium, multi-episode children's television show *ever* in Russia. "It's like we're doing a moonshot," I exclaim.

Deadpan, Misha says, "Well, the Russians were the first into space."

Everyone laughs, including me.

At dusk, Misha invites me for tea at his apartment. He and I will be working closely for the next sixteen months, and it'll be good to get to know each other better.

We drive in Misha's car to his studio apartment, which is tiny. Stepping over the half-folded futon bed, he jokes about how he and his wife have to climb over the furniture to get to the bathroom. "It's tricky when the bed is pulled out at night and it's dark; sometimes it's a struggle to get to the toilet in time."

I laugh, trying to hide my shock at such living conditions.

I'm even more surprised when something on the floor starts buzzing.

"What's the fax machine doing here?" I ask, confused.

Misha explains that he had moved it from our office to his apartment so that when messages come in overnight, he could answer them right away. "Also, it's safer here." He shrugs matter-of-factly. "The television station isn't secure— someone's always trying to take it."

I feel guilty, imagining how the noise must wake the couple every time we fax documents from America when it is the middle of the night in Moscow. Misha's dedication to the production touches me.

We drink tea while Misha regales me with stories of his time in Japan. He points to a photo on the wall of himself dressed in an XXX-Large kimono, towering over three Japanese businessmen in dark suits.

"I did not take off my kimono for three months," he recounts. "I ate, drank, slept, and traded metals in it."

I wasn't aware that in addition to his credentials as a prosecutor, race car driver, and now television producer, that he also engaged in metals trading in Asia.

Later that night, on my way back to my hotel by taxi, it's snowing and pitch black. The government has halved the budget for lighting streetlamps in Moscow. The taxi passes sheared-off monuments with only their granite bases remaining. On such a dark night, the city looks depressing and war torn. My mind turns to how much of Russia's identity is being stripped away at break-neck speed. The endless philosophical arguments over music, the Muppets, and the production process itself may be a response to this rapid change. Maybe I'm imagining it, but each conversation I have with my Russian colleagues feels tinged with wounded pride. A desperation to preserve the country's history and identity is making it difficult for them to embrace the creation of something new.

But when I get to the office the following day, Katya informs me that she's agreed to meet with Sasha Sklyar at a nearby café in the afternoon. Perhaps she's doing it just to shut me up because she seems no less doubtful about his raucous music and how it cannot benefit Russian children. But I notice something else. A few hours before her scheduled meeting with Sasha, Katya seems nervous. She looks paler than usual and flustered. I'm certain she's never been in the same room with someone like Sasha.

"Do you want me to go with you?" I ask.

"Oh, no, no, I'll be fine," she says, as though trying to convince herself.

Two hours later, it's clear that I should not have worried. A beaming Katya returns to our office from the meeting. "You know, Natasha, he's nothing like what I thought he'd be," she declares. "He knows so much about music."

I'm relieved. Sasha came through, just as I'd suspected he would. Somehow, perhaps using the diplomatic skills he'd developed in North Korea, he's converted Katya to the other side.

"We spoke about our children, who are about the same age," Katya tells me, far more effusive than usual. "You know he studied classical piano before he played the guitar?"

Throughout the week, Katya can be heard quoting Sasha as though he's her newfound musical oracle. "He says rock music doesn't have to be tough and that he can develop a musical language that is as relatable to children as classical music." This marks the beginning of a metamorphosis that will cause Katya to entirely revamp her approach to *Ulitsa Sezam*'s music.

She invites contemporary musicians from all over the city to submit compositions, creating opportunities for established artists like Sasha and younger, unknown musicians who have never experienced the kind of creative freedom found at *Ulitsa Sezam*. I watch these funky, long-haired artists streaming into our temporary office, and sometimes, playing their songs on guitars, spilling into the corridor. The atmosphere is intoxicating, and our production draws a lot of attention from ORT employees from neighboring offices. Katya becomes a champion of all musical genres from classical to Russian rock, punk, jazz, and even heavy metal. And the melodies and lyrics of the new music submissions are extraordinarily playful, including original parodies of Russian poetry, folk ballads, and Soviet hymns.

Robin and I are dumbfounded but ecstatic.

One songwriter uses the melody of a famous Russian love song, "*Ochi Chernye*" ("Black Eyes"), while changing the words to a hilarious ode to *kasha* (Russian porridge). In another tune, a composer takes a recognizable patriotic Soviet hymn about "world peace," rhyming the word "peace" with the name of a yogurt drink. Without understanding Russian, it's impossible to grasp the absurdity and humor of these verses poking fun at the Soviet way of life, but it works.

The songwriters catch on quickly, learning how to write lyrics that will appeal to both children and adults. So, while youngsters might be clapping their hands to a catchy song glorifying oat cereal, their parents will appreciate the musical parody—*Sesame Street*–style musical comedy at its best.

Still some musicians have trouble writing short, snappy lines. We try to help by screening American television commercials with famously catchy jingles. One such commercial advertising hotdogs, "I Wish I Were an Oscar Meyer Weiner," catches their attention.

After hearing the jingle only once, the Russian songwriters can't stop reciting it around the office.

Laughter and singing fill our days as artists drop off their songs for review. When the final mix of the first five songs is done, the team's excitement is explosive. Even though we are working out of a cramped temporary space, the team members are becoming friends and the production is humming along nicely.

The following afternoon, Katya shows up at our office with a cassette tape of Sasha Sklyar's first recorded song for *Ulitsa Sezam*. She pops the tape into the player, and his bouncy chord progression fills the room. I'd been at my desk, but I stop working, as do others in the office until we are all gathered around the tape player, listening to "*Ruki Pomoi*" ("Washing Hands").

The song has a catchy melody, and the vocals include an upbeat chorus, "*Rump-Bum-Bum-Bum . . . Ruki Pomoi.*" I'm astonished to hear Sasha's recognizable deep bass voice belting out such cheerful, light lyrics: "After washing one hand, don't forget the other one," he croons sweetly.

Robin starts singing along, waving her arms like a conductor, directing us all to sing. Laughing and blushing like a teenager attending her first rock concert, Katya initially resists but eventually joins in. As we belt out Sasha's lyrics in unison, air-washing our hands on the chorus, I feel sure that *Ulitsa Sezam* will be a hit—if we can ever get the show on the air. We still need to find a broadcaster.

Katya is justifiably pleased with herself. And when Robin tells her, "Sasha's song is as good as the best of any songs on *Sesame Street*," she confidently responds, "Well, I'm not that surprised because Sasha told me he has a small son and just imagined that he was singing to him."

The next day, I'm still at my hotel at midday. I'd stayed up late reviewing budgets and reading the latest scripts and am still reading them now. Robin stops by and excitedly tells me that she may have found a producer to help us dub the fifteen to twenty hours of live action and animation video clips from the American *Sesame Street* library.

I'm delighted, because I desperately need a broader range of *Sesame Street* clips to introduce the American show to potential collaborators. Leonid and I have been using the subtitled videos, but we prefer the clips be dubbed. I'm hopeful that when my ORT producing team sees these hilarious *Sesame Street* clips dubbed in their language, they will be more accepting of the Henson-style Muppets.

For quite some time I'd been anxious about finding a producer with voice-over experience. Larissa Chernova, the producer Robin tracked down, was the longtime former director of the prestigious Gorky Film Studio, responsible for dubbing nearly all foreign films imported to Russia between 1930 and the 1960s.

I arrange to meet Larissa late one evening at her tiny one-room apartment in central Moscow. At seventy years old she is beautiful, her white hair pulled back in a neat bun. But I see she was always beautiful. She walks over to a scarred and dented piano and picks up a picture frame with a faded black-and-white photograph of her younger self. She's standing in front of a spanking new German editing machine, dressed in a *halat* (a quarter-length white smock with a matching cap typical of Soviet film technicians). In the bottom corner of the photo, "1950" is scrawled. It's a stunning photo, and it's only a little bit eerie that she has kept the same hairstyle.

"Doing voice-overs was my life's passion," she shares, gazing at the photo with nostalgia.

With a clipped, formal intonation, Larissa uses a more sophisticated Russian vocabulary than I'm used to. "You may not be aware," she explains softly, enunciating each word and stretching out her vowels in a singsong pattern, "that synchronized dubbing, where different actors recite the voiceover for each character, has not been done in Russia since the 1960s."

She tells me that today's foreign films are dubbed by a single announcer reading the dialogue for all the characters in the same monotone voice, without any effort to differentiate characters.

She glances again at the photo, seeming to want to jump into the frame and return to the past. "It's a travesty that studios have reduced the quality of performance in this way."

She sets the frame on the piano and sits on the green velvet couch. "The single-voice narration of today doesn't allow the audience to truly *feel* the actors' emotions." When she utters "feel," she emotes with her entire body. "Instead, the annoying narrator's voice interrupts the emotions onscreen, and audiences are left feeling empty." She makes a sad mime face.

It takes little to convince Larissa to help with the dubbing of the American show segments. She offers to assemble her old team from Gorki Studios and audition actors to dub the voices of Bert, Ernie, Elmo, and Cookie Monster. Her energy is remarkable. This lovely woman is a testament to a lost generation of talented artists.

———————

Two days later, Leonid, Robin, and I meet Larissa and her two voice-over actors at ORT's front entrance. We must sneak into the recording studio late at night; it's the only time when the edit rooms are free. As foreigners, Robin and I must get a new stamped pass each time we enter the TV station. Leonid hands cartons of Marlboro cigarettes to the two sleepy uniformed guards at the entrance to smooth our entry, and we're in that easily.

Inside the recording studio, Larissa directs the editor to cue up the first *Sesame Street* clip. Bert and Ernie, dressed in their matching pajamas, lay on twin beds, unable to fall asleep. Before dubbing the clips, we must come up with Russian names for Bert and Ernie that coincide with the Latin letters "B" and "E" that appear on the foot posts of their beds. After throwing around names that don't sound at all Russian, Robin suggests that Ernie become *Enik* and Bert *Vlad*. (In Russian, the Cyrillic letter *B* sounds like *V*.) All of us agree. (Later, Bert's name is changed from *Vlad* to *Vlas*.)

Larissa is fond of stories. We learn that the man who did the monotone narrations for most of Russia's bootleg foreign films held his nose while recording the dialogue—"so he could protect his true identity." She smiles mischievously. "His nasal voice kept him from being arrested." I wonder if this is true.

A perfectionist, Larissa directs the two actors standing in front of microphones in the recording booth. "Watch the next American clip again and note how perfectly the actors' dialogue is in sync with the movement of the puppets' mouths."

Larissa replays the audio through the speakers in the edit room, and we all watch the episode of Ernie sitting in his bathtub, his orange body buck naked as he plays with his yellow rubber Duckie while singing the famous "Rubber Duckie" song.

Suddenly Leonid jumps out of his seat, grabs me, and we start waltzing furiously around the studio. Everything stops as Larissa, Robin, and the actors enjoy the scene of these crazy producers dancing to "Rubber Duckie."

The actors then voice-over the lyrics in Russian. When the editor plays back the new dubbed recording with Vlas and Enik on the screen, speaking Russian, it's pure magic. Two American icons have been reborn as Russian Muppets.

9

JUST WHEN YOU THINK IT CAN'T GET ANY WORSE

The editing session lasted late into the night, and Leonid and I get a late start the following morning, missing breakfast or any chance to read the news. Traffic on the road leading to the television station is slower than usual. It's March 2, 1995, so not a holiday. As we approach ORT, we see a large crowd gathered, facing off with police.

"It looks like some kind of demonstration," I remark, confused.

As we draw nearer, we hear shouting and one protestor yells at the police, "You are to blame!" Others nearby are huddled together. Some look as though they are crying.

Leonid stops and jumps out of his car. He grabs a stranger, demanding to know what has happened. Through the car window, I watch as Leonid listens—then grips his head in his hands.

Exiting the car, I rush over to him. He's so upset, he can barely describe what has happened, but I soon understand that Vlad Listyev, the towering newsman who was made the head of ORT last month, has been murdered. I can't believe it—this charismatic, courageous man can't possibly be gone.

"He was assassinated in cold blood—the bastards," Leonid moans, inhaling deeply between sentences. "They shot him in the entryway of his apartment building as he was returning home after taping his show," he adds angrily.

I feel sick, recalling our conversation only three weeks earlier when Vlad had committed to helping us broadcast *Sesame Street*.

Leonid and I return to the car and park in the lot. We then shove past the crowd, battling our way into the building. Inside, employees fill the hallways, wailing and expressing outrage that this brave man had been cut down in his prime. For many Russians, the assassination of Listyev—who'd appeared several nights a week on TV screens in their living room, fighting for a free and uncorrupt Russia—crushes their hopes that anything can change.

Days after the horrific murder, rumors spread about who was responsible. Many blame powerful media moguls like Berezovsky, who would have lost millions if Listyev's moratorium on advertising had gone through on April 1 as planned. No one knows for sure why he was killed, but we do know it was an execution, not a robbery or a random killing. All of Vlad's valuables, including a large amount of cash, were left untouched on his body.

I haven't been able to reach Ken all day. Finally, at one in the morning, he calls my hotel room. As soon as I hear his voice, I start crying, telling him about Vlad. "He was so young, and he has children," I moan. "He wasn't afraid to stick out his neck to help us." I tell Ken Vlad's death is a huge blow to *Sesame Street*. "Everyone at ORT is frightened now," I whisper.

"What about you?" he asks worriedly. "Are you still going to ORT every day? Are you safe?" Ken hadn't worried about me in the past and his concern now makes the violence feel closer somehow.

I describe how any semblance of order is breaking down—on the streets, in the city, and at the TV station.

"And it's not just media moguls like Listyev who are getting shot; everyone's feeling vulnerable." A sob escapes from my lips.

Ken is silent, then asks, "Do you think the communists could come back to power—I mean, through popular elections?"

"Yes, it's possible," I say, sounding deflated.

I tell Ken about Gennadi Zyuganov, the Communist Party candidate running for president of Russia who has been gaining support throughout the country.

"It's getting harder for me to appear positive in front of my team when I feel like everything is falling apart," I say. "I doubt anyone at ORT will take a risk on anything new, and especially not on an American show."

Ken consoles me. "I'm so sorry, love. You've given so much to this production. I know Russia's insane, but you have to believe the show will be all right in the long run."

His words help me realize I've grown to need his comforting.

I don't want to hang up, but I mumble, "I have to go." I know I need sleep. Tomorrow will be another tough day.

When I arrive at the TV station early the next morning, a crowd is still gathered. The day before, no programming aired at all, and instead the network showed a screen with the words: "VLAD LISTYEV IS DEAD." I don't know if national programming has resumed today. I navigate past the crowd in front of the building and into the lobby, where employees are still walking around dazed, holding each other, and some crying.

Misha is already at the office when I arrive. He proposes closing the office for a short period of mourning. I agree. We'll resume in two days' time. Meanwhile, I fly to New York, feeling more dejected than ever.

—————

I rarely make the monthly International Production Group (IPG) department meetings at the workshop because I'm in Moscow. But this time, I'll be there, and I have no choice but to tell my coworkers the news about Listyev.

I listen as the other producers make their presentations about their mostly untroubled productions in Europe. With every new report on how well things are going, I feel increasingly nervous. When my turn to speak finally comes, I deliver the shocking news. The room goes suddenly quiet. The head of international production sighs wearily, as though he expected something like this would happen. "This production is so ill-conceived that, should it go south, the reputational damage to the workshop and the *Sesame* brand could be catastrophic," he says.

I glare at him, feeling the heat rising in my cheeks. I had hoped to elicit his sympathy, not his reproach. Since the day he hired me, he's harped on the incredible risks of operating in Russia, a perspective that is shared by others at the workshop.

He must realize that it's absurd to go into Russia in the first place without expecting to face enormous risk. But he has the power to shut us down.

"We shouldn't give up on the Russians in their hour of need," I plead.

My colleagues eye each other across the conference table and look from my boss to me.

"The team in Moscow is making tremendous personal sacrifices," I say. "They're as committed to *Sesame Street* as you all are."

My colleagues shift in their seats. They fully understand the numerous challenges involved in working overseas but do not relish witnessing a showdown.

My boss is not a pushover. He's confident in his convictions and shoots back, "As I've said before, I think realistically we should revert to doing *Open Sesame*, which requires a much smaller amount of original production."

Folding my arms across my chest, I hold my ground, insisting that Congress earmarked funding for a full coproduction of *Sesame Street*, with training and a majority of content produced in Moscow—not a production that is mostly dubbed from the American show.

Abruptly, my boss pushes his chair back, stands up, and announces he has to attend another meeting and will have to speak with Baxter about this issue later. He then excuses himself, leaving me to deliver the rest of my report to the others.

After the meeting, Cooper Wright, the executive producer of *Sesame Street* in South Africa, hangs back to speak with me. She's a friend and the only other woman producer in our department.

"You know, Tasha, I understand what you're going through in Russia. I have the same situation with *Takalani Sesame* [*Sesame Street* in South Africa] where the post-apartheid television station is in the throes of change. Just like Russia, I have no idea who are the right people to talk to and who I can depend on."

She walks me out of the conference room, her arm around my shoulders, trying to comfort me. "Everything will be okay," she says. Cooper has been a producer at the workshop much longer than I have and her success in navigating disagreements with my boss gives me confidence that I can get through this period. Tilting her head and smiling, she adds, "After all, Natasha, we are on the right side of history."

That afternoon, the phone in my office rings. It's Ken, who's returned from Frankfurt, Germany, where he had presented an academic paper at the Bundesbank. My words spill forth, full of emotion, as I tell him what's going on. He urges me to take a break and come to Princeton Junction—one hour from the city—for the weekend, an invitation he's made many times.

Up until now, I've begged off visiting Ken's home. And he's made it easy by coming into the city and letting me pretend our relationship is more casual and carefree than it is. But now, as the train leaves Manhattan behind, racing past exploding cherry blossoms and lovely houses with big yards and white picket fences, I feel comforted by the idea of temporarily abandoning my anarchic life in Moscow to be with Ken in these bucolic surroundings. I catch myself fantasizing about marrying Ken, moving to this blissful place, even (Gahd!) starting a family.

I spot him on the platform as the train rolls into the station, smoothing down the tufts of hair on his head against the blowing wind. When he sees me, his face lights up and he waves.

I don't realize how tired I am until that evening. Ken has prepared a beautiful meal, but I'm almost too exhausted to eat. Ken understands.

On a long walk the following day I bend Ken's ear talking about my work. I lament to him how embarrassingly naive I must have sounded to my workshop colleagues—pleading to save my production. So often, I feel at odds with Sesame Workshop's risk-averse culture. Ken gently offers a different perspective, suggesting that my boss is just doing his job—rationally weighing the risks and deciding how best to proceed. In my gut, it doesn't feel right to abandon our Russian ship so soon. But Ken's sympathy for my boss helps me take a step back and acknowledge the corporate politics at play. Although I don't agree with everything Ken says, he does give me one particularly excellent piece of advice—proposing that I ask to change my reporting structure so that I can report directly to Baxter instead of the VP of international production.

By the time Sunday night arrives, I feel rested and have a plan. On Monday morning I arrive at work and head straight for Baxter's office. I love that his door is literally always open. He waves me inside, asking, "What's up?

Baxter hates confrontation, and I want more than anything else to please him, but the situation with my boss is unsustainable and I argue my case.

He listens but I can sense his guard is up. He's often blocked previous efforts to scale back the scope of the Russian production—but when he hears my proposal that I directly report to him, he defends my current boss, commending him for consistently working in the best interests of the company.

"But he's obstructing me at every turn," I plead.

Baxter and I both know I'm indispensable to this production, especially now, when we are about to host the Russian team for training at *Sesame Street*. He promises to see what he can do.

Two days later, Baxter calls me back to his office. As of now, I'm to report directly to him. I'm so relieved I throw my arms around him. He takes a step back, laughing. "You aren't going to make me regret this, right?"

I can tell he's not entirely comfortable with his decision, and I feel bad about going over my now-former boss's head, but I also don't feel as if I had a choice.

———————

I feel invigorated by my new freedom and that the Russia team will soon be arriving in America. I'm also excited that Leonid will soon fly to New York. He will meet with Baxter and *Sesame Street*'s lawyers to discuss alternate broadcasters to ORT.

———————

When Leonid arrives at the workshop a week later, he comes to my office, and before his rendezvous with Baxter I fill him in on details about the upcoming training session. He seems more focused on making sure he gets some R&R away from Moscow and asks, "What are we going to do on the weekend?"

He invites Ken and me to join him at Rasputin's, a Brooklyn nightclub popular with Russian immigrants, prostitutes, and flashy mobsters. An American journalist friend of Leonid's picked the place because she's writing a story about the Russian criminal infiltration of the American Mafia for the *Washington Post*. The reporter believes Rasputin's attracts the crowd she's writing about, and, for some reason, she believes Leonid has valuable information.

We arrive at the Brighton Beach club on Saturday night. A striking young hostess in a shiny gold lame halter top and black leather miniskirt glances at the reservations book and shoots us an irritated look—most likely because we are an hour late for our reserved dinner seating.

She swishes her hips like a metronome as we follow her long, lean, fish-net-stockinged legs perched on stiletto heels into the restaurant and to our table. Thrusting her chin and looking at us with disdain, she says with a thick Russian accent as if commanding a dog, "You—sit."

The reporter is waiting for us at the table. The first three courses of appetizers—fried pork dumplings, oily cabbage soup, and cold blini with mountains of caviar stacked, one on top of the other, on large white platters—are dried and crusty.

Ken looks at the platters, confused. "Why would the waiters serve all the courses at once?"

"It's just like in Russia: if you pay for something, then it's yours, whether you want it or not," Leonid chuckles. "That's Russian capitalism," he says with a wink.

Ken forces himself to smile, but he wears a stunned expression as he takes in the gaudy red velvet curtains and oversize gold chairs. He sees the four bottles of Stolichnaya Vodka that the waiters had left on our table—one bottle per person—and whispers to me, "Remember I don't drink much." I make a sad face and insist that tonight will be different. He can't refuse.

Foraging beneath the plates, I find four shot glasses and pour.

"*Na Zdorov'ye*," I toast, laughing.

Suddenly the lights dim. On an elevated stage opposite the dining tables, a chorus line of muscular blond men in matching pinstripe suits and white fedoras begin singing and dancing wildly to "The Jet Song," the raucous number from *West Side Story*.

Next is a drag queen with big hair and bigger breasts who kicks her legs in the air while lip-syncing Marlene Dietrich's "The Boys in the Backroom." None of the dancers sing well, but the audience adores them.

Leonid's reporter asks me about my experiences with the Russian Mafia.

I explain, "We have no idea who in Moscow is Mafia and who is not. It's hard to tell the difference, really." I turn my attention to Ken, who, seemingly uncomfortable with the topic of conversation, quietly kicks back a couple of shots.

I joke with Leonid that my boyfriend might not survive the night.

We don't leave the club until three in the morning. Back at the apartment, Ken is so drunk that he can barely take off his shoes. To my surprise, he's deliriously silly, completely unlike his sober self. I try to put him to bed, but he keeps standing up, insisting he has an important question to ask.

Slurring his speech, he looks squarely at my face with his bloodshot puppy-dog eyes and says, "Natasha, will you marry me?"

I burst out laughing because I think he's kidding around.

I pull him playfully onto the bed. "Trust me, you do not want to marry me!" I say more emphatically than I feel.

He grabs both of my hands, declaring his love. Realizing he is entirely serious, I embrace him, surprised at how terror and elation can inhabit my body at the same time.

He holds me closer, promising he will make me happy.

My eyes start tearing. "I want to make you happy too," I softly mumble, reaching for him. I feel exhausted and a little nauseated from the alcohol. "We should go to sleep," I whisper, promising to give him an answer in the morning.

This seems to satisfy him, and he passes out.

I stay awake much of the night, imagining how my life would change if I married Ken. I love him, but how would it work? Ken also travels a lot for work. Would I be able to continue filming overseas? How would we take care of kids, if we decided to have kids? We haven't talked about any of this, and I didn't expect a marriage proposal, *especially* not after a night at Rasputin's! We've been dating less than a year, and I've been overseas for a good portion of it. I tell myself that by morning, he won't remember even broaching the subject. Just as dawn approaches, I finally fall asleep.

I wake to sunlight streaming through the window and open my eyes to see Ken, fully dressed in a suit and tie, standing over the bed, lightly touching my hair. He's got an early flight to Washington, DC, where he'll be presenting his latest research at a Federal Reserve conference.

"I have to go." Ken seems unaffected by last night's drinking. "But I want to know your answer, my love," he says, looking down at me with the most tender of expressions.

Now I'm fully awake, and I realize his drunken proposal wasn't a dream.

I rub my eyes. Still standing, he says, "Sweetie, I know you imagine I'll constrain your freedom, but you don't need to feel that way at all. You will have incredible freedom *and* all my love forever."

I scrunch down under the covers and playfully ask, "Would you mind getting down one knee and asking me again? I'd love a proper, sober proposal, please."

As confident today as he was last night, Ken smiles and drops to one knee. I can see only the top of his balding head peeking above the comforter when he asks again.

This time I say yes.

Ken falls onto the bed in a mock swoon. "I guess I'll have to get used to constantly feeling disoriented, because that's how everything is with you."

I smile, knowing it's going to get a lot more disorienting when Ken comes back to New York to meet my Russian colleagues who are arriving from Moscow in two days.

10

BOOT CAMP WITH SERGEANT ELMO

After a long flight on Aeroflot, Russia's national airline, eight members of my Russian team, accompanied by Robin, emerge from customs at JFK airport, looking a bit worse for wear but thrilled to be in the Big Apple.

Except for glamorous Irina Borisova, this is everyone's first time visiting America. The Soviet government had strictly regulated international travel, not permitting average Russian citizens to travel to capitalist countries. Since the collapse of communism, foreign travel is slowly becoming easier.

Once outside, the group is startled by April's warm temperatures compared to Moscow. The van is too small to fit everyone, so Irina takes a separate car that we'd arranged. The rest of us pile into a van, and there erupts some grumbling about Irina's having flown first class while the rest of the team flew in economy steerage.

"How is it possible that this rich lady can afford to fly first class but isn't able to pay our salaries?" Lida mutters under her breath. "And it's not right that Irina hired a private car, so she wouldn't have to ride in the van with all of us."

I tell them that I'd arranged the separate car for logistical reasons and remind them that Irina Borisova paid for their plane tickets (the first production expense she's paid for so far).

As the van careens down the Van Wyck Expressway, one of the producers exclaims, "Look at this road! It's gorgeous." I have to laugh; most New Yorkers would hardly call the Van Wyck gorgeous.

Manhattan's Oz-like skyline comes into view as we cross the Fifty-Ninth Street Bridge. All the complaining about Irina stops at once. My passengers gape at the barges cruising down the East River and the spire of the Empire State Building in the distance.

"*Hoo-pah!*" Midhat shouts, ceremoniously opening a bottle of vodka brought from Moscow. He pours shots into the plastic cups he'd stolen from the flight attendants' cart on the plane and, spilling some on himself, passes them around the van. Dr. Anna Genina, the director of research for *Ulitsa Sezam*, and Katya flatly refuse, while Robin argues with Midhat to put away the bottle.

Raising his cup, Midhat says, "*To Amerika—di land of di free and the braayve.*"

As the van moves through midtown, Dr. Genina, ever the stickler for rules, taps the driver on his shoulder and gestures toward the backseat.

The driver indifferently mumbles, "No alcohol in a moving vehicle."

Dr. Genina translates, looking triumphant.

Midhat knocks back another shot and screws up his face in an apology to the driver while raising the bottle, showing him that you can't put the cap back on a Russian bottle—its design makes that impossible.

Bumping along in the van with my entire team, speaking Russian in the middle of Manhattan, feels surreal. For me, it's like we're a Russian version of a 1960s sitcom, *The Beverly Hillbillies*, with Midhat as Jed. I stare at them in disbelief, their faces framed against the backdrop of *my* city, *my* home.

The sightseeing is interrupted by quiet sobbing from the van's back row. Everyone turns toward Katya, who swivels her face toward the window, trying to hide her tears. Dr. Genina, the group's mother hen, tries to offer comfort, but the kindness only makes Katya wail even louder. Through sobs, she explains that she's never been separated from Masha, her four-year-old daughter, not even for one night, and she misses her little girl.

But the sights on Madison Avenue seem to quiet Katya as she stares in awe at couture fashions in shop windows and fancy apartment buildings with uniformed doormen. Everyone is oohing and aahing as we inch forward in heavy traffic. Having been told all their lives that life in the Soviet Union is better than the decaying West, the group appears to be in collective shock.

The van drops them off at a hotel on the Upper West Side, where they'll be staying for the week. When they find out that they each have their own room, an unexpected luxury, their mouths drop.

The following morning, the Russians arrive bright and early at *Sesame Street* headquarters on Sixty-Fourth Street—except for Irina. She will be meeting instead with *Sesame Street*'s legal and financial executives, with Leonid, to discuss *Ulitsa Sezam*'s coproduction agreement. The contract is *still* not signed.

The weeklong training workshop will feature a conga-line of veteran *Sesame Street* professionals, in addition to Ed Christie, the Henson Company's supervisor for Muppet character design and collaboration with *Sesame Street*'s international coproductions. I'm not sure who's more excited: the Russians or my American colleagues.

Jet-lagged but enthusiastic, the Russian producers take their seats around an oblong conference table on the fourth floor. I want my now close friend, Arlene Sherman, *Sesame Street*'s senior producer, to speak first because her experience with the day-to-day supervision of the American show's studio production and creation of live-action and animated films is vital.

"Animation should only be used when an artist wants to achieve something that cannot be done in real life," she begins, as an interpreter translates her words for our Russian guests.

She shows the group an example on a large TV monitor. In the video clip, a cartoon boy stands at a bathroom sink brushing his teeth. As the water from the bathroom faucet runs, the sink fills, and the screen becomes a split image. The new pane shows a fish in a pond next to the boy's house. As the bathroom sink fills in one frame, the pond drains in the adjacent panel, and the fish realizes that his life is in danger. The fish then picks up a telephone beside the pond and calls the boy. "Please turn off the faucet," he begs. When the boy hears the fish's pleas to conserve water, he dutifully turns off the faucet. Water immediately flows back into the pond, and the fish happily swims away.

It's a lesson in conservation, and most of the Russians like the segment—except Lida.

"This would never work in Russia," she smugly objects. "We are not rich, like you Americans, and our children don't have telephones in their bathrooms."

Arlene doesn't miss a beat. "Well, in America, our fish don't have telephones in their ponds." Laughter ripples through the room, and even Katya chuckles heartily. Lida turns bright red.

The Russian team responds to Arlene's passion and generosity. When she's done, they give her a boisterous round of applause, unusual for Russians.

But not everything goes easily. Although grateful for the opportunity to come to New York, the producers seem uneasy. *Sesame Street* may be new to them, but they have decades of film and television experience. As forthright and helpful as my American colleagues are speaking about children's television, the Russians don't like being lectured on how to educate Russian children. They feel it's humiliating. Lida expresses what perhaps many in the group are feeling: "We know we have a lot to learn, but we know best what our children and our country need."

I admire her for speaking up.

Despite some moments of cultural insensitivity, I also see sparks of camaraderie. During coffee breaks, the Russians ask their new colleagues about America's school system, health care, and cost of apartments in New York. In return, they offer tales of life in Russia.

But mostly, we work for hours, inside the windowless conference room, where even lunch is brought in. We move glacially through *Sesame Street*'s bible, a fifty-page translated handbook outlining every step of doing an international coproduction.

Sergei, the live-action director, asks, somewhat irritated, "Are we going to have to take these two kilos of paper back to Moscow?" "Yes," I say as we plow on. I'm concerned that if they don't absorb this information now, it will be much more difficult when we're back in Moscow. The only parts of the training they seem to find faintly pleasurable are the coffee breaks.

By late afternoon, we've hit a wall. The Russians are saturated. They want to get outside and explore the lauded wonders of New York City. I stop the session an hour early and, once they've scattered, go to my office to get some work done.

Leonid, who'd been in a meeting down the hall in Baxter's office, pushes open my door and warns, "Natasha, you have to change the dinner location." I'd booked a lovely Italian restaurant where it's hard to get a reservation. "Why?" I ask.

Leonid rolls his eyes. "The group will be insulted if you take them to a place that serves only noodles."

Apparently, pasta isn't a real meal.

"Only poor people eat noodles," Leonid adds. "Find a steakhouse, Natasha."

Thanks to Leonid, dinner is a success. The team relaxes, thrilled by the quality and size of the meat cuts. Leonid presides over the table, regaling the group with funny stories about his life in California when he first arrived. I'm grateful for his irrepressible energy after such an exhausting day.

By the time dessert is served, we realize Midhat has disappeared. During the first two courses, he fidgeted in his chair, complaining that he was not allowed to smoke. "How can you Americans be so uncivilized, depriving your own citizens the pleasure of smoking in public places?"

Thirty minutes pass, and I'm starting to worry. I race outside, zigzagging up and down Columbus Avenue, yelling his name. Leonid joins me, but we have no luck. After forty minutes, I'm panicking at having lost a Russian national in Manhattan.

Leonid returns to the restaurant, collects the group, and accompanies them back to the hotel. I continue circling a one-mile radius, figuring Midhat could not have made it that far—unless he took a cab, which is possible because we gave him a per-diem in American dollars.

From a phone booth on the street, I call the restaurant again. They tell me a man appearing to match my description is sitting on the bench outside the establishment. I run the twelve blocks back to the restaurant arriving in a sweat.

Midhat is seated next to the maître d' sipping scotch. He holds up his glass, nodding approvingly. "*Khoroshiy Scot-ch*" ["Good scotch"], he says. He looks entirely at home, as though he's been sitting on this bench, drinking tumblers of malt for decades. But I can't be angry. He's too lovable.

Walking back to the hotel, I ask where he'd gone.

"I went for a little walk."

It's late now, and the city has quieted down. We walk in silence for a while as Midhat takes drags from his cigarette. "People here seem so free," he observes with some sadness. "Everyone looks happy. Even beggars walk around with silly smiles on their faces. They crack jokes when they ask for money."

He inhales, then stubs out his cigarette butt. Several minutes later, as Midhat regards a window display, he pauses. "I wonder what I might have accomplished as a young man if the choices in my country had been greater." I don't know what to say. "Maybe I would have been a clothing designer," he adds, puffing himself up and pulling on the lapel of his white suit. I smile and slide my arm around his back, and squeeze. He murmurs, his voice cracking slightly, "Natulya, I hope you realize how lucky you are that you grew up here."

I think about my grandpa Nathan. If the tsarist government hadn't chased him out of Belorussia in the early 1900s for being Jewish, I wouldn't be an American.

We reach Lincoln Center just as the New York City Ballet is letting out. Elegantly dressed New Yorkers spill onto the grand plaza, congregating around the fountain. Their faces are illuminated by the shimmering lit columns of frothy water shooting into the dark sky. Midhat and I pause to watch the crowd. They do look happy.

I feel lucky—fortunate to have been born in America.

On day two of boot camp, Michael Lohman, *Sesame Street*'s executive producer, introduces the Russian team to the process of designing new puppet characters. My hope is that Lohman will put an end to the Russian team's pesky opposition to the Henson-style Muppets and inspire them to adopt a similar process when developing their own Muppet roster for *Ulitsa Sezam*.

Lohman breaks down the process the American writers and producers recently used to develop the physical and personality characteristics for the newest female *Sesame Street* Muppet character, Zoe. He explains that *Sesame Street* is a bit of a "boys club," where most of the puppeteers and Muppet characters are male. But he says this is changing. The original sketches for Zoe, we learn, didn't have any typical "girlish" features—no big eyelashes, no jewelry, no cute pink barrettes—because the American writers, especially female script-writers, didn't want to perpetuate gender stereotypes.

As the Russian team listens with rapt attention, Lohman describes how the American show's researchers tested the original Zoe sketches with children. The results showed that the little girls in the focus group preferred the drawings where Zoe wore cute hair bows and jewelry and played with dolls. So much for the writers' attempts to counter female stereotypes.

The Russian team seems to enjoy hearing about how educational research influenced the creative process. The final Zoe, Lohman reveals, wears a purple and red hair clip and a necklace.

At our midmorning break, Lohman sidles up to me and asks to meet the executive in charge from Russian television. I fumble, making excuses for Midhat, who for some reason did not show up this morning. I have no idea where he is, and I'm angry that he's skipping the training, especially after taking off last night without telling me.

At eleven o'clock, Lohman resumes his presentation, and suddenly Midhat appears, standing outside the glass wall of the conference room dressed in a freshly pressed, cream-colored linen suit and a Panama hat, and waving.

I gesture to the empty chair next to me and give him a warning look *to get inside now.*

Midhat comically slinks into the conference room, imitating a prowler step-ping lightly. He squats beside me, and stage-whispers in Russian, "I have to go to Atlantic City *now.*"

I glance up at Lohman, who pauses his presentation at the interruption.

Grabbing Midhat's arm, I pull him outside into the hallway.

He stammers, "Leonid is taking me in a taxi to the casinos."

"No, he's not," I say. Leonid has said nothing about this to me, and anyway, none of the Russians are allowed to cross state lines.

I march Midhat to my office and have him wait while I call Leonid's hotel room.

After several rings, Leonid answers, "Allo," he says groggily.

"Are you still in bed?" I ask.

Leonid starts complaining about how badly he feels after a late-night drinking session with Midhat. Apparently, after I'd dropped off Midhat at the hotel last night, they did more nocturnal drinking until the wee hours of the morning. Leonid makes excuses. "Midhat had jet lag," Leonid says, "What was I supposed to do?"

Yelling into the phone, I unleash a flurry of epithets, some in English, some in Russian.

"Midhat *can't* go to New Jersey. His visa won't allow him to leave New York State!"

Seated at their cubicle desks outside my office, my American colleagues gape at me.

Meanwhile, Leonid is silent.

"Hello? Leonid? Are you still there?" I ask.

"Are you crazy, Natasha? he says finally. "Do you really expect Russians to come to New York and *not* go to Atlantic City?"

"Midhat is not fucking allowed to cross state lines!"

"But Natasha—"

I hang up.

Midhat is the titular head of the Russian team, and I have relied on his wise counsel throughout the production. He often helps usher the production over critical stumbling blocks; however, he's not essential to moving forward. If he wants to get drunk and gamble, I doubt there's anything I can do about it. But Leonid's sabotaging of our workshop by aiding and abetting Midhat is infuriating.

Several hours later, long after the day's session is over, Leonid and Midhat return from New Jersey to the hotel, apparently a few hundred dollars richer.

Leonid phones me that night at my apartment to apologize. "I'm sorry," he says. "But this is Midhat's first time in America, and he's like a father to me. You know, Natasha I couldn't say no when asked to go." I hear him drag on his cigarette. "Friendship is a twenty-four-hour concept."

Although fuming inside, I also understand that Russian friendship means never saying no.

———————

On day three of the training, I've arranged a delayed start at one in the afternoon, giving the Russian team the morning to be tourists and shop, and allowing me to invite Irina, Midhat, Robin, and Leonid for brunch at my new apartment. I'd finally saved enough money from working at *Sesame Street* for two years to move from the apartment Leonid called my "rat hole" to a one-bedroom on the Upper West Side with my boyfriend—I mean fiancé.

While I set out coasters and napkins on a coffee table to prepare for the brunch, Ken washes the dishes I had left in the sink. I look at him feeling tenderness and anxiety at the prospect of my two worlds colliding: Planet-New York, and Planet-Moscow. For most of our nine-month relationship, Ken has been deeply curious and perhaps even slightly suspicious of my other life, five thousand miles away. Although apart for weeks, we trust each other. Still, I sometimes catch him looking at me as though he's questioning how exactly it's all going to work. I guess I'm a little worried too.

The sound of the doorbell catches my attention.

I'm grateful Leonid's arrived first. He walks through the door and Ken holds out his hand. Ignoring it, Leonid pulls him forward into an awkward embrace, then heads to the kitchen to see what food will be served.

Robin arrives, and I sit her on the couch next to Ken so they can get to know each other. Leonid waves to Robin from the kitchen, where he's "taste testing" the food to make sure I'm not "poisoning anyone."

A few moments later, the phone rings. It's Midhat telling us that he will be an hour late, blaming his hangover left over from "got-damn-ed Atlantic City." It seems he's picked up some colorful new English words.

Irina arrives with a bouquet too large for any vase I own. She looks stunning in what appears to be a new red Chanel suit with white fringe. Enjoying the attention, she gives us a twirl and giggles. I've never seen her so happy. New shoes, new bag, new makeup. She must have spent the last two days shopping. I introduce her to Ken.

When I tell her we're engaged, she screams, does a dance on her high heels, and hugs me tightly. "He has to come to Moscow before the wedding," she insists. "For my birthday next month in May. That is the perfect time in Moscow." She tilts her chin up, and steps closer to Ken, putting her arm in his. "So it's decided then, we will see you for my celebration."

Ken looks at me a little desperately but I can only reply, "Well, love, Irina Borisova always gets her way."

He doesn't seem averse to the idea. And maybe it will be the right time for him to cross through the looking glass into my mad Moscow world and see how and why I'd spent most of the past decade in Russia.

Forty minutes later, the doorbell rings, and Midhat walks in, wrapping his arms around Ken's torso. Seven inches shorter than Ken, Midhat cups the back of Ken's head and kisses him three times, alternating cheeks. I had already told Midhat about the engagement.

I enjoy seeing Ken *way* out of his comfort zone, a feeling he surely hates but wears well. Everyone is speaking only Russian.

"*Nakonetsto, Ken-chic!* [Finally, Little Ken!] Congratulations," Midhat says. He scans the coffee table, his face lighting up at the steaming coffee, fresh lox, bagels, and croissants laid out on a Russian lace tablecloth, and then, just as quickly, his expression changes to disappointment.

"Natulya, don't you have anything stronger to drink than coffee?" he chides me for being a lousy hostess.

I reach for a bottle of scotch from the built-in oak liquor cabinet and pour drinks for all of us, including Ken, who holds the glass out in front of his chest, the way you might a rare object.

My Russian friends are so intense. I worry Ken is overwhelmed as they bombard him with questions, including why he never visited Russia during his chess career. By the time my guests leave, the bottle of scotch is empty and Ken, who has barely sipped his drink, looks like he needs one.

That afternoon, the team (except for Irina and Leonid) gathers for a meeting with Dr. Valeria Lovelace, the director of research and a longtime veteran of *Sesame Street*. Valeria is African American, in her midthirties, and holds a PhD in social psychology. She encourages multiculturalism and has made it her life's goal to ensure that children's television portrays positive images of people of color.

The Russians file into Valeria's office, where the only seats available are Lilliputian chairs for preschoolers. The Russians perch on them hilariously and uncomfortably.

Valeria speaks animatedly about the historic racism African Americans have faced and *Sesame Street*'s efforts in battling racism on television and in the real world. "Four years ago, in response to rising racial unrest in the U.S. in 1989, we launched a race relations curriculum designed to model racial harmony," she explains. "We did this after conducting a study where children of many races were asked to play a game in which they drew their concept of a neighborhood. The results showed white children significantly segregated African American children when drawing homes, schools, playgrounds, and churches. To try to counter this racism, *Sesame Street* showed white children visiting the homes of their African American friends."

I'd hoped my Russian colleagues would take Valeria's talk to heart, relating it to racial discrimination in their own country, but the Russians look at each other, confused. To my horror, I overhear Lida whispering to her husband, the creative director, "Doesn't she know we don't have any blacks in Russia?"

This is actually untrue; many African black students from Soviet satellite countries come to study at Moscow's famous Lumumba University. And Paul Robeson, the well-known African American actor/singer and self-declared communist, often spent time in Moscow and was a vocal critic of American black exploitation. I imagined the Russian team members would be familiar with Robeson and other black American socialists who viewed Soviet Russia as a beacon of freedom.

The Soviet Union had always positioned itself as a country free of racism and black exploitation. Images of American social injustice—white police officers beating African American citizens—filled Soviet newspapers and television to demonstrate the superiority of socialism. In reality, Russia's relationship with minorities has always been complicated. Soviet society included more than 120 distinct ethnic groups. And even now in the 1990s, some Russians use the word *chernie* (black) as a derogatory slur to describe people of color from former Soviet republics such as Azerbaijan, Chechnya, and Tajikistan. Ukrainians and Armenians are generally spared this slur, perhaps because some Russians do not consider them distinct nations, even though each has its own long history, culture, and language.

Valeria speaks for thirty minutes, and I wait for an opportunity to discuss how *Ulitsa Sezam* could potentially address discrimination against minorities in their own country, including Jews. In Soviet Russia, anti-Semitism was common and Jewish people were considered a distinct ethnic group. The word "Jew" was stamped on their passports.

Valeria is called out of the room for a few minutes, and the Russians begin talking among themselves.

A debate erupts regarding what to do about the vast number of clips from the American show with African American child actors. Lida contends, "When selecting segments to dub for our show, we will have to eliminate any video clips with American *chernie* [black] children. Russian audiences will not accept seeing such children on *Ulitsa Sezam*."

I cringe. The idea of excluding segments based on race is horrifying.

Fortunately, not all my Russian colleagues agree with Lida.

This painful conversation makes me realize how much work I have ahead of me. I must convince every member of our team not only to be more inclusive, but also to have a genuine change of heart. I want them to *choose* to include segments with African American, Latino, and Asian children *and* to create new segments with children representing various nationalities from their own former republics.

Valeria returns and concludes her talk.

It dawns on me that rather than bridging the gap between our cultures, Valeria's talk on American racism may have inadvertently widened it, with the Russians barely recognizing how the discussion relates to their own country.

There's a break for lunch, after which everyone will head to a preschool in Harlem to participate in a research testing session that Valeria arranged. The Russian team will see the research process firsthand and take part in evaluating the appeal and educational efficacy of several *Sesame Street* segments.

At a nearby café, the Russian team continues the conversation about race over lunch, debating whether *Ulitsa Sezam*'s lead roles should feature exclusively ethnically Russian actors.

Lida argues, "Including minorities in *Ulitsa Sezam* just to model racial harmony is as bad and hypocritical as the communists pretending our nationalities all get along."

Some of her colleagues continue to object, insisting, "It's even more important now to show different nationalities living together in peace."

I am keenly aware how *Ulitsa Sezam* could show children of all nationalities playing together in an effort to foster peace at a time when former Soviet republics are being torn apart by ethnic strife as they fight for their independence from Russia. The debate is postponed as we move on to our next event, the research session in Harlem.

I fear the trip may be a disaster.

Due to a logistical mix-up, instead of a van, two shiny black stretch limousines pull up outside the entrance to *Sesame Street* headquarters. Valeria looks horrified. The Russians, who've only seen luxury vehicles like this in movies, can't believe their luck and pile inside, along with Robin and the two American translators accompanying us. I watch as they stroke the leather seats admiringly, taking turns pressing the button to make the glass partition move up and down. As the limo takes off, they open all the cabinets and drawers, marveling at the complimentary liquor, water bottles, and candy.

Valeria's assistants hand out pink T-shirts with the words, "Sesame Street Research." The Russians slide these over their heads, now a part of the American research team.

As the chauffeur crosses the park and cruises uptown, along Madison Avenue, the Russians press their faces against the windows looking at the high-end stores. But as we drive further uptown, Vika comments that the faces in the crowds have changed from white to various shades of brown and black. The contrast between parts of the city visibly disturbs the group. Vika points out the homeless people sleeping on the street, shaking her head in disbelief.

They stare wide-eyed at the poverty often described in the Soviet press but never seen up close. For once, they're silent. Russia also has a homeless problem, of course, but until recently, their government denied homelessness even existed. The image didn't fit with its myth of social equality. But I shift uncomfortably in my seat, embarrassed by the conditions in my own country.

The limo stops in front of the preschool, a two-story brick building surrounded by a chain-link fence. The school's director stands out front, astonished to see our mode of transportation.

Valeria and I hop out of the car first, earnestly trying to apologize and explain the mix-up. Meanwhile, our guests, completely unfazed, jump out of the vehicles and start snapping photos of themselves with their Soviet cameras—against the backdrop of limousines and the chain-link fence.

Inside the school, fifteen adorable, pint-sized preschoolers are waiting for us. Everyone is excited. For most of the Russian producers, the sight of an entire group of dark-skinned children is a novel experience, and for me, seeing the Russians in Harlem is just as strange.

Each Russian producer is paired with a child—a buddy system of sorts. As they pair up, the kids lead their Russian to round tables with two tiny chairs. They begin playing with Play-Doh and Mr. Potato Head, both of which are entirely new to the Russians. The adult visitors giggle in delight, putting Mr. Potato Head's feet where his ears go, waiting for the children to yell, "No, not like that!" The language of laughter appears to be universal as the Russians horse around with their buddies, leaving the translators to stand by idly.

Getting the group's attention, the American researchers begin by asking if the children can recognize the letter B and whether they can write the letter. They record the children's answers. Then the researchers set up a video camera to film the children and a monitor on which they will show the children several new *Sesame Street* clips, including one teaching the letter B.

After the children view the video clips, the researchers, including the Russians, interview their assigned child through a translator, asking the child what they understood from watching the video clips. The Russians are astounded that, after viewing the segments, many of the children have learned the letter B. Moreover, the children who recognize the letter can also write it and recite several words beginning with the letter B.

From the expressions on my colleagues' faces, I can tell our excursion has exceeded their expectations. Even the usually subdued Sergei cannot stop grinning and patting the cornrows of "his" little girl as she hugs him. A playful, competitive debate breaks out over whose child has a better understanding of the letter B. Sergei lifts his child in the air as she squeals in delight.

Finally, my Russian team is having fun.

When it comes time for us to leave, the adults and the children alike take silly photographs, embracing each other so tightly that I fear we will have tears when we depart—and I don't mean the children. As the limousine pulls away from the preschool, I notice Sergei looking out the window with a wistful expression. He waves to his child partner until she's out of sight.

I hope the experience convinces my colleagues of *Sesame Street*'s potential to educate children of all colors—in America and Russia. I give the team the rest of the afternoon off to sightsee or shop. Meanwhile, I book a reservation for them to have dinner in my favorite part of New York City, Greenwich Village, and then plan to introduce them to their first taste of classic Irish Guinness at McSorley's pub.

That evening, I'm waiting at the Columbus Circle subway station entrance when I catch sight of my Russian colleagues confidently darting across the busy city street, adroitly navigating buses, bike messengers, and taxi drivers—laughing all the while, like genuine New Yorkers. America is no longer intimidating to them.

We gather together and I buy train tickets for everyone. The group is shocked by the cost of public transport—at least five times higher than what they pay for state-subsidized transportation in Moscow.

As the subway rumbles and squeaks through the tunnels, one of the producers asks, "Why is it that America's roads are so great, but the subway is terrible?"

Once again, I'm embarrassed. Compared to Moscow's metro system—with its impeccably clean and ornately decorated stations with marble walls, mosaics, stained glass, and chandeliers, and trains that run on time—the New York subway is a dump. Over the din of the car, I say, "I *dunno*, every New Yorker asks the same question."

The train lurches, finally stopping at West Fourth Street, and we all pile out. As we spill onto the street, a group of African American teenagers in black-sock caps and low-slung jeans begin loudly shouting at us from about thirty feet away. The Russians look confused, and I must too.

Within seconds, our group is overtaken. "Hey, Yo! Yo!" one young man yells, coming nearer. One of the young men points at the back of my black leather jacket. "Yo, Bert and Ernie, all right, my main man!" He grins ear to ear.

My mouth falls open, and I start laughing. I had completely forgotten about the giant orange and yellow Bert and Ernie faces embossed on the back of my bomber jacket, a gift from *Sesame Street*. The Russians are astonished to see these grown men giggling and slapping each other while sharing their favorite Bert and Ernie episodes with us, with me translating.

Running into the group is serendipity. As much as the group has been immersing themselves in the folklore of *Sesame Street* for several months, until this moment, they hadn't fully understood the affection *Sesame Street* evokes in Americans or the show's prominence in the pantheon of American culture.

Before we head off, my teammates and the young men take turns shaking hands and some venture an embrace. This random encounter also shows my team the colossal appeal of the Muppets and seems to convince them of the potential reach *Ulitsa Sezam*'s Muppets could have in Russia. For the first time, I sense we all want the same thing—for *Ulitsa Sezam* to steal the hearts of Russian children the same way it stole the hearts of the young men we encountered. As we walk through the narrow streets in the Village, I realize how thoroughly this trip to America has changed my team's views about race, the Muppets, and *Sesame Street* in general. They'll be returning to Moscow in three days as very changed individuals.

I don't arrive back in Moscow until two weeks later, on May 1—International Worker's Solidarity Day. Today, the holiday is less about worker solidarity than about enjoying three days off from work, basking in the warmer temperatures now that the sun stays longer in the sky. Heading into the city, many streets are blocked off for the oncoming parade as families, carrying balloons and Russian flags, stream into the city in the direction of the Kremlin.

But for *Ulitsa Sezam*, there's no break. Spring and summer are our critical seasons; we must complete the bulk of live-action filming while the weather is decent. I check into the Palace Hotel and discover that Vika Lukina, the show's animation director, has left a note with the concierge, asking to meet me first thing in the morning.

The morning after the holiday, I get up early to meet Vika in the hotel restaurant. Robin arrived even earlier so we could go over everything that's happened in my absence. She begins grumbling about how the head writer has been exercising dictatorial control over the scriptwriting process. She also reports the Russian team's continued aversion to adopting Henson-style puppets for their show, despite the positive views they'd expressed while in New York. Immediately, the group's obstinance makes me feel like Napoleon—unable to extricate himself from Russia's muddy bog.

Robin leaves before Vika arrives, fuming. The hotel security guard at the entrance had taken her for a prostitute and tried to stop her from entering the premises. I want to laugh, but it isn't funny and it happens all the time to single women when they walk into these new fancy Moscow hotels. It's offensive.

While catching her breath, Vika takes a seat at my table, and I apologize for not meeting her at the entrance. I gesture toward the lavish buffet of hard-to-get fresh fruits—pineapples, pomegranates, and kiwi—and ask if she'd like anything to eat. "No," she responds, pouring herself coffee.

I feel awkward stuffing my face when Vika isn't eating. I explain to Vika that it's impossible to find food as a vegetarian, and I don't get a chance to eat all day. "Breakfast is my only meal until I get back to the hotel late at night."

Vika nods. She knows how difficult things are right now with food in Moscow, also for herbivores.

"I want to thank you for meeting me," she opens. "I love *Sesame Street*, and I believe *Ulitsa Sezam* can become a huge hit in Russia—but not with the production team we have."

For quite a while, I've sensed tension between Vika and the ORT producers. Vika owns her own company and is incredibly entrepreneurial compared to the rest of the team. She's had opportunities to make money that the other producers, who are state employees, have not.

Vika tells me she's upset because some team members are not showing her the respect she deserves. She feels they resent her and are dismissing every suggestion she makes.

I stop eating. "Please, tell me more."

Vika sits straighter in her chair and gently suggests that the way I'm going about convincing the Russian team to include the Muppets in *Ulitsa Sezam* is all wrong. "You Americans ignore a fundamental truth about us: that this Soviet socialist way of life is the only life we have ever known. Changing our system offers the promise of something better, but for many, change is frightening. My coworkers, like me, grew up under communism, and we all want our TV show to re-create the warm memories that we have from childhood, but also to introduce something new. Most Russians don't know what that new thing is."

She continues, "The team needs to understand that *Ulitsa Sezam* can help our children become less afraid of change. We need to show children how to take the initiative and try something different—on their own, as I did," she ends proudly.

Vika offers to speak with the producers about how the *Sesame Street* Muppets could be this new thing. I agree and thank her.

The next day at our ORT office, I ask the team to stop working and have the writers leave for an hour to allow for a private discussion. Once they've gone, I encourage the team to show Vika the respect she deserves—the same respect they should be giving to all the freelance artists who do not come from recognized state TV and film circles. I emphasize how important it is to welcome the newcomers who will be joining our team in greater numbers.

I then turn the floor over to Vika.

She begins confidently. "When we visited New York, I bought a whole bunch of different American toys for my eight-year-old daughter to play with, including two Muppet dolls. When I got home, my daughter played with all the toys, but she took Elmo and Big Bird to bed with her every night, and she continues to do so." Vika goes on, "There's something magical about the American Muppets, something uniquely appealing that our children have never seen. Don't we want this for our children? We have a chance to create something wonderful and new so our children can experience a wider world than we did."

Vika's story about her daughter strikes a chord, and the producers vaguely agree to try to develop Henson-style puppets for the show, but based on Russian aesthetics.

Could the Muppet blockade finally be lifted? If so, I feel like getting down on my hands and knees and kissing Vika's feet! In an hour, she's achieved what was impossible for me for months.

But the following weeks are long and arduous as we work toward developing sketches of the Russian Muppets. I try implementing some of the brainstorming strategies Michael Lohman had recommended to the team when they were in New York.

I gather the producing team in a conference room at ORT TV and show some video clips of *Sesame Street*'s other international Muppets. I then set up a wooden easel, attaching a large white pad to the front with a clip. In the center, I draw a line creating two columns: one for character and physical traits of the American *Sesame Street* Muppets, and the other for the characteristics my team would most like to see for their own Russian Muppets. After the video is over, I invite the group to come up and write their character preferences for their Muppets on the pad.

Based on the preferences listed in the right-hand column, the Russian team appears to want their Muppet to be a wise, benevolent human-looking older man who lives in the forest, inside a tree. Their inspiration for this character is *Domovoi*, a six-hundred-year-old spirit from Russian folklore whose omnipotent knowledge allows him to protect hearth and home.

One of the writers, a talented artist, begins drawing rough sketches of Domovoi at once, depicting him as a gray-haired old man with flashing eyes who looks a bit like *Ded Moroz* (the Slavic Father Frost). One of the producers suggests adding a skullcap to the drawing, making the old man resemble a religious figure. Another suggests giving him a traditional Russian quilted felt jacket and felt boots. As the writer-artist fills in more details, the drawing of the puppet looks more humanoid than Muppet-oid. It also doesn't look like any Muppet I've seen in the Henson menagerie. And his personality, as the Russians describe it, more closely resembles an omnipotent authority figure than a playful child.

"Wouldn't it be more entertaining to have a puppet who is the same age as our young audience?" I say, gently. "A character who does not know *everything* already and more like a four-year-old who makes mistakes? And isn't so . . . um . . . scary-looking?"

I explain that young viewers typically identify with the Muppet characters because they are like children themselves—with oversized child-like heads, big eyes, and endless curiosity, making discoveries and learning.

Lida barks back, "It is ridiculous to expect children to learn from children in a children's show. Learning is *not* a discovery process. It's information to be heard and absorbed."

Oh, God.

There's some more debate, but in general, the team is content with their design of Domovoi. I agree to submit their drawings to Ed at the Jim Henson Company, although I wish we had something better. Unfortunately, we've no time left to discuss design ideas for the other two Slavic Muppets. Vika sweetly hands me a stack of Russian fairytale books to share with the American Muppet designer. She looks a bit disappointed about the results of her pep talk.

I've not seen Leonid for several weeks and when he shows up at my hotel, he shares that things are not going well for the business side of *Ulitsa Sezam*. Although Irina spent a week in New York negotiating with *Sesame Street*'s lawyers, she left without signing a coproduction agreement. And without a signed contract, she cannot begin paying Moscow production costs, and Leonid cannot seal any deals with broadcasters.

I ask Leonid to drop me off at Video Art, so I can confront Irina. Leonid begs off due to his other appointments. I don't look forward to this; Irina has a way of making you feel bad about asking her for what she owes. Right now she owes two months' salary to our core Russian production team, and she still hasn't provided us with an office space large enough for our growing *Ulitsa Sezam* team. We are splitting at the seams, working in the tiny temporary office Midhat provided when we first started the production.

Irina's recently spent a fortune renovating *her* office, and I haven't seen it yet. When I walk into Video Art's reception area, I'm nearly blinded by the sea of milky whiteness: white leather couches, white carpets, marble coffee tables, and oversize white throw pillows. No expense appears to have been spared. Although today is Irina's birthday, I feel myself getting angrier that she's spent so much money while not paying my team.

In the waiting area, people holding flowers and gifts are waiting their turn to wish the woman of the hour a happy birthday. The advertising side of Irina's company has grown in the last months. Other employees and clients continue to arrive, bearing more presents. I realize today maybe isn't the day to face up to her.

The door to Irina's office is open, and I can see her on the phone, resting the handle in the crook of her neck as she motions for me to come in and sit down. Irina looks stunning in a taupe-colored midriff jacket and matching miniskirt with knee-high brown leather boots. I wonder if this outfit is a souvenir from her shopping spree in New York City.

While still on the phone and without skipping a beat in her private conversation, Irina makes eye contact with the others waiting in her office, making sure each person feels special and important. Still, something isn't quite right.

Irina's arguing loudly. She is obviously talking to someone too important for her to hang up on, despite the entourage.

"Dearest Volodya, you must help me," she pleads into the phone. "Today of all days. It's my birthday. Can't you give me this teeny weenie little birthday present?" she coos.

I walk over to her wisp of a secretary and ask who's on the phone.

"It's Vladimir Zhechkov."

My stomach turns. I'm pretty sure he's in charge of Premier SV, the advertising company that sells Video Art its airtime as part of an arrangement with

Berezovsky's advertising company, Reclama Holding. Premier SV sells airtime at discounted prices to select independent companies, like Video Art, who then produce programming and sell the advertising slots surrounding the shows they create.

I overhear Irina arguing about revenue that Reclama Holding owes Video Art for advertising spots her company had produced and sold. Irina had once told me her arrangement with Zhechkov was supposed to be good for both of them. But it hasn't gone so well lately. From what I can hear, his firm owes Irina a lot of money—and this, I suspect, might be why Irina can't meet *Ulitsa Sezam*'s payroll or rent us an office. But of course, I can't be sure. Nothing in Russia is transparent.

"Volodya, *my dear*, you know the tax collectors have no mercy. They demand their pound of flesh, my dearest, you have to help me," she pleads seductively. "If you don't pay me, I will go bankrupt."

Hearing "tax collector" and "bankrupt" makes me even more nervous. Tax collection in Russia is unregulated. Laws make it virtually impossible for any business to operate legally and honestly. If a Russian company were to obey all the government requirements, the tax liability would exceed its revenues.

Finally, Irina hangs up the phone and comes around to the front of her desk. Even though a moment earlier she had been begging Zhechkov and declaring her imminent bankruptcy, she's smiling and glad-handing everyone in the room, accepting gifts and heartfelt toasts with a glass of champagne.

I watch her soak in all the attention, moving through the room with the air of a movie star, yet somehow without seeming the least bit inauthentic. Her desperate pleas for cash moments earlier are forgotten.

I embrace Irina and tell her how beautiful she looks in the suit. She struts a few steps like a model on a catwalk, then kisses me three times.

"I have a surprise to share," I say excitedly. "Ken is arriving in Moscow tomorrow, and he will be coming to your birthday party!

Irina throws up her hands, "Excellent!" She hugs me again.

Then, rising on her tiptoes, like a mistress of ceremonies before the assembled, Irina announces with glee, "Dearest people, our little Natasha is going to get *married*!" Although most of the people in the room, Irina's business associates, are strangers, each one of them comes up and warmly congratulates me. In Russia, the concept of "the friend of my friend is my friend" goes much further than it does in America. I'm surprised by how much I enjoy being fawned over as the bride-to-be.

Irina and I are both self-made women who work eighteen-hour days, and both of us have had to carve a path for our careers through a maze of sexist men. Still, certain things make us critically different. Irina's life is undoubtedly much harder than mine, having to care for a nine-year-old daughter and a husband, on top of running a company in a crazy country.

Because of this, I hate nagging her for money. As angry as I am, I know she's not maliciously withholding funds from the production. She wants *Sesame Street* to succeed and stands to make a substantial profit if it does. But I must ask about the office space situation and her company's financial commitment to the production.

An hour later, surrounded by the massive pile of gifts and bouquets from all her admirers, we are alone at last. Sitting beside her on her plush leather couch, I take a deep breath. "Even with it being your birthday, it sounded from your side of the conversation that Zhechkov would not honor his contractual agreements with Video Art, is that right?"

Irina smiles and looks down at her skirt, smoothing the wrinkles without saying anything. Getting impatient, I implore, "Irina, do we have a money problem?"

She sighs. "Natasha, my dear, paying taxes in Russia is like a game of cat-and-mouse, and the cat always wins—usually pocketing more for himself than he gives to anyone else." She pauses and then adds, "And in this case, the cat is asking for a lot.

"We have a little misunderstanding with Premier SV. They want me and everyone else to pay more for commercial airtime, but I don't have the money to pay them, the tax collectors, *and Ulitsa Sezam*'s production at the same time." She adds that Reclama Holding is an unreliable partner. She explains that they are months late or entirely delinquent in reimbursing Video Art for advertising spots produced and paid for by her company. "I have no recourse," she admits with a beleaguered expression.

Listening to Irina, I can't help worrying how all this will play out. *Sesame Street* can only use U.S. government funds to pay for training and technology costs in Russia, and Baxter wants me to move the production along, but that's impossible without money.

Softly, I argue, "Irina, the bottom line is that we can no longer function unless you furnish us with an office. We can't go on like this."

Irina makes a sympathetic face. "You look so tired, Natasha, and you've gotten engaged. *Dusha Moya*, I apologize about the office."

I want to shake her. Instead, I take her hand in mine. "Irina, between the team at ORT and the additional freelancers, we have over two hundred people working at *Ulitsa Sezam* now. You can't expect us to produce the TV series out of one tiny room at ORT."

She looks down at her boots, brushing off an invisible speck, and then, tilting her head, says, "Natasha let's not talk about *biznes* anymore. Let's talk about your wedding!" She pats my thigh. "I am so deeply happy for you. This is such a big step in your life." She asks, "What does your gown look like? How many people are coming? Will it be a religious service?"

Listening to her rattle off all these questions about the wedding that I haven't even started to consider makes me even more anxious than our money problems do.

"Irina, I promise to share all the wedding details with you, but right now we need an office and *Ulitsa Sezam*'s payroll met." I say, patting her thigh back.

She grins mischievously, cocks her head to the side, and jests, "Maybe as a wedding gift, Natasha, or—"

We're interrupted by Irina's waif-like secretary, who pushes open the door just a crack and slides her head into the room, timidly. "Irina Borisova, you have another call."

Irina stands up, making an apologetic face, and her secretary ushers me out the door.

As I head to my car, I think, "Well, that went horribly."

11

THE GRANDMASTER IN MOSCOW

The next morning I head to the Moscow airport to meet Ken. Standing in the crowd at international arrivals, I feel giddy, like a mail-order bride waiting to meet her betrothed for the first time. So much of my life in Moscow is a mystery to him. If he doesn't fall in love with Russia, it will crush me.

Ken emerges from customs, looking frazzled but happy to see me. He puts down his luggage to hug me, blocking passengers trying to push their way forward. Ken's patience has already been severely tested. He tells me that in baggage claims a "cart Nazi" refused to rent him a luggage cart.

"I had to pay in rubles," he says, exasperated. "But I didn't have any rubles because you can't buy rubles from any banks in the West and there are no currency-changing kiosks until you clear customs." A perfectly normal Russian rule, but it made no sense to my logical fiancé.

When we get to the Palace Hotel, I give Ken rubles, and he finds it hilarious that the bills still bear the words "State Bank of the USSR" even though the USSR no longer exists. I'm amused *this* is what an economist notices in his first hours in Moscow. After that, he takes a quick nap to rest up before we have to leave for Irina's birthday party.

That evening, just as a torrential rain arrives, Ken and I take a taxi along the River Embankment Road to a docked Korean restaurant houseboat where Irina's birthday party is already in full swing. Fifty or so guests, elegantly dressed in sparkly cocktail dresses or tuxedos, mingle in a dimly lit cabin below deck. Wide-eyed, Ken takes in the scene: red silk tablecloths, gold tea candles, and gifts piled on every banquette, leaving no place to sit down. Korean waiters in starched white shirts and bow ties carry silver trays with blini and caviar and fluted glasses of champagne. It's a class-A shindig.

Ken whispers to me that he feels underdressed. "Don't worry," I tell him, "You could be dressed in a loincloth and Irina would be happy to see you." My assurances do not put him at ease. Holding the bouquet of flowers we brought in one hand, I slip my other arm into the crook of his elbow and lead him to search for Irina.

A pounding rain rattles the windows and with each swell, the barge sways, causing wine glasses precariously hanging on a ceiling wine rack to clink like chimes. During one giant surge, Irina's presents—boxes of chocolates, flower bouquets wrapped in purple and pink cellophane, and bottles of champagne—tumble to the floor. All the men gallantly scramble, like a football scrimmage, reaching for the champagne bottles to stop them from rolling across the deck or shattering. Women in their stiletto heels struggle to maintain balance by clutching the boat's wooden masts or gripping table corners.

Irina spots Ken and rushes over to him. "You came! It is so wonderful you are here for my birthday." Irina looks at Ken with such warmth that I'm afraid he might melt. She kisses him, then rubs her lipstick smudge on his face with her finger as Ken stands ill at ease.

He bravely compliments Irina in Russian, smiling, "You look lovely in your dress."

I beam with pride.

At the signal, a chime, we all take our seats at a long rectangular table. I'm touched to discover Irina has placed Ken and me in seats of honor beside her. On my other side is Irina's accountant, a heavyset Russian-Korean man. Irina trusts this man with her life. He knows all her deep dark secrets, financial and otherwise.

Mid-dinner, a handsome, broad-shouldered man in his late thirties arrives late, carrying a bouquet of peonies. Judging from Irina's conspicuous flirtation, I wonder if he's her Don Juan or simply a Don paying his respects. It's certainly not her husband, whom I've met, and who is conspicuously absent tonight. While eavesdropping on their conversation, I hear the words "Premier SV" and "Reclama Holding," and I realize the handsome man is Volodya Zhechkov, the advertising executive Irina had been pleading with on the phone in her office the day before.

He leans down and whispers something into Irina's ear that makes her giggle. Irina tilts her head, resting it for a moment on Zhechkov's shoulder, and he says something else that I cannot hear.

I look at Ken meaningfully, trying to get him to pay attention to the unusual exchange playing out, but he's oblivious. Irina is behaving oddly and submissively. I wonder if this performance is about money or something else.

The man doesn't sit down but kisses Irina again on her cheek and leaves.

Irina's charm works on almost everyone, but perhaps not on him.

After he's gone, I turn to Irina and ask, "Was that Zhechkov?"

"Yes. I'm sorry I didn't introduce you, but he was in a hurry."

"He's very handsome," I say, raising my eyebrows, hoping to elicit more information.

With a twinkle in her eye, she responds, "Yes, he's the perfect specimen of Russian masculinity—as ruthless in his business dealings as he is tender with the many women in his life."

We both burst out laughing, and all the men at the table, including Ken, have no idea why.

I glance across the table and catch Ken looking at me in a new way. I like to think he's impressed with me, hearing me speak Russian and seeing how relaxed I am in what is an unbelievably bizarre social setting for him. Of course, it is a serious event for me. Irina is foremost my business partner, and I want to make her happy. Having Ken here helps. And he's getting a front row seat to my Moscow life. It would be hard to explain this scene to him—or anyone.

As the first course is served, toasting begins, and continues for the next four hours. Toasts in Russia conform to strict rules: they must be heartfelt, witty, and, most importantly, provoke meaningful reflection. Attempting to preserve his sobriety and health, Ken occasionally lifts his shot glass and sips, but eagle-eyed Irina nods at him to drink to the bottom.

Ken is jet-lagged, fading, and desperately wants to leave, but Irina will not allow it. "It's time for Korean karaoke!" she shouts, jumping up from the table. The guests gather in front of a giant TV monitor on the wall. On the screen, a Korean woman dressed up like Madonna begins singing the lyrics to "Material Girl" while English subtitles flash across the screen. The Russians loudly sing along in broken English, trying to drown out the Korean-accented verse.

After a few more pop hits, the men drunkenly put their arms around each other, swaying back and forth as the barge lurches, and then they launch into a traditional Russian folk song. Pulling Ken into their group, they belt out the lyrics to the Russian love song, *Ochi Chernye*.

Oh, you dark black eyes, full-of-passion-eyes.

Oh, you burning eyes, how you hypnotize. . . .

Substituting the lyrics "Black Sea" for Black Eyes, they boisterously belt out a ridiculous ode to the Russian empire's beloved Crimean Black Sea, reveling in their shared patriotism.

When the men in their drunken haze realize suddenly that their beloved Black Sea no longer belongs to Mother Russia but to newly independent Ukraine, they change the lyrics back to black eyes.

The singers encircle Irina as they dance. She's ecstatic at being the center of attention again. Ken stealthily slips out of the ensemble and I pull him toward the exit. For a moment before stepping off the boat, I stand, watching Irina. She looks so happy. I adore her.

———————

Back at the hotel at 4 a.m., I ask Ken what he thought of the party.

He thinks for a moment. "I don't know anyone who could have scripted a party as wild as that one. They all seem to be living on the edge."

That's all he has to say, and I'm a little disappointed he's not more effusive. Doesn't he understand that the wildness is what I love most about it here? Russians embrace life as they do because history has taught them how just one false step can plunge them into unimaginable misfortune; therefore, they live more passionately than most people living in free and open societies.

I want to explain this to him, to tell him all the things I've learned about these people I love. But I must let him sleep. He's been awake for nearly twenty-two hours.

Sensing my disappointment, he mumbles, "I'm beginning to understand what's so appealing about the Russians, but I'm not sure about spending a lot of time here." Just before nodding off, he says, "I love you. If you'll let me, I'll try to find other ways to make you as happy."

While Ken sleeps, I lay awake scheming how best to hook Ken on the seductive chaos of Russia.

———————

Today I plan to play hooky and take Ken sightseeing to Red Square, Lenin Hills, and the statue graveyard. At breakfast, he surprises me with the news he had been saving for the right moment. He's booked a venue in New Jersey for our wedding on June 25, two months from now.

"They had an unexpected opening," he offers brightly, "It's just a backup, in case you don't have time to look at options."

I'm speechless—first because I'm embarrassed that I haven't lifted a finger to plan our wedding, and second, because I love him so much for having taken charge. What other man would do this without the slightest resentment?

He chuckles and says, "I figured if I booked a location that we might have a chance of actually getting married." Ken's become wiser, aware the only stable thing in Russia is instability, and you have to plan for it.

Just as we are about to leave the hotel and head out for the Kremlin, Misha calls, insisting I come to the office. After three months of requests, Irina has finally agreed to review *Ulitsa Sezam*'s budget with the actual intention to pay out what is owed. Perhaps our conversation, or Ken's attending her birthday party, softened her into resignation. In any case, I cannot miss the chance to get my team paid.

Our sightseeing will have to wait.

Because getting a pass to enter the TV station for a foreigner is time-consuming and complicated, I leave Ken sitting on a hardwood windowsill in the lobby of ORT. He says it's fine, and he'll read a book. I feel terrible about leaving him suddenly like this.

It turns out to be a busy morning. I send Misha's secretary to the entrance to tell Ken that I will be an hour. The secretary takes messages to Ken three times, making him aware that I'm still stuck in the office dealing with various crises. Each time, my sweet fiancé sends back the same message: "Take the time you need."

By the time I finish, it's late afternoon. I apologize to Ken, who again says, "It's no problem." I feel awful. I want Ken to see more of Moscow, and we need to talk more about wedding plans, but now there's no time. We can only visit Red Square, and then we must head to the airport so Ken can catch his plane back to the States. Sadly, I realize that the only memories Ken will have of his trip to Moscow are the cracked linoleum floors of the television station and drunken Russians singing karaoke.

At the airport, before Ken passes through the sliding glass doors, he hugs me tightly. "I know it's going to be a great show, but stay alive so we can get married," he teases with a sardonic look. As he walks off, he looks back and smiles, waving wearily.

Watching him go, I know we'll be ok, but I doubt he'll return to Russia. And now, I won't see him for another three weeks—not until I'm back in New York. I've had to extend my stay in Moscow because we are getting close to finalizing the designs for the Russian Muppets and I need to train some of the new free-lance directors who've come on board. We're still way behind schedule producing live-action and animated film storyboards and scripts for this month.

Meanwhile, our search for talented scriptwriters is turning into a comedy of errors. Robin has been collaborating with Lida, the show's head writer, on script development for the past two months. Scriptwriting is the backbone of any television production, and for *Ulitsa Sezam* we need to write hundreds of scripts, filling about fifteen hours of original content. We need more script-writers, but Lida has been excluding all the younger writers, refusing to consider their spec scripts.

———————

A few days later, I'm at ORT with Robin and Lida for their morning review of any new spec scripts. A disheveled man in his fifties shows up at the office, dripping wet and carrying a brown, rain-soaked cardboard file folder. The reek of his cologne follows him into the room, hovering like an unwelcome guest. Lida already knows him, so he introduces himself to Robin and me as Boris.

Shuffling through his files, he picks out a crumpled piece of paper: a storyboard for a script called "Courage." A storyboard is a drawing with different boxes showing what happens in each scene of a script. The first box of his storyboard shows a split screen—depicting a skydiver about to jump out of a plane, juxtaposed with a close-up shot of a dentist drilling into a child's mouth. A series of images shows the dentist at work and the sky diver jumping. The tagline at the end of the segment, intended to encourage dental hygiene, is: "Have courage. Do not be afraid."

Robin shoots me a horrified look. I cringe in response. The script would give children nightmares, I imagine, and ensure they'd never want to visit a dentist again. Furthermore, the parallel action is too conceptually abstract. Preschoolers will not understand the connection between jumping out of a plane and visiting a dentist.

But Lida finds nothing wrong with the script and wants to approve it. I'm beginning to see why Robin has been so frustrated with her.

Boris leaves and we open the windows to air out the office.

"*Now* do you get it?" whispers Robin to me.

When I return to the hotel that evening, I continue reading through the stack of new scripts. I'd expected marrying the fun, goofy, mostly slapstick style of the American show with Russia's tradition of typically dark, satirical comedy would be cumbersome, but these submitted scripts are downright depressing— way too bleak for a children's comedy show.

I should not be as surprised as I am. Comedy as a genre flourished in America following the end of World War I. Buster Keaton, Charlie Chaplin, and the Marx Brothers dominated the silver screen with their slapstick antics over the next decade. Meanwhile, Soviet cultural life during this time was dedicated to glorifying the "worker's paradise" through polemical works, often at the expense of slapstick comedy. Vladimir Lenin even wrote, "Art for art's sake has no place in Soviet Russia." And I guess the worker's paradise had no place for slapstick comedy.

In truth, Russians have a wonderful sense of humor in both literature and cinema. But it is mostly based on irony, parody, and wordplay. This type of humor is difficult for young children to understand as compared to physical humor.

The next day, after arguing over more poorly written scripts, Lida admits she has a problem with her chosen union member scriptwriters. She suggests hiring the "Black Hen," a newly formed group of for-hire writers who produce anything from political speeches and advertisements to pornographic novellas. Although the Black Hen sounds like the name of a Brazilian street gang, Lida is taken with the group because—naturally—they are all members of the esteemed Union of Writers.

We invite Anton Lepin, the forty-year-old head of the Black Hen, to show us his work. He arrives at our office dressed like a preppy Westerner in a white Oxford dress shirt, chinos, and loafers. His demeanor is modern and entrepreneurial. Anton is quick-witted, and his irreverent jokes make me and everyone else laugh. We hire him and several of his Black Hen colleagues.

Over the next two weeks, our little office turns into a machine, churning out dozens of spec scripts and storyboards. As scripts get approved, filming begins. But the team is not thrilled when I inform them that in three weeks, they will have to put aside their pressing production work for a few days to attend the curriculum workshop hosted by *Ulitsa Sezam*'s research team.

In response, Misha starts yelling, "We cannot waste valuable days with these education experts."

"The curriculum workshop is mandatory," I tell him.

The day before I am scheduled to fly back to New York, I discover that Irina hasn't met the payroll for the Russian team after promising some weeks earlier that she would. Even worse, Misha informs me that the key members of our producing team are now suddenly refusing to attend the curriculum workshop because they have not been paid.

This is a disaster.

The curriculum workshop is the most critical component in creating any *Sesame Street* coproduction. During the past three months, the show's

American and Russian research directors have worked tirelessly to organize the seminar, where the research experts and the creative team are supposed to come together to determine the educational content of *Ulitsa Sezam*. If the Moscow producing team doesn't show up, my research colleagues will be livid.

The next day, I leave for New York, determined to convince Sesame Workshop to loan Video Art some funds so my team will return to work and attend the curriculum workshop.

––––––––––––

At *Sesame* headquarters, Baxter makes time to see me. When I walk into his office, he gives me a hug and excitedly asks, "Hey, you want to see the prototype for our newest toy?" He holds up a cardboard box with Elmo's half-moon face staring through the cellophane cutout window. Pulling the plush doll from its packaging, he pushes the toy into my hands, urging me, "Press his tummy, press his tummy!"

I hold Elmo in one hand and hesitantly squeeze his belly, not sure what's going to happen.

The Muppet toy emits a high-pitched squeal. "That tickles!"

The words take me by total surprise, and I nearly drop the toy.

"Squeeze again," Baxter encourages.

When I do, Elmo yells out, "Oh boy!"

Three squeezes in a row send the doll into a laughing, shaking, vibrating frenzy.

"It's 'Tickle Me Elmo.' Isn't it great?" Baxter tells me the toy is going to be a huge Christmas breakout success. I'm no judge of kids' toys, but I imagine any toy that can make me laugh like that will make a lot of money. I also figure this is a great segue to ask Baxter for more of the same.

I share the depressing information about Irina's temporary cash-flow problem and my team's threat to skip the curriculum workshop. Baxter tells me there's no way we can allow these obstacles to get in the way of the Moscow workshop. He promises to help. As I walk out the door, he throws me a box with "Tickle Me Elmo" inside and says, "Keep it, looks like you need it."

I love having him as my new boss.

That afternoon, I head across town to the Muppet Mansion to speak with Ed Christie, the Henson Company supervisor assigned to work with me on developing the Russian Muppets. I've only met him once before, at the New York training workshop with my team.

When I ring the doorbell of the tiny Upper East Side townhouse on Sixty-Seventh Street, an attendant instructs me to wait in the entryway, gesturing toward a single row of antique upholstered theater seats with red velvet fold-down cushions. A giant mural painted on the wall behind depicts various Muppets characters in an old-style movie theater, frantically clambering over one another to get to their seats. Sitting in the chair, with the Muppets drawn on the wall behind me, I feel like an audience member in the theater. The perspective is ingenious and fun.

I'm excited to work with Ed Christie, who has won multiple Emmy Awards for his wizardly Muppet designs as part of the team at the Henson Workshop. He greets me and quickly leads me to the elevator. He seems to be in a hurry or maybe just distracted. When I try to make small talk, he only grunts in response.

Arriving at the fourth floor, he motions me to follow him through a labyrinth of workshop tables. In his silence, my anxiety grows about showing him the Russian concept for their "Domovoi" puppet.

I step carefully around plastic roller carts filled with feathers and pieces of foam. Various body parts hang from the ceiling, swinging above our heads, including Elmo's limp torso attached to a hook. Swatches of fur in nearly every color are stacked on tables like animal pelts. We pass an open drawer filled with variously sized eyeballs and noses and, in another, a giant pile of red and green legs jumbled together like toy snakes.

When I catch sight of ten Miss Piggies hanging on the wall, I yell, "Oh my *God*, Miss Piggy!"

Several artists working silently at tables nearby look up, then ignore me. They've heard it before, perhaps every time someone new enters this enchanting lair.

When we finally reach Ed's workstation, he gets right to the point, asking me to show him the Russian sketches. I'm intimidated by the surroundings and mortified to show him, fearing the work is subpar, but I have no choice. Gingerly, I pull the drawings out of my backpack and hand them over.

Ed looks at the drawings of Domovoi and makes a sour expression. "This design will not work," he says flatly. "The Russian full-body Muppet should be more childlike, like Big Bird. Children relate to Muppets because they are playful, flexible, and open." He thinks the Russian spirit of the home looks terrifying.

He gestures toward the drawn skullcap that Domovoi is wearing and asks with a sarcastic tone, "Do the Russians expect Domovoi to give the children communion and take confession?" It's a joke, but he asks it without cracking a smile.

I confide in Ed about the difficulties I've been having trying to convince the Russians to accept Muppets of any kind. He tells me he will draft some rough sketches that the Russians will like, and I can bring them back to Moscow.

"Oh, I almost forgot." I pull out the fairytale books Vika had given to me. "These may be helpful in your creative process," I offer, optimistically.

For the first time, Ed smiles. He walks me to the elevator; I'm still embarrassed about Domovoi. "I promise the next time we see each other you will be more impressed by the Russian designs."

"I hope so," he says, as the doors to the elevator close.

I'm on pins and needles the next few days, waiting to hear what the workshop will decide about fronting Video Art funds, if only temporarily, so the curriculum seminar can proceed as planned.

Meanwhile, I've *got* to buy a wedding dress. I remember seeing the perfect A-line, off-the-shoulder, white satin gown in a bridal magazine that I had bought in the airport. Serendipitously, I find one just like it—only cheaper.

At the bridal shop, the sales attendant fawns all over me as I stand in front of the full-length mirror, watching myself, turning this way and that. The dress is everything I'd hoped but the image still feels off somehow.

"Something is missing," the attendant mutters and then runs off. She returns with a fake pearl necklace and clasps it around my neck. "There!" She says, inspecting me the way a pastry chef might the fondant on a wedding cake she'd made.

Unfortunately, the overpriced phony jewelry doesn't have the same effect on me. The frilly, feminine woman in white staring back from the mirror seems incredibly far from my self-image of a sleep-deprived puppet director who negotiates deals with oligarchs, navigates murders, and defuses political strife. I want so desperately to believe I *can be* the woman in the mirror—passionately in love and a wife. But how does marriage and maybe a family fit in with my life? Will I lose my edge as I walk down the aisle?

I feel disoriented—like a fraud—my identity dissembling. Returning to the changing room, I take off the dress. I feel safer with it zipped into its plastic hanging bag and I'm back to being the self I recognize, for now.

Two days before I am supposed to return to Moscow, I'm copied on a memo in which Baxter writes, "I think it's best for the workshop to commit the USAID money for the next phase of the Russian project to keep the project moving forward and the staff working." In his folksy style, he adds, "Sure, it is a gamble, but it is a show of good faith and, if we are wrong, then we will know that Video Art is not the right partner."

I thank my lucky stars Baxter has pulled us out of the fire again. "We have money to pay our team!" I yell into the phone to Misha who's been waiting to hear from me. He seems surprised by the good news and promises to make sure the producing team shows up at the curriculum workshop in Moscow, which is now only two weeks away.

12

BIG BIRD'S BIBLE

Sesame Street uses a proprietary research-based approach to creating children's television that was developed by the show's original creators. The cornerstone of this model is the curriculum workshop, which involves bringing child education experts together with TV professionals to develop specific educational goals that also reflect the culture and values in the countries where the show is being produced.

It's an enlightened idea and I have seen the positive impact of *Sesame Street*'s research, but the research model can also feel a bit doctrinaire, bordering on cult-like. During their training in New York, the Russians referred to the fifty-page tome detailing *Sesame Street*'s production-research bible as the "Muppet Manifesto."

I sense that the Russian producers and directors generally romanticize the creative process, and they have not been shy about expressing their views—finding *Sesame Street*'s research process "cumbersome." And I've heard one or two of my *Ulitsa Sezam* colleagues describe research efforts as "meddling in the artistic process."

I share some of their feelings at times—especially coming from the rough-and-tumble world of independent filmmaking, where flexibility and spontaneity are critical for success. It's hard enough to come up with original ideas and get preschoolers to laugh without having to conform to educational guidelines set down by academics from twenty years earlier.

On the other hand, *Sesame Street*'s academic researchers see themselves as enlightened purveyors of young television viewers. I respect them immensely but worry that if educators determine the show's content, *Ulitsa Sezam* could be dull, without offering entertainment. But as a newbie to children's television, I especially need the researchers on my side. Whatever happens at the Russian curriculum seminar, I tell myself I must trust the process.

On the first day of the curriculum workshop, Moscow is experiencing a record-smashing heatwave for mid-June. My team gathers outside the Danilov

Monastery, the headquarters of the Russian Orthodox Church, which dates back to the thirteenth century. The monastery is a fortress on the banks of the Moscow River, surrounded by freshly painted white stone walls. The guards at the entrance wave us through to an interior courtyard where blue onion-domed churches with golden spires rise spectacularly from the ground as in a pop-up fairytale. Dr. Genina, the director for *Ulitsa Sezam* research, selected this site for our workshop—not for its spiritual significance as I had thought, but because it was one of the few places large and affordable enough.

Our motley crew shuffles past wilting flower beds while our eyes lock on monks in black robes pacing the gardens with pensive expressions. I watch them, imagining how much they must be sweating beneath their heavy robes. We pass a giant stone crucifix in the center of the compound; worshipers slowly circle the cross, murmuring prayers. I feel the ghostly presence of tsar Ivan the Terrible, who graced these grounds almost four centuries ago. A vengeful tyrant, it's rumored that he blinded the architect of the magnificent St. Basil's Cathedral so he could never produce anything so beautiful again. I shiver.

The group proceeds in silence to the Monastery Hotel, the site of our workshop. After climbing four flights (the elevator is broken), we arrive breathless and sweating at a cramped conference room where I discover there's no air conditioning. The temperature in the room must already be well over a hundred degrees.

"We'll roast like chickens," someone shouts from the back of the room.

To prepare for the curriculum workshop during the past months, Dr. Genina made several trips to far regions of Russia, recruiting experts to help shape the educational framework for the show. On one occasion, Dr. Charlotte Cole (Chary), *Sesame Street*'s American director of international research, joined her in Ekaterinburg. Together, they interviewed Russian teachers and academics specializing in early childhood development, psychology, mathematics, ecology, health, music, and ethnic and gender studies. Based on these discussions, they then selected a group of ten to attend the workshop in Moscow. They also invited several educators from former Soviet republics such as Georgia and Ukraine. Dr. Genina told these educators that the goal of the curriculum workshop is to find a middle ground between Western liberal values, typical of the *Sesame Street* brand, and post-soviet Russian culture and spiritual values.

Dr. Genina expects a large group at the workshop, including members of *Ulitsa Sezam*'s research team, representatives from the *Sesame Street* international research department, and key members of my production team.

I feel fortunate to have gotten to know Dr. Genina better during the New York training some two months earlier. After graduating with high honors from Moscow's Pedagogical University, she'd worked for twelve years at the Moscow State Academic Children's Musical Theater. Her background in both education and theater impressed me, as did her commitment and tireless efforts improving the lives of Russian children.

Many of the educators had arrived the night before and are now gathered around the amenities table getting coffee and meeting each other for the first time. Dr. Genina moves through the crowd, enthusiastically greeting the forty-three participants. Some of the teachers and academics recognize each other while others, visiting Moscow for the first time, stand uncomfortably off to the side, shyly eyeing their colleagues.

Dr. Genina, smartly dressed in a lime green jacket, powder blue dress skirt, and sensible walking shoes, is making all feel welcome—and I expect her poise and diplomacy will be needed over the next few days. From across the room, she nods to me and smiles slightly. She's the ideal facilitator for today's discussion.

She looks nervous, as though steeling herself for the upcoming battles.

I see Misha already seated at the conference table. The first *Playboy* just hit Russian newsstands, and he's discreetly reading it inside the fold of one of the binders that has been placed in front of each chair. Other members of my team politely engage with the academics, inquiring where they are from. Despite earlier objections to attending the seminar—not only because of money issues—they now seem to welcome the hiatus from our grueling fourteen-hour workdays producing the show. The free coffee also helps.

Chary arrives. She's one of *Sesame Street*'s rising stars and a brilliant American researcher with a PhD in children's education from Harvard. Tall, bookish, and intense, she works unimaginably hard, traveling extensively and often to dangerous locations for Sesame Workshop.

Dr. Genina announces the start of the meeting, inviting participants to sit along one side of four rectangular folding tables that form a square, with a space in the center. She explains the workshop will be conducted in Russian with translators interpreting for English speakers. Excitedly, the participants pick up the pens and plush Elmo and Cookie Monster dolls placed at each seating for them to take home.

"This is so professional," one academic says, in Russian, as he picks up the pen, examining it and clicking the top before straightening the placard with his name in front of his seat. He screws the cap off the water bottle and takes a swig, nodding approvingly. The labels on the glass water bottles say *Svyatoi Istochnik* (Holy Springs), and in tiny Russian print, "Manufactured by the Russian

Orthodox Church." I laugh out loud. It's incredible that the Orthodox Church runs a bottling plant. It's a good business. Most Russians consider bottled water a luxury and this blessed water is more precious than most.

After initial introductions and a review of the agenda by Dr. Genina, we watch a video of the American show's segments. Even before the subtitled clip of Cookie Monster is over, one of the participants, a mathematics professor, raises his hand, impatient to speak.

"Our preschoolers are much smarter than American children. We will need a more advanced curriculum for our show."

The educators on each side of him nod in agreement.

I sit quietly, aware how such a statement will sound to every American in the room. Education is one of the Soviet Union's most outstanding achievements, but it's not as though the kids have finished calculus by kindergarten.

But most of the Russian experts appear to agree with the math professor. To an assemblage of bobbing heads, a history teacher adds, "We must figure out how we will speak about our country's difficult past and how to present it in a positive light so that we can restore faith in our country for future generations."

A music expert suggests focusing on Russian culture as a way to "bring to light Russia's glorious past—showing our music, our literature, and our faith." His poetic words evoke beaming smiles.

Then the math teacher stands up, slaps his hand loudly on the table, and says, "We must remember that above all, we are still a superpower, and our children must not feel humiliation about our past. On the contrary, they must be proud of their country!"

Dr. Genina allows this free-form discussion, encouraging others who had not yet spoken to do so, but also reminds them, "It's true that we are a superpower and that our children excel at learning letters and numbers compared to children in other countries, but they also need new skills and a new way of thinking to prepare them for a successful transition to a democratic society." She emphasizes that the curriculum goals for *Ulitsa Sezam* will naturally differ from the U.S. show, but "not because Russian children are smarter."

A history teacher raises her hand. "The show's too fast-paced for Russian children." Another adds, "The characters act too hysterical and behave [*nekulturnyy*] in an uncultured way." I have to work hard not to react, recalling the puppet Petrushka in Midhat's office, beating the daylights out of another sock puppet.

The educators speak at length, uninterrupted, and I sense they feel respected and valued. Dr. Genina tells the group, "Based on earlier recommendations from all of you, I have selected topics to focus on during the seminar:

education, economics, social issues, gender, and nationality issues. But there will be plenty of time to consider the issues you've raised and expand to other topics as well." She emphasizes that while the Russian show is expected to be distinctly Russian, *Sesame Street*'s experience will be useful in helping the group develop concrete ideas for their show.

Dr. Genina halts the first session at eleven o'clock for a break.

Thank goodness. I need coffee after a morning listening to so many comments bashing American education.

Sipping my coffee in a corner of the room, I overhear a Russian physicist apologizing to Chary in English, explaining that he's considering leaving soon. "You are tasking us with developing this curriculum to help kids learn the skills they need for an open society, but how can we do it if we haven't lived in an open society?" There's sadness in his voice.

I move closer.

Chary gently touches his shoulder, encouraging him to stay and engage in the multiday process and see what happens. He does.

Later in the morning, we broach the thorny topic of teaching children the skills needed to thrive in Russia's new free-market society.

The physicist talks about how capitalism cannot meet the needs of ordinary Russian people who are used to socialist state protection and security. "Those who are less capable or weaker should not be penalized just because they don't know how to make money. It's not humane, and we shouldn't teach such ideas to children."

The health expert agrees, "We do not want our children to envy people who have material things and are rich."

A preschool teacher with brown hair disagrees, "*Ulitsa Sezam must* include lessons about the free market. Otherwise, our children will not know how to survive."

Across the table, one history expert exclaims, "Business should not be a bad word in Russian. We need to teach our children to respect people who are doing business because they are a creative part of the new society."

The antipathy toward capitalism that some educators express is understandable. Most Russians are suffering economically, and no one disputes that inequality in Russia has risen, far surpassing levels experienced under communism. Russian life expectancy has plummeted, along with teachers' lifetime savings, including many in this room. It's not surprising they are frightened.

The math teacher shouts across the chasm between the tables, "Russia's strengths are in math and science, and above all else, we must preserve this strength. We must not succumb to the West's destructive obsession with capital."

Another teacher argues, "If the show focuses on money in any way, our children will grow up paying attention to making money, instead of focusing on being socially responsible people."

The group's concern about how wealth will change their society is valid. Many of my Western friends in Moscow, and possibly even me, are guilty of evangelizing free markets while ignoring escalating economic inequality across the former Soviet Union. As I listen to the intense exchanges, I find it startling how many of these ideas about capitalism resonate with ongoing debates in America, between liberals on the left and neoconservatives on the right.

Natalia, a psychologist, raises her hand. Her voice is sweet and sincere.

"But our children already know all about money. Three-year-olds in my preschool class can tell me the ruble-to-dollar exchange rate even though it changes practically every day." She pleads, "We can't just ignore it. If we don't help them understand what a free market is, our children will be left behind."

These educators face a significant dilemma; few of them even know what a free market actually is. Three years earlier, these teachers were standing in front of their classes, waving wooden batons, conducting their pupils in songs glorifying socialism.

Raising my hand, I propose that *Ulitsa Sezam* could feature, for example, a segment showing children running a lemonade stand as a way of teaching about business and teamwork.

The group is horrified—not only by the idea of children selling items on the street but also at the thought of showing children engaged in what one participant calls "dirty mercantile activities." "Only desperate, poor people sell stuff on the street to survive and it's dangerous," one educator argues. Another admonishes, "It's not right to show children trying to earn money—it encourages individual greed." I hadn't anticipated my example would provoke such reactions. Of course, though, it makes sense—in Soviet times, selling items on the street was illegal, and only the poorest Russians or Mafia resorted to street commerce.

Skillfully changing the subject, Dr. Genina tells the group how *Ulitsa Sezam*'s research team canvassed teachers, librarians, and heads of nursery schools and orphanages in several regions of Russia for their opinions on what preschoolers should learn. "We were startled to discover that many Russian educators are unsure about the ideals and history they should teach children."

For example, she says, one of the teachers interviewed said, "Thousands of children's textbooks glorifying the Russian Revolution and its leaders had to be discarded, and there are no new books for us to use to teach children."

In this stifling room, it's hard to keep everyone focused, but Dr. Genina has the group's rapt attention and presses on.

The next speaker is Dr. Elena Lenskaya, the head of the international relations department at the ministry of education. She's well known among the other educators. Three years earlier, at Sesame Workshop's request, she'd traveled to Washington, DC, to advocate for Russian *Sesame Street* before the U.S. Senate Foreign Relations Subcommittee.

She stands up to speak. "The Russian education system is certainly in a state of crisis," she says. "We at the ministry do not have enough money to pay teachers' salaries, let alone create new textbooks."

Her voice softens, and Dr. Lenskaya addresses the elephant in the room: "The Soviet education system was set up to excel in science and mathematics, and we accomplished this beautifully. But today our education system is no longer tenable, and *Ulitsa Sezam* can help us by giving us an alternative tool to help educate our children while we redesign our curriculum for a new Russia."

Many shift uncomfortably in their seats. They seem embarrassed to hear a government official acknowledge any weakness in Russia's education system in front of the American guests. Dr. Genina offers a gentle statement of support, "All countries go through difficult times and being able to admit weakness is the first step to changing things."

I feel grateful to Dr. Lenskaya and Dr. Genina for framing *Ulitsa Sezam* in a positive light. Although I'd anticipated *some criticism* of *Sesame Street* because our program is foreign, I'd hoped the Russian educators would recognize the artistic brilliance and universal humanity of the Muppets and understand the show's potential value for their country.

Although I've been having discussions like these with my team for months, the penetrating insights raised on this first day of the seminar impress us all. I now realize why *Sesame Street*'s research-production model and the curriculum workshop are essential to the production process. The workshop is key to reaching a consensus on how to meet the actual needs of children and produce content that is relatable, relevant, and compelling. Despite this, the attendees appear immobilized by their differences, and I worry they will not come to a consensus. Chary assures me that she's seen it before and encourages me to be patient.

13

AN ANGEL DESCENDS

Things get more heated as the Russian educators turn to a discussion of how *Sesame Street* promotes inclusivity. We watch a clip about a boy in a wheelchair. In the segment, the boy meets a friend on his way to the park and the two of them play catch and fly a kite while a whimsical song with upbeat lyrics called "Me & My Chair" plays in background.

Surprisingly, the sweet and touching segment elicits a harsh response.

"How can you show children in wheelchairs? It's so *exploitative*," reacts one teacher.

"It's shameful showing this poor crippled boy trying to act normal by playing ball and flying a kite," says another.

A third educator shakes her head. "Why would normal children ever want to watch *nenormal'nye* [not normal] children in a TV show?" I'm shocked to hear "not normal" used to describe children with disabilities.

I play dumb. "So, are you saying that *Ulitsa Sezam* cannot show any disabled children?"

The teacher who'd spoken first nods. "Yes, exactly—allow children to forget about these hardships; at least while watching the television show, let them escape the hell we live in."

I feel deflated. How can *Ulitsa Sezam* teach empathy and understanding if these distinguished and enlightened educators express such archaic views? But the conversation takes a further turn when a child health expert suggests that it is insensitive to show a child in a wheelchair because most Russians cannot afford such an apparatus. With great sympathy, she explains that many handicapped children are trapped in their beds, and when they see a child in a video with a wheelchair, they will feel sad about what they do not have.

I hadn't thought of this, but ignoring Russian children with disabilities also seems wrong.

From the corner of the room, a middle-aged woman with a soft, round face speaks in a quiet voice. "My name is Ludmila Chapurina. I teach children in

Cheboksary, the capital of Chuvashia, one of our poorest regions in western Russia."

Drawing in a long breath, she continues, "For decades, the communist government used our town, populated mostly by Turkic people, as a dumping ground for hazardous chemicals. Not surprisingly, the rate of birth deformities in the Chuvash region is among the highest in Russia." She speaks slowly and calmly but with sincerity and intensity that mesmerizes everyone in the room.

"I work with wheelchair-bound children every day. They laugh with me, paint pictures, play music, and have a wonderful time. But you can't imagine how much these crippled children long to play with normal children—how they long to live in a world where they are not treated with contempt. Don't you people understand that just because a child has a problem with his legs doesn't mean he can't be talented in other areas? These children are so sensitive. We need to help healthy children see these other children as equal to themselves and valuable in society."

It's as if an angel has descended into our presence. The harsh language poisoning the atmosphere moments earlier evaporates into thin air. The math expert stares at his hands, tightly cupped atop the table. Several participants appear close to tears. My eyes become watery and I wipe at them, hoping no one sees me. I'm surprised at my emotional response, but after months of pressure building up to this moment, I feel overwhelmed.

I sense everyone realizing that something otherworldly is taking place. As a group, we are overcome with a deep awareness of our responsibility and an understanding of how *Ulitsa Sezam* can help fight prejudice and encourage tolerance, first on a television screen and then in real life. Ludmilla has cast a spell on us all.

Dr. Genina decides to break for lunch. As the attendees gather around the buffet, I grab a sandwich and head out the door.

Outside the building, I can breathe again, even though the heat is suffocating. I need time to collect myself. A group of soldiers dressed in army fatigues and carrying machine guns traverses the garden. An older woman wearing a tattered green dress with sweat-stained creases stands in front of St. Daniil church, holding out white wax candles, pleading with her eyes for a sale. Her candles are identical to the ones sold inside the church for the same price. I don't understand how she is making any money. I buy two candles and bow my head slightly. She gives me a toothless smile.

A small wooden bench overlooks a pond where a family of ducks shade themselves beneath a giant willow. Sun-scorched, yellow-brown grass along the embankment offers the scrawny fowl nothing to eat. I sit down as they paddle in my direction and throw bread from my sandwich into the water. They dive for it, attacking each other. The ducks' desperation to find food reminds me of an orphanage I visited a few months earlier in Novosibirsk. Malnourished babies were wrapped in dirty rags as diapers, crying incessantly in their metal cribs.

I'd pushed these images out of my head until the moment Ludmila started describing the children in Cheboksary. It's as though a dam inside broke and I realized how numb I've become to Russia's suffering. I've buried myself in work and ignored what was right in front of me.

It's only the first day, and I'm already feeling emotionally drained. I put my head between my legs and take several deep breaths.

The ducks nibble at my lunch, and when I look up again, I notice a priest dressed in a black habit and miter circling the pond, the gold cross dangling from his neck swinging rhythmically with each step. He walks with an almost mystical grace, placing one foot in front of the other, moving toward me. I realize to my utter amazement that it's Patriarch Alexey II, the head of the Russian Orthodox Church. I recognize his face from the press.

Accidentally running into the Russian patriarch is like having a chance encounter with the pope in Vatican City. The presence of His Holiness after the morning's emotional catharsis moves me. It does not feel coincidental. As my friends know well, although I am not religious, I *am* superstitious.

He pauses at the edge of the pond, close to my bench, and I rise, inching closer to him, awkwardly half bowing and nodding at the same time, unsure of the religious protocol.

Suddenly I hear myself start speaking to him. "Your Excellency," I address him, in Russian. "I am American, collaborating with a group of educators from all over Russia and we are here creating a new educational television show for Russia's children." As soon as the words leave my mouth, I feel embarrassed for talking about my business before this holy man.

But he is gracious. "I guess even godly places have to rent out facilities to support themselves," he says with a nod.

Trying to recover, I bow my head again and ask if he could bless me and our endeavor. He extends his hand and blesses me with the sign of the cross. For a moment, I can barely breathe, struggling to process whether I am daydreaming or this is really happening.

The patriarch turns to go, and I slowly make my way back to the workshop, struggling to transition back to the secular world.

Back at the conference room, the remnants of lunch have been cleared away and the participants are huddled in small groups, chatting and drinking coffee. In the sweltering heat, the room is thick with smells of cigarettes and sweat. I get a coffee and join Misha's conversation. He's debating with one of the participants whether *Ulitsa Sezam* should include scenarios where children play competitive sports. Misha urges, "This will engender a positive attitude toward competition, which is important in a free market." On my other side, I overhear our live-action director asking a teacher from a Moscow elementary school for permission to shoot a video at her school for our show. Seeing my creative team engaging with the educators makes me feel the workshop is already a success.

Misha moves to the conference table and resumes reading *Playboy*. I interrupt him, recounting my random encounter with the patriarch.

At first he doesn't believe me. But then he sees how flushed my face is and realizes I'm telling the truth. In a hushed tone, he whispers, "You are fortunate to have spoken to His Holiness because he rarely speaks to people." Misha stares at me—I suspect, looking for evidence of how the encounter has changed me.

There's a commotion toward the front of the room as two participants burst into the room, breathlessly describing how Chechens have taken over the city of Budyonnovsk in southern Russia. The Chechen separatists—whom the Russians refer to as "terrorists"—are holding more than a thousand Russian nationals hostage.

The news is almost too shocking to absorb. Several educators lean on each other for support while others gasp or swear. This is the first violent incursion by a former Soviet republic targeting civilians in a Russian city since the collapse of the USSR.

Aside from worrying about the fate of the hostages, I fear this new situation might make it impossible to continue our workshop. How can we expect the academics to focus on a puppet show when their compatriots are being rounded up at gunpoint?

Amid such alarm, it takes incredible skill to get the participants to resume the meeting, but Dr. Genina manages exactly that. "While our people, including our children, are under siege and terrified in Budyonnovsk, we must still do what we came here to do," she says. "Through our work, we must ensure that violence like this does not happen again. Our role is to teach the next generation how to get along and have peace." She continues, expertly maneuvering the group's attention back to *Ulitsa Sezam*.

Despite a television news blackout in Budyonnovsk, the seminar participants arrive the next day knowing a great deal about the attack. The outpouring of collective grief is palpable and a nationalities specialist who writes about the problems of integrating ethnic minorities in Russia shares what he's heard with the group.

"The Chechens have taken at least fifteen hundred people hostage, including many children, and are holding them inside a city hospital." His next pronouncement almost made my heart stop. "The Chechen commander of the raid has told Russian authorities that for every Chechen soldier shot, they will kill ten hostages."

As horrible and tragic as the crisis is, sharing this experience brings our group closer together. The Americans in the group express sympathy over what is happening, and this seems to soften the educators toward the show. Our Russian colleagues are beginning to trust us and accept that we don't want to impose our values on Russia—that we genuinely seek to accommodate Russian views in choosing the show's goals.

In the wake of the Chechen attack, it doesn't seem optimal to discuss how *Ulitsa Sezam* should address minorities and diversity, but this is one of the most important goals of the series. Bravely, the group appears to have made a tacit pact not to speak about Budyonnovsk during the seminar so the necessary work can proceed. I am deeply moved by everyone's sheer will not to let their despair eclipse what they came to achieve.

Dr. Genina reminds the participants that *Ulitsa Sezam* is being made for children of many ethnicities. "We expect that our program, if aired on ORT, will be transmitted all across the former Soviet Union to Georgians, Armenians, Azerbaijanis, Ukrainians—and," she pauses, "Chechen children as well." Continuing in the same calm voice, Dr. Genina maintains, "Our hope is that *Ulitsa Sezam* can heal some of the divisions between feuding ethnic groups and provide conflict resolution skills at an early age."

The nationality question is acutely felt by many Russians, including people in this room who feel deep pain and a sense of betrayal about the breakup of their country. They resent their former "Socialist brethren," who, despite having benefited under Socialism—gaining education and opportunities—are now taking up arms against the motherland. More than half of the fifteen former USSR republics are now fighting for their independence from Russia.

A nationalities expert says, "In war zones today, like in Chechnya, it is the children who suffer the most." She urges the group to accept that even though children look different, they are all "God-created and none are bad." She entreats, "Do you want our children to live in a world where they grow up to hate other nationalities, where our world is divided into enemies and friends within our own borders?" I want to hug her for saying what I am sure many of us are feeling in the wake of this recent attack.

Dr. Genina encourages the group to try to put aside the hostility they may feel toward the Chechens so we can have an objective discussion. She begins, "Should *Ulitsa Sezam*'s storylines feature ethnic minorities from the former Soviet Union? How will the show present diverse cultural traditions like music, dancing, and national costumes from the former republics?"

In the last hours before lunch, a consensus is reached. The group resolves to include actors from different ethnic nationalities in the television show and incorporate elements from each of their cultures. It's a wonderful moment but it ends abruptly when one attendee who had left the room to check on the latest news now pushes through the door, yelling, "Russian TV just reported that Chechen rebels have shot five hostages." We all stare at each other in disbelief.

It's a tough afternoon, not only because of the growing crisis in Budyonnovsk. We have a challenging agenda ahead of us—including tackling issues like gender representation and sexual identity that not all of us will agree upon. I wonder if alternative families and same-sex partners will be part of our discussion. These subjects are still very much taboo in Russia, despite the country's recent liberalization.

I'm pleasantly surprised to see a gender expert present, a petite Russian woman with short blonde hair and a soft voice.

Dr. Genina shifts the conversation to a discussion about gender stereotypes. "For generations, there have been feminine men and masculine women. *Ulitsa Sezam* needs to defy traditional stereotypes for men and women," she begins. "Russian women are still the primary caregivers, doing childcare, laundry, and cooking. Therefore, it's important that *Ulitsa Sezam* show male characters as more involved in cooking and taking care of children." I gather we will not be discussing sexual identity at this gathering, but I'm pleased she's challenging these stereotypes.

Dr. Genina continues. "Right now, what we have is mothers raising children, but we need to model parenting with both the mother and the father together."

One of *Ulitsa Sezam*'s young female writers, invited to sit in on the seminar for the day, raises her hand to speak. "The New Soviet Woman was supposed to be a heroine of the workplace *and* a paragon of motherhood, but legislation meant to liberate women only gave women the freedom to work more—outside *and* inside the home." A ripple of laughter is heard.

The men in the room say little, perhaps feeling that they don't have the right to object. The writer proposes the husband character in *Ulitsa Sezam*—a leading role—do all the cooking in the fictional family home. This is a popular suggestion, and I love the direction they're taking.

However well the conference is going, the crisis in Budyonnovsk means the mood remains somber. During breaks, participants share whatever details they have about the hostages. At one point, one of the conference participants reports that the Russian military has dispatched troops to the region. The room erupts in cheers, then just as quickly quiets down as we consider the horror the hostages must be enduring.

After only two days of intense discussions and hard work, I find it incredible that these strong-willed participants have found common ground and are looking more relaxed and comfortable with each other, often exchanging warm smiles. Even more impressive: the curriculum for *Ulitsa Sezam* is beginning to take shape.

———————

Dr. Genina begins the final day's discussion by summarizing the goals the group has coalesced around, which will determine the show's content. "*Ulitsa Sezam* will focus on helping Russian children understand the values of an open and democratic society. Children will learn that their role and place in society is determined not by any closed social system, but by their personal choices, self-initiative, and actions."

Bucking decades of Soviet educational aims, she reiterates the group's collective wish that the show highlight self-actualization and individualism for all children, including non-ethnically Russian children and those who are disabled. At this, everyone in the room turns to Ludmilla.

Dr. Genina admonishes the group that such tolerance will require a delicate balance. As evidenced by the Budyonnovsk massacre, self-actualization means independence from Russia for many Muslims. To address this issue, Dr. Genina again mentions *Ulitsa Sezam*'s goal of including stories about cooperation among diverse ethnic groups, helping children develop the tools they need to live in a country where there may always be ethnic turmoil.

Glancing at the mathematician, Dr. Genina continues. "Russian children who grow up on *Ulitsa Sezam* will be proud and appreciate that they live in a great nation that has contributed generously to world knowledge and culture. They will be raised as healthy, happy, open, and curious people who are sure of themselves and believe they have a positive future."

When she finishes speaking, the group is silent—no boisterous clapping or smiling. Their serious expressions seem to acknowledge the importance of the work accomplished.

The conference attendees mill around for a long time afterward, exchanging phone numbers, promising to stay in touch. The physicist who had spoken earlier with Chary and stayed for the entire workshop pulls her aside. "I was so skeptical about this seminar at the beginning and doubted that we'd be able to develop an adequate curriculum to help our children. But after participating in the process, I now see that relying not on one, but on many diverse views from all the different experts, together we are somehow able to come up with a plan that might work."

I share his awe at our collaboration and credit Dr. Genina and Chary for its success. As I walk with my team through the monastery grounds toward the exit gate, I wonder if our productive discussions in this sacrosanct citadel will eventually change Russia. Maybe Patriarch Aleksey II's blessing played a part in our success.

The day after our conference, watching TV in my hotel, I'm horrified to learn that hundreds of hostages were killed in Budyonnovsk. I feel the loss deeply, almost viscerally. My only comfort is knowing that the crisis in Budyonnovsk imbued those at the seminar with a deeper appreciation of how our show might foster peace among future generations.

14

B IS FOR BLACKLIST

Shortly after the curriculum workshop, Dr. Genina writes up what becomes the final curriculum document outlining the show's educational goals based on recommendations from the curriculum workshop. The writers find this framework extremely helpful, and script submissions increase threefold. Regrettably, though, our high hopes for the Black Hen writers have been dashed. Lida's hand-picked writers seem unable to conform to *Sesame Street*'s three-to-five-page standard format, often submitting tomes of more than ten pages. And these Black Hen scripts, while well written, are often shockingly sad, violent, racist, and sexist.

At one meeting in our office with the Black Hen gang, a writer proposes a live-action storyboard to teach the letter *D*. His storyboard depicts a sad furry Muppet slowly mopping a linoleum floor and the letter *D* comes up on the screen as a voice narrates: "*D* for *Depressia*." Lida and the writers find this funny. I wouldn't be surprised if next, they propose a script where a Muppet throws herself under a moving train, à la Anna Karenina—teaching the letter "*J* for Jump."

Script meetings involve writers taking turns reading from their work. We'd asked the writers for scripts that teach the prescribed goal from the curriculum document and specified that the writing should be *relevant* and relatable for young children. But more than half of the Black Hen writers, each of whom wrote in isolation, submitted scripts with escapist themes—sending their characters off to outer space or to foreign lands where they have extraordinary adventures.

In one script called "The Map," meant to teach geography, the storyboard shows a child escaping in a flying saucer from Russia to France, where the boy feasts on a banquet of fine cheeses and foie gras.

Since citizens can now travel more freely, it's only natural that they would write about places they'd dreamed of visiting. Apparently, the Black Hen writers feel that what children would find most exciting *is to leave Russia*.

Robin and I glean another problem with our *Sezam* writers, which is that they don't fully grasp that television is a visual medium. It requires more action than words. Our young children viewers are just learning how to use their bodies to relate to the world physically. Children will laugh hysterically at a person scrunching up their nose or pretending to fall over a ball but are less interested in verbal description. One submitted script about a Russian folk orchestra includes a sentence about musicians feeling "sadness in their souls as they play a song of suffering." How can the writers expect children to understand the word *dusha* (soul) in this abstract context? But when I challenge Lida on this, she defends her writer. "From the time Russian children are two years old, they understand the word soul."

It seems incredible that Lida insists on championing these scripts. And then one night, when Robin and I stay late at the office, Robin looks through a stack of scripts on Lida's desk, discovering a piece of paper with the names of Robin's film school classmates who had submitted spec scripts for *Sesame Street*.

"This is a blacklist!" Robin yells—horrified to see the names on the same page with the authors Lida had rejected. I don't want to believe Lida would keep such a thing, but it is: a list of names.

The next day, Robin confronts Lida at the office. When I intervene, proposing Lida make amends by interviewing some of Robin's classmates as potential scriptwriters—in the spirit of giving everyone a chance—Lida defends her position.

"There's no point. These are useless, infantile children without any scientific understanding of writing or any status or recognition by the Union of Writers," she argues.

Robin, standing beside me, snaps back, "It's irrelevant whether writers are members of the Union of Writers or how old they are. All that should matter is if writers have an imagination, a good sense of humor, and can write well."

That afternoon, Robin invites some of her film school cohort to our office— many of whose names appeared on Lida's blacklist. However, when they arrive, Lida refuses to shake their hands and storms out of the office in a huff. This is incredibly embarrassing for Robin. I listen to her apologizing to her classmates for wasting their time as they head out the door.

When Lida returns to the office, Robin turns on her. "You are afraid of my generation because in *your* generation, everything was about politics and connections, but now, success depends on ability and talent." Robin is now shouting. "And you don't like the young writers because they won't bow down to you."

Robin seems to have crossed a line. Everyone in the office stops working, including me, waiting to see what will happen next. Lida shoots Robin a laser glare and storms out of the room.

After a moment, Misha, who has been listening at his desk, walks over to me and coolly interjects. "We need Lida. We must produce more than a hundred scripts quickly, and we don't have anyone else. She's managing the writers, and they are an unruly bunch."

Later, I ask Robin to get a drink after work with me. We arrive to a bar full of American and European men, some accompanied by prostitutes hanging on their every word.

We find two empty stools.

"I don't understand why you don't fire Lida. Then everyone would be welcome to submit scripts," Robin protests.

I see so much of my younger, idealistic self in her. Robin is fearless and approaches her job with dedication and professionalism beyond her years—impressing everyone except Lida. Some of the difficulties between Robin and Lida transcend opinions and values. I'm sure it's not easy for Lida to take direction from someone so young—and a foreigner.

After a few drinks, I encourage Robin to be more patient. "Lida is accustomed to working with the writers she chooses and trusts. In Soviet times she had to be careful," I say, noting that a few years earlier, if Lida vouched for people she didn't know at the TV station, it could lead to betrayal or worse. Instinctively, she's wary of hiring people she doesn't know personally.

Hearing myself defend Lida makes me have more empathy for her than I'd imagined I possessed.

Robin isn't buying it. She's still mad. "That's irrelevant now. Things have changed in Russia," she insists. "My generation doesn't have to play by the rules that people like Lida were forced to live by. We should be given a chance."

"That's all true," I say. "But there's also a practical reason it's difficult to fire her." I explain that Lida already traveled to New York and attended the *Sesame Street* training workshop paid for by U.S. taxpayers; it would be politically awkward for Misha and me to fire her right now. I remind Robin that Lida and the other producers have been working without receiving a regular salary. "And, if any of them leave, then we'll have no team at all."

"Lida is only interested in power," Robin exclaims.

I admire her youthful passion.

We order another glass of wine, and I promise Robin I will speak with Lida and Misha and do whatever is necessary to let the twenty-somethings submit spec scripts.

When I visit the office the next afternoon, Lida is working with another Black Hen writer. I ask her to meet Misha and me in Midhat's office. She struts in and plops herself down on the couch without a word.

I begin, asking Lida if she knows how Joan Ganz Cooney came up with the original idea for *Sesame Street*.

"No," she says disinterestedly.

"She was walking down a grocery store aisle in the 1960s and observed how children shopping with their mothers all asked to buy products that they'd seen advertised on television. Cooney thought if children could remember the brand names of detergent and toothpaste, then the same advertising techniques used to sell products could be used to create impactful educational messaging teaching children cognitive skills.

"What does this have to do with us?" Lida asks, unsure where this conversation is going.

I explain that since we are having so much trouble finding decent scriptwriters, perhaps she'd consider changing her tactics. If she won't hire the film students, maybe she'd consider approaching young writers working in Russia's new advertising industry?

Lida rolls her eyes. "It's not our custom to hire people off the streets."

When I pressure her further, she quits. Unfortunately, Piotr, our creative director and Lida's husband, quits in solidarity. Misha and I had not anticipated that.

Our office is so tiny, everyone already knew anyway, but Misha gathers the team and formally announces the couples' departure. Misha and I exchange glances. "This situation creates more problems," he says. But, despite the catastrophic loss of both our head writer and our creative director, the whole team seems to feel enormous relief.

Robin suddenly starts dancing around the office, singing, "Ding dong, the Wicked Witch is dead."

I'd underestimated Lida's effect on the atmosphere in the office. All the constant disagreements have taken a toll, even on Misha. He is now convinced of the need to hire a new crop of writers; he and I decide that Robin should take the lead coordinating the scriptwriting process, at least until we find a new head writer.

———————

A few days later, I'm getting ready to return home once again—I can't quite believe it, but my wedding is in four days. It's time for me to wrap up reviewing the latest scripts and instruct Robin and Misha on how to prepare the monthly estimated budget and payroll.

I arrive at the office the following morning and the entire production team yells, "Surprise!" Misha opens a bottle of champagne, putting a splash into each person's glass, then makes a toast, "*Ni pukha, ni pera*," a Russian expression equivalent to "Break a leg." I am touched.

Our parting is quite emotional. I joke that my teammates must think my future husband will put me in chains and prevent me from returning to Russia.

Before heading out the door, I remind Misha that he must fax me the month's production budget before the end of the week, so I can get it approved in New York and bring more money back to Moscow after the wedding.

On the way out the door, I hug our office mascot, Elmo. Looking into his Ping-Pong eyeballs, I say, loud enough for everyone to hear, "The next time we see each other, Big Elmo, I'll be a married woman!"

Everyone laughs and, for the first time in many months, I relax.

15

STEALING ELMO

The popular stereotype in the media of women spending endless hours fantasizing about their wedding applies to many of my friends—but for me, not so much.

I barely had time to get myself from the airport to our apartment and then to the Manhattan store to pick up my wedding dress. And although I had promised Ken that I would get back five days before the wedding, I only managed three. When I walk into our apartment, I discover my sweet fiancé is fretting about various last-minute wedding details. Later, he's upset that I'm on the phone speaking Russian, focusing on work instead of helping him, which had been the plan.

On the big day, Ken and I discover that the limousine we've hired to transport us to the Princeton chapel is too small to fit us *and* my gown without wrinkling the frock. So, my silk dress rides in luxury in the limo while we follow behind on the New Jersey Turnpike in my beat-up Honda. This is the opposite of romantic, but while most men would have found this all incredibly annoying, Ken appreciates the humor, and I'm grateful to have time alone with him to decompress.

Ken begins reciting the names of his distant relatives who will be attending the wedding. He correctly assumed I've forgotten. It suddenly hits me that I'd skipped most of the cardinal steps a bride is supposed to take while planning a wedding. Ken chose the date, location, and dinner menu, while I only requisitioned the vodka and wooden children's toys as our centerpieces from Russia. I feel like the worst bride ever—like an actress stepping into a role for which I'm completely unprepared.

I reach over and press my hand into his leg and tell him how grateful I am.

His eyes meet mine. He knows what I am thinking. "Sweetheart, everything is going to be fine." He leans over and plants a kiss on my forehead.

We arrive at the venue thirty-minutes late. But at least my gown is wrinkle-free. My bridesmaids stuff me into it in an alcove off the nave.

In addition to having a maid of honor, I asked Leonid to be my best man. He knocks on the door inside the church where I'm getting ready. He looks very handsome in his tuxedo while taking in the scene as my sister Emily fixes my veil and adjusts my white, strapless gown. He smiles at me. Leonid's presence magnifies the reality that this is happening, and my heart skips a beat.

He leans over, asking, "May I?" and helps to clasp the pearl necklace around my neck. He wears a bittersweet expression, as though he knows something that I don't—perhaps how much my life is about to change. With a grin, he tells me that our honored guest Irina has just arrived—putting a sarcastic emphasis on "honored." She still hasn't gotten us an office in Moscow or signed the agreement with *Sesame Street*, but she made it to my wedding.

I had invited Irina as a courtesy, mainly because she was constantly peppering me with questions about what American weddings look like and whether Jewish weddings are as long as Russian Orthodox ones. She pestered me to show her pictures of my dress, and when I gave in and showed her a photo of me wearing it, she placed her hand over her mouth and gasped. "Oh, my dear Natasha, you look like a Tsarina." I could tell she was angling for an invitation, but I had never thought she'd come. It seemed ridiculous that she'd be so invested in my big day, but now that it's here, I get it. Weddings are hopeful, and we all need hope. I'm happy Irina came.

It's a sweltering ninety-nine degrees, and due to our late arrival from the city, our one hundred guests have been perspiring in the uncomfortable hardwood church pews for the past forty minutes. The building's organizers did a beautiful job transforming the nondenominational Gothic-style chapel into a place of Jewish worship. Replacing the pulpit is a *chuppah*—a canopy supported by four tall poles, beneath which the ceremony will take place, symbolizing the home that Ken and I will build together. All the crucifixes on the altar are covered with white velvet fabric.

The choir begins singing, and my seventy-year-old father escorts me down the aisle, grinning as though he's just pulled off the Great Train Robbery. We all stand under the chuppah and I stifle a feeling of sadness, wishing my mother were among us. Vows are exchanged, the rabbi gives his blessings, and Ken breaks a wine glass wrapped in cloth with his foot, as is Jewish custom. The rabbi says, "Mazel Tov," and we're married!

We glide down the aisle, hand in hand. I feel deliriously happy. Ken looks relieved. I pass my four siblings seated together in a pew. They seem astonished that someone tied the knot with their crazy sister.

Outside, in the receiving line greeting guests, I spot Irina wearing a gorgeous pink, short-waisted jacket and tight black silk pencil skirt. She rushes over to embrace me, exulting, "This is one of the best days of my life."

Irina's joy is so immense and genuine, and I can't believe I almost didn't invite her. She appears totally at ease with my wacky relatives. I watch her talking to my sisters and brothers. I wonder what she's saying about me that's making them laugh so much. Circulating like a pro, she schmoozes with Ken's friends, celebrated economists, and his mother.

At one point, Irina raises her glass and makes a toast. "Natasha, now that you are married and have a husband to take care of, I will make sure that *Ulitsa Sezam* will not cause you any more problems, and my wedding present to you will be a new office!"

I can only hope.

Ken booked us a three-night honeymoon—our *mini*-moon—at a bed and breakfast not far from the chapel, figuring that I wouldn't want to go anywhere too far because I travel so much for work.

Not even twelve hours after saying "I do," the room phone at our romantic B&B rings. It's Moscow calling. I look at Ken, guilt-ridden. "I had to give Robin the number in case of emergency," I reveal sheepishly.

My husband shakes his head in disbelief.

As soon as I pick up, I hear Robin's usually cheerful voice reduced to a terrified whisper. Gruff male Russian voices are shouting in the background. She speaks into the receiver frantically and incoherently, "Our floor is overrun with soldiers with machine guns. They're forcing us to evacuate the office."

Ken catches a few words. He pushes his ear toward the receiver as I listen, straining to understand the soldiers' voices through the receiver. "What's going on?" he whispers.

I hold the phone away from my ear because the voices on the line are now very loud, shouting, "Everyone get out *now*!"

Through the clamor, I recognize Misha's deep voice as he calmly argues with the militiamen, "We have nothing to do with politics; we're making a children's television show."

I feel the tension flood my body. Ken touches my arm. "What's going on?" he says. But of course, I have no idea. We sit on the bed, our heads bent toward the phone receiver, listening together as the voices get louder and more aggressive.

Robin yells into the phone, "Soldiers are taking over our office and they've got AK-47s."

"Who are they?" I shout back. "Can you tell if they're military or police?"

Robin sounds confused and scared. "I don't know. They're going down the corridor and storming every office. Everyone is grabbing whatever they can before getting kicked out."

I hear screaming and can decipher Misha pleading with soldiers to give him and Robin five minutes to fax something to America. I can't imagine what they want to fax in this moment of crisis.

Then there's a thump, as if Robin has placed the phone on her desk. Next I hear the furious tapping of computer keys. I realize, ridiculous as it is, that Robin must be trying to finish typing up the production budget so she can fax it to me—probably with a machine gun pointed at her head. *Sesame Street* will not send cash to Moscow unless they receive the written budget estimate. Without this money, production will come to a grinding halt. I listen to Misha pleading with the soldiers for more time. I feel helpless.

Suddenly, a soldier shouts, "You have ten minutes to collect what you need and get out."

Oh my god, I think, looking over at Ken. I wonder if this is happening because conservatives are trying to take over the television station again, as they did in 1993.

He looks back at me, concerned. This is not the honeymoon we expected, and I can tell he's afraid for Robin, Misha, and the other producers. It's different now that he knows who they are. "This is awful," he says.

Finally, Robin is back on the line, dazed and disoriented. She keeps apologizing while continuing to type.

"Robin," I yell, "get out of there."

"I'm so sorry, so sorry. . . . I'm taking too long typing. I'm so sorry."

I look in bewilderment at Ken. "Why isn't she leaving the office?"

"Robin, forget about the budget!" I scream into the phone. I hear Misha continue trying to stall the soldiers. His booming voice is getting angrier and angrier, and then—

The call drops.

My heart nearly stops.

I try redialing our Moscow office with the B&B owner's help making the international call, but the line is dead, as is the one in Midhat's office on the same floor. Panic spreads through my entire body. Robin is twenty-two. What will I say to her mother if something happens to her? Ken looks at me, worried. Our romantic mini-moon is over. We start packing up our clothes and wedding gifts to return to Manhattan.

———————

Later, Misha calls me in the middle of the night. Ken is asleep. I whisper as I talk to Misha, who confirms that no one got hurt and everyone is safe. I let out my breath, near tears.

When I ask him what happened, he reconstructs the day's events.

"Robin was a superstar," he narrates proudly. "After the guards pulled out the phone cords to the phone/fax machine in our office, she snuck past them to the neighboring office, where their phone lines were still working, and started faxing the budget to New York. When two soldiers spotted her, she threw herself in front of their guns—blocking them from accessing the fax machine. Only after she heard the *beep-beep* of a successful transmission did she step away with her hands up."

That Robin took such a risk to send a fax seems insane to me.

Misha continues, "The soldiers put locks with wax seals on every office, and now we have no access to any of our equipment or scripts."

"Were you guys able to save anything from the office?" I ask.

Misha laughs. "Well, we tried to save Elmo but one of the soldiers took him."

"They stole Elmo! Incredible," I exclaim.

"Yeah," Misha says, "I tried to save Elmo by grabbing him out of the soldier's arms, but the commando yanked him from my grasp." He describes how he and Robin sadly watched as the soldier shifted his machine gun to the side, stuffing Elmo under his armpit as he marched down the long hallway.

"We watched Elmo's half-moon smile bouncing up and down, until the soldier disappeared through the swinging doors," he says. "It was terrifying."

"Why take Elmo?" I ask.

Misha sighs, "Maybe for his kid?"

I tell Misha everything will be all right, that we've probably just gotten in the crosshairs of some random battle at the television station. "What's most important is that no one got hurt."

"But without scripts, equipment, or an office, how can we possibly produce anything?" He's got a point. And hearing the defeat in his voice nearly crushes me.

A day later, Irina phones me from Moscow. She had flown back immediately after my wedding. Fortunately, she was at Video Art when our office was raided. Before I can get a word out, she laments how perilously close we'd come to placing our employees in danger.

"Do you know why this happened?" I ask.

"It's Russia," Irina replies, unfazed. "Someone is always fighting with someone—what do you expect?"

I suppose, setting up shop inside ORT was bound to get us in trouble. I remind her that we wouldn't be in this situation if she'd gotten us the office promised months ago.

Irina confides in me that, sadly, the TV station has once again frozen her bank accounts, and although she'd hoped this month to meet *Ulitsa Sezam*'s payroll and set up an office for us, it's no longer possible. "I know you understand, *Dusha Moya*," she coos, sprinkling salt on the wound.

I want to scream. How can I run a production with more than two hundred people when we don't have a suitable office, a budget, or any semblance of stability? It's like trying to make a children's puppet show in the middle of a war zone.

16

WILL *SESAME STREET* SAVE THE DAY?

I'd expected to take off two weeks after my wedding, but now I will have to return to Moscow sooner. The situation with the ORT office takeover and Irina's frozen bank account is catastrophic, much worse than the other crises we've weathered. It could shut down the entire production. I call Misha again and direct him to tell the team to continue working from their homes as best they can while I try to resolve the crisis.

In the middle of the night, the fax machine in my New York apartment spits out a sheet of paper with "HELP! HELP! HELP!!!" across the top. Since we got kicked out of our office, it's a struggle for Robin to communicate with me. She travels for an hour on public transport to Misha's apartment and uses his fax/phone, or she goes to the central post office and books an international call, which is crazy expensive and involves hours of waiting in line. As I read Robin's fax, which is handwritten because she has no computer, I thank every higher power for Misha's foresight in moving a fax machine to his home. The fax reads:

> We won't last long like this! We are completely cut off from all our producers and directors! The writers who have scripts ready to turn in don't know where to find us or how to contact us, and no one has phones, and even if we did, we have nowhere to meet. HELP! PLEASE!!! It's like we're being thrown out into the street. The situation is DIRE.

Sesame Workshop's lawyers are going to have a field day when I tell them about the takeover—how *Ulitsa Sezam* exposed the American company to unprecedented risk. Unfortunately, the larger picture is even more disheartening: if the television station is no longer safe, then who's actually in charge of Russia?

On Monday morning, I return to Sesame Workshop in time to attend the monthly international production group meeting. I feel a strange cognitive dissonance, observing my American colleagues streaming into the conference room, carrying coffee cups and commenting on nothing more than the unusually humid June day.

When called on, my voice is shaking. My team had experienced other crises in the past, but not like this one.

My newest tale of woe is met with looks of shock. Unfortunately, in my efforts to evoke sympathy—giving a blow-by-blow description of my brave Moscow colleagues facing down machine guns—I am suddenly aware that I may be digging my professional grave. I feel the eyes of my ex-boss, who is still in charge of the international production division, boring into me. When I finish, he points out that this situation could jeopardize government grants for *Sesame Street* in the future.

There's nothing I can say. Lightning has struck our *Ulitsa Sezam* production for the third time.

He looks annoyed. "Maybe we should consider postponing the Moscow production entirely, Natasha?" adding that he will discuss the sad state of affairs with Baxter and his senior colleagues. What does he mean by "postponing?" For how long? Unfortunately, Baxter is away and apparently will not be back for another day. I worry about getting other execs at the workshop involved.

I let out a slow breath, recognizing that if the CFO—who is not a fan of Russia—hears about this, *Ulitsa Sezam* is doomed.

The meeting is over, and everyone scatters.

That night I am an emotional wreck. Ken tries to comfort me, but I'm inconsolable. With all the effort invested into this production, I must face the reality that we may fail. I think of the promises I've made to my Russian colleagues and begin to feel sick, knowing how ending production will crush them. And yet, I understand it's a lot to ask of a corporation like *Sesame Street* to continue accepting such enormous risks in Moscow.

Ken says, "Imagine if someone had gotten hurt or even killed during the office takeover." He tells me I shouldn't personalize every defeat. "*Sesame Street* has properties all over the globe; they have to consider how corruption or Russia's collapse might potentially harm the company."

In my heart, I know Ken's being sensible, but I'm still upset. Doesn't the company understand that *Ulitsa Sezam* is about so much more? Every day, I see how my brilliant and creative colleagues are transforming into independent and fearless warriors battling to bring openness and light to Russia. I envision our show will carry these same messages to millions of children throughout the former USSR. The *Sesame Street* Muppets model the very best of what America has to offer.

When I wake up, I see a bouquet of roses left on the kitchen table by my sweetheart.

Robin calls my New York office later that afternoon. A friend of hers who works at an American company has let her use his phone. From five thousand miles away, through the crackling phone line, her laughter momentarily reassures me that all is not lost. "We're all still *aliiive*," she sings, making light of what she and I both know is a catastrophic situation.

It's wonderful to hear Robin's voice. She tells me things have improved slightly since her all-caps-ridden fax. She's managed to round up team members and they're meeting daily in her tiny dorm room. "Although the crew is demoralized, not one person wants to give up on the show," she says.

I breathe a sigh of relief.

However, in the confusion of the takeover, our shooting schedule is completely disrupted. Robin frantically asks what to do about the scheduled film shoot with twenty kids later this week and if we should cancel it.

The line buzzes as she waits for my answer. I have no idea what to tell her. If we temporarily halt production, the talented team we've assembled may not wait for us; they'll have to take new jobs if we aren't back up and running soon. I ask Robin if the city is now safe. Robin says the attack was limited to the TV station so there's no danger filming the kids in their school.

"Does the director have the equipment he needs?" I'm worried that it might have been seized in the office assault.

"He's borrowing all the equipment from VGIK, and we can pick it up tomorrow."

"Go ahead and shoot then," I say, while aware that we still might have to shut down our entire production soon.

Everyone is scared about what will happen to *Ulitsa Sezam* and their jobs, including me. I feel terrible that I'm not there but also very proud of Robin for holding the team together. I want to offer assurances that everything will be okay, but of course I can't.

The next day I'm told Baxter's back in town, and I'm supposed to meet him in his office. That afternoon, I take a seat in my regular oversize chair and wait. My lower lip begins bleeding from my picking at the skin. Though nervous, I'm cautiously optimistic. Baxter lives off the anarchy in Russia the same way I do, and he's never failed to come through for us. But this time may be different.

He arrives in the doorway. I steel myself for whatever devastating news he's about to deliver. Instead, he looks at me with an impish smile.

"Natasha, we all agree that *Ulitsa Sezam* may be on life support, but it's not dead yet. The good news is that C-suite has decided to resuscitate the patient."

Standing with his hands on his hips, he adds, "Corporate will commit to covering Irina's costs for the next two months, until she can get on her feet again."

I feel such relief, while gulping in air so I don't cry in front of Baxter. "That's more than enough time for Irina to get the bank to remove the hold on her money." At least, I hope so.

Baxter puts his palms on my shoulders and looks me in the eye. "Natasha, I've stuck my neck out for you. If you fail, it'll be my head on the chopping block."

"We will make it work," I promise, not quite knowing how.

Outside Baxter's office, walking down the hall, my hands are shaking.

I need to get back to Moscow and see if we still have a team and a production.

17

THE SCRIPTWRITERS AND GROUCHO MARXISM

On the flight back to Moscow, I feel happy, constantly touching my wedding ring, beaming. My good mood was no doubt being helped along by the two scotches I ordered. I need to prepare for what's ahead. My team is shattered, but I'm also grateful for the wedding present *Sesame Street*'s executives gave me: a bailout for *Ulitsa Sezam*.

Leonid meets me at the airport. On the way to my hotel, once again, we talk about the storming of the TV station. He tells me, "The public is growing intolerant of so-called democratic freedom—too much freedom for Russia." Apparently the atmosphere has become aggressively anti-Western and anti-American. "It's not safe for foreigners." Leonid lowers his head to light a cigarette as he's driving. "You remember my friend, Eduard Uspensky? The famous children's author I told you about?"

I shake my head no.

"Well, he's just published a vicious attack against Russian *Sesame Street* in *Ogonyok*." This is a culture magazine that is popular among Moscow's elite.

Keeping his eyes on the road, Leonid pulls the periodical out of his satchel between the seats and shoves it toward me. I begin reading aloud: "Everything in the country has been turned upside-down, no one knows about tomorrow, and as we speak, another danger approaches—a large American educational entertainment television series called *Ulitsa Sezam* is seeking to replace Russian education with 'American chewing gum for the masses.' *Sesame Street* will seduce Russian children . . . and poison Russia by getting people to buy toys, candy, and anything else you can think of."

"How is this even *possible*?" I say. "How can anyone blame *Sesame Street* for the chaos Russia is experiencing? That's absurd."

Leonid is quiet, navigating a difficult intersection. I consider whether Uspensky's hyperbolic article is at all accurate. Some of my Russian friends with kids have been complaining about American culture hijacking Russian childhood. One mother told me, "All my kids want now are Power Rangers." I know the flood of Western children's toys into Russia's consumer-starved market is fanning further resentment because parents can't afford to buy these products for their children.

Leonid tells me to continue reading. "Is capitalism destroying what is left of Russian culture? Attacking the very heart of our TV production? Why should we give the Americans our airtime to make money and profit from our children? Television could be saving our country and our children by uniting people and the republics, as well as the government; but it is doing just the opposite."

It's a damning indictment.

"We need more Russian allies," I tell Leonid. "We've got to fight back and as-sure the Russian public that *Ulitsa Sezam* will be Russian, and not just another distasteful American import."

Although dreadfully hot, the hour-long car ride provides an opportunity to plan. We come up with a strategy to find an established director with gravitas in Russia's TV and film industry—someone who can be the public face of our coproduction and, we hope, appease the critics.

Leonid drops me at the Palace Hotel and speeds off to another meeting. I race toward Misha and Robin, who are waiting for me in the lobby. Hugging them tightly, I feel overwhelmed with relief that they weren't harmed in the attack. I'm embarrassing them both, but they allow it.

We work in the hotel restaurant for the next four hours, trying to wrap our heads around coordinating future filming and production activities without an office, equipment, or phones. Losing the office has put us deeply behind schedule. The biggest problem is now figuring out how to reproduce all the seized scripts. Moreover, after losing our head writer and many of her most loyal scribes—actually not a great loss—we also need to train the new crop of young screenwriters from the film school who've joined us and give a re-fresher course to the more senior writers who've stayed on. More than half of the writers are new to *Ulitsa Sezam*.

Over the past weeks, Robin has been triumphant in her new role as script coordinator; but as an American, even as culturally fluent as she is, Robin can't continue exercising so much control over the *Ulitsa Sezam* scripts. That's not the *Sesame Street* way. Anton, from the Black Hen group, had prepared some pretty decent scripts compared to the other union member writers, so Misha and I appoint him head writer. We promote Robin to resident producer and she takes on a bigger role in production coordination.

However, to start off the new and old group of writers on the right foot, I'd arranged for Luis Santiero, an Emmy Award–winning *Sesame Street* writer, to travel to Moscow.

Luis arrives at the Palace Hotel two weeks later, jet-lagged and anxious about leading the writer's workshop. He's also jittery about being in a country that until recently was communist. He has good reason.

Luis immigrated to the United States from Cuba with his family in 1960, the year Fidel Castro's Marxist regime nationalized private property and seized Luis's family estate. His great-grandfather, Gerardo Machado, had been the president of Cuba from 1925 to 1933—a past that proved problematic for him and his descendents in the years following the Cuban revolution.

Luis and I meet in the hotel restaurant. At forty, Luis is trim and handsome, with dark eyes. Over dinner, he asks whether I think the writers will be responsive to his advice. I describe the recent raid on the TV station and the firing of our head writer, so he understands the atmosphere he's walking into. But I reassure him that he's arrived at the perfect time, and I have faith he can impart some of his scriptwriting genius to our beleaguered group of writers, still traumatized by the takeover. "With you here, the new scriptwriters will have a distinct advantage over the last group," I offer optimistically.

On the first day of the writer's workshop, the rag-tag *Ulitsa Sezam* writers— about thirty men and women of various ages—file into the Central House of Authors, a legendary club on Povarskaya Street, frequented in Soviet times by famous writers like Mikhail Bulgakov and Yevgeny Evtushenko. The young scribes chatter excitedly as they pass through the gilded, oak-paneled central dining room with crystal chandeliers. Unlike the union member writers, who in Soviet times had visited the exclusive club on numerous occasions, the younger generation is seeing the inside for the first time.

In a room adjacent to the dining room, the writers take seats around a long rectangular table. After introductions, Luis reassures the group his workshop will provide the skills they need to create engaging scripts filling approximately fifteen hours of children's television. I explain that we have a team of translators working around the clock to translate the Russian scripts into English, and vice versa.

Luis begins by describing the three different types of *Sesame Street* scripts: animated, live-action, and studio, where the Muppets interact with human actors in what will be a Russian-style neighborhood. In the interest of bringing everyone up to speed, I show the group the latest Henson Company draft sketches of the proposed Slavic Muppets based on earlier discussions with *Ulitsa Sezam*'s producers.

"These aren't fully fleshed out," I say. "In fact, the largest Muppet, a full-size body puppet, is the only one with a name—*Domovoi*."

Luis and I lead an open discussion, inviting comments on the proposed puppets. "I hope with your ideas, we can bring these characters to life," I chirp.

Right away, an older man named Oleg takes issue with the proposed drawings. "The body puppet shouldn't be blue because people will think the puppet is a homosexual." In Russian, *Goloboi* (blue) is a euphemism for gay. He says this as though being gay is wrong.

This is not how I wanted to begin the workshop—embarrassed in front of our Western guest. Also, I'm aware that some people in the room may themselves be queer, if closeted. I want *Ulitsa Sezam* to be a place where all can feel welcome.

My attention shifts back to Luis, who has turned to face Oleg.

"Muppets don't really have sexual preferences," he says with a straight face. "Or sex for that matter."

The rest of the group laughs uproariously, and Luis earns points for this joke. I adore him for keeping his cool.

One of the younger writers, who has been scribbling on a piece of paper, raises her hand. "Why don't we call the Domovoi Muppet *Zeliboba*?" The writers seem to like the whimsical, nonsense name.

Another writer, part of the senior collective, dislikes the proposed character of the girl puppet. "She should not be active, but shy and passive, while the boy puppet should be the active one," he states decisively.

"Yeah," agrees another colleague. "The female puppet should be more like a traditional character from Russian fairytales: sweet, docile, obedient, and feminine."

Nana Grinstein, the outspoken woman with short dark hair and black eyes who had come up with the name Zeliboba, scoffs at the men. "That's a ridiculous stereotype. Instead, we should be figuring out how to help little girls discover how to be more assertive and fulfilled in new Russia."

Luis looks like he needs a break. We step outside the building to get some air. I can tell he's upset, but when he speaks his words are measured and calm. "I can't believe how conservative some of the writers are." He sighs and then gives me a bemused look. "They're worse than the Cuban exiles I grew up with in Miami." Luis looks past me, and I see his eyes settling on a crowd of older women standing in a line that wraps around a building across the street.

"What's going on there?" he asks.

"It's a Russian bank. The women are waiting to trade in their old ruble bills before the government takes them out of circulation." I explain that most Russians don't keep their savings in banks because they don't trust banks to keep their money safe. I joke that by the age of these women, some of their bills might date back to World War II. This isn't actually possible because a few years earlier, the Russian Central Bank had invalidated all Soviet currency issued before 1993. But if they don't change the bills, they'll lose their life savings.

Luis shakes his head in disbelief and tells me he remembers when the same thing happened in Cuba after the revolution.

When we get back to the room, the writer who objected to *Ulitsa Sezam*'s largest puppet being blue has consulted with some of the older male writers and apparently they've reached a consensus. He proposes replacing the boy and girl puppets with a scarecrow and a tumbleweed puppet. The tumbleweed will roll around from place to place and gather information for the scarecrow. "This way, we will have no issues with the puppets' genders," he says, pleased with the idea.

I can't stop myself. "You mean the tumbleweed puppet will gather information like a KGB agent for the scarecrow?"

Everyone laughs except the writers who came up with the idea. I propose we table further conversation about the Muppets because it's taking up too much time. Luis moves on to a discussion about writing structure.

Most of these young writers are familiar with standard comedy structure: set up a joke, and then build it and deliver the punchline. To test their skills, Luis splits them up into groups. As the day progresses, the writers present their sketch ideas, reading aloud. Luis provides on-the-spot critiques while sending them off to do rewrites.

Luis brings the group together again to discuss one of the scripts that aims to teach the concept of sharing.

The script is called "Sharing Apples." Vadim, the author, begins reciting the dialogue between two hypothetical Muppets:

MUPPET 1: Look at these apples. I picked them myself. Isn't that great?
MUPPET 2: Great? Maybe for you! Now, what are you going to do with them?
MUPPET 1: Well, eat them, of course.
MUPPET 2: Eat them—all by yourself?
MUPPET 1: More for me!
MUPPET 2: Can't you think of something better?
MUPPET 1: When I eat apples, I think there is nothing better.
MUPPET 2: Well, better for you, but what about me?

"Do you think the dialogue is perhaps too aggressive?" Luis asks politely. When the group stares at him, confused, Luis tells them he notices a pattern in the conversational exchanges between characters in nearly all the proposed scripts he's read. He picks up another script and quotes various phrases used, such as "Give that to me," "Stop bothering me," and "Go away."

Luis suggests toning down some of the more commonly used impolite phrases. To demonstrate an alternative, he shows several clips of Bert and Ernie in which they tease each other mercilessly but with gentleness and warmth.

Luis turns off the video player. "Do you think this approach could work in your scripts?" Not all the writers agree, with some looking away from Luis or down at their notes. Anton begins huffing, then mutters loud enough to be heard, "The only reason the Americans came to Moscow is to insult our writing."

Luis is normally polite and mild-mannered, but now looks ready to take off his kid gloves. Glaring at Anton, he says, "Any writer who cannot deal with this kind of editorial critique isn't worth his salt."

I want to applaud, but recognize that this is Luis's boxing match, and he's doing just fine throwing his own punches.

Red-faced, Anton glares at Luis and crosses his arms over his chest. Some of the writers—mostly the younger scribes—appear almost relieved to see Luis standing up to Anton. They agree to work on developing a lexicon of kindness and compassion in future scripts.

At the end of the day, Luis whispers to me that Anton is getting on his nerves.

"That's too bad," I smile, "because Anton and his wife have invited you to dinner tonight."

Luis is exhausted but can't say no. Robin goes with them to translate.

———————

That night I meet up with Leonid at a popular Jewish restaurant near Mayakovski Square. Between servings of gefilte fish, potato latkes, and the world's best chicken soup, Leonid complains, "No one, at any of the TV stations, wants to air an American show right now."

I grumble in turn about the issues we're having with the writers.

He shrugs and says, "Tasha, walk down the street, any street in Moscow. Have you ever noticed when someone bumps into you, they never smile or apologize? Russians seldom smile—why should they? They don't feel very friendly. Life is too hard."

I protest that this is not always the case; Russians are the kindest, most generous people in private.

Leonid nods. "Yes, that's true, until they're not."

Sometimes Leonid's too dark for me.

Luis joins me for breakfast at the hotel buffet. I'd expected to hear him grouse about his night with Anton, but instead he sounds surprisingly upbeat. Before getting food, he tells me that he had an unexpectedly pleasant evening with Anton and the writer's wife and then stayed up, reviewing the scripts the writers had completed in session the day before.

"Although I can't quite tell what the translated scripts sound like in Russian with their rhymes and wordplay, they are incredibly original. I think they're getting it!" he says excitedly. We chat throughout breakfast, and I'm relieved to hear how some of the writers are producing the funny, goofy, carefree scripts with clear educational goals that are typical of *Sesame Street*.

On the workshop's second day, the atmosphere appears more relaxed. Even Anton chats easily with the younger writers and seems cooperative.

As soon as the writers take their seats, Nana raises her hand. "After yesterday's discussion about tone of voice and aggression, I want to talk about why I think we scriptwriters are having trouble writing upbeat, positive scripts like the ones we've seen on the American show." She explains that every time they try to write sweet scripts like the American show, they end up feeling too cloyingly sentimental. "As writers, we are afraid of writing anything that feels false, that does not reflect the reality in our country. But also, above all else, we want to avoid writing scripts that become a sad reflection of our current reality."

Although Luis is unaware of Nana's tragic personal background, many of her classmates from VGIK know her story. At age seventeen, Nana, along with her parents, a mixed Armenian and Jewish couple, were forced to flee Baku, the capital of Azerbaijan, after ethnic tensions erupted. Hundreds of thousands of Armenian Christians, Jews, and Azerbaijani Muslims were displaced, just like the Tartars before them. Nana and her family had feared for their lives.

Nana continues. "Luis, I'm not being critical. I think we are doing the best we can, and we want our show to make Russian children happy, but I am not sure how to do this and remain true to myself."

I jump into the discussion. "Russia's situation is not that dissimilar from America in the early 1960s when violence and racial discrimination dominated the social landscape. Even though we had terrible discrimination against people of color, *Sesame Street*'s writers portrayed harmonious race relations on the show, which impacted generations of children and parents." I tell them *Ulitsa Sezam* can do the same in Russia. "Your prose can change the future."

Luis nods, seeming to appreciate the support. He explains that a typical *Sesame Street* script is written on two levels, playing between the reality of adult shared experiences in popular culture and political life and the child's point of view. "Through this intersection of realities, the script becomes genuine and true."

Nana is not convinced. "We cannot write humorous parodies or ironies about our past because it is too painful to joke about things that have only recently broken down or are continuing to break down in front of our eyes."

Nana is very articulate. She continues as several of her fellow writers nod their heads. "So many of *Sesame Street*'s videos spoof popular American culture, and everyone understands the jokes. In new Russia, we have no new shared culture, and the jokes about our new society haven't even been invented yet."

The discussion has veered into an area where we need greater expertise. I offer to bring Dr. Genina to the later afternoon session.

As the day progresses, Luis reviews the scripts he read the night before. His analysis touches on the differences between Russian-style comedy and American slapstick humor. Focusing on the Marx Brothers as an example, he explains that Groucho Marx and his gang routinely use a stream of puns, wordplay, and malapropisms, but they also incorporate physical humor, leaving audiences rolling on the floor in laughter. He points out that Russian-style humor is typically droll, sarcastic, and not physical.

One writer raises her hand. "We call our humor 'laughing between tears.'"

I hadn't thought about this before, but now I realize that it's rare to see Russians explode in belly laughter as many Americans do while watching slapstick films and TV shows like *Airplane* or *Dumb and Dumber*.

After lunch, Dr. Genina tells the group that her talk this afternoon will focus on two crucial goals for *Ulitsa Sezam*: racial tolerance and positive social behavior.

She repeats what some writers already know: the show's storylines will include Russians as well as actors representing different nationalities from former Soviet republics.

I inhale slowly, worried how this group may respond to a conversation about race and nationality. It was difficult enough broaching these topics with our producers in New York, and now we have it all over again with the writers.

One of the writers shares his conservative views. "We have more important things to address in our show than nationality issues. These minorities should be more grateful. If it hadn't been for the Soviet Union, they'd be living in mud huts."

Another writer says, "While it's important to focus on minorities, we have more pressing lessons to teach our children, like how to navigate in a competitive market. They will have to learn to take risks and not be afraid."

Once again, Nana saves the day. "Of course, we have to include non-Russians in our show because that's what new Russia looks like today. Anything else would be a lie."

As the group debates, Dr. Genina patiently lets the discussion unfold.

After a while, Luis joins, encouraging the writers to conform to the educational goals outlined in the curriculum document. He reminds them, "It's the writer's job to write the scripts and the researcher's job to set the goals."

Dr. Genina smiles and uses this transition to move on to the next issue.

"Many Russians have forgotten how to be polite," she says, then suggests, "The television series should create storylines that demonstrate good manners and show people talking politely to each other and being civil. For example, when a store clerk serves a customer, she might say, 'May I please help you?'" She worries that under communism, the deprivation so many experienced may have eroded any semblance of civility between people.

But Dr. Genina points out that rudeness in Russia is really only a recent historical development, and one that she hopes can be reversed. She describes how traditional Russian forms of address changed as societal norms changed. In prerevolutionary Russia, she explains, many forms of address conveyed respect but also communicated class status, gender, military rank, and marital relations, for example, *Gospodin* (Mr.) and *Gospozha* (Mrs.). In an attempt to rid forms of address that suggested societal status, the Soviet government had declared such exchanges to be "too bourgeois" and consigned them to the linguistic garbage heap, replaced by the more egalitarian: *tovarish* (comrade) and, later, *muzhchina* (man) and *zhenschina* (woman). "To the Russian ear these greetings sound unnatural and weird," Dr. Genina says. She turns toward me and asks, "Imagine if in America, you could no longer address people as Mr. and Mrs. and there was nothing to replace them."

I understand the problem she's spelling out. Soviet-imposed forms of address are no longer needed or wanted but there's nothing popularly accepted to replace them.

She shakes her head with some exasperation. "We are in a kind of language limbo," she says.

Luis listens as the writers brainstorm about how to create scripts that reflect what Dr. Genina called "a kinder, gentler world." The group then rewrites their scripts, taking into account recommendations to soften the tone and language.

We reconvene later in the day and the writers take turns reading their new scripts aloud. All of them reflect a real effort toward politeness and care. One script in particular perfectly illustrates Dr. Genina's recommendations.

At a local bakery, Zeliboba holds open the door for his neighbor, Aunt Dasha, who in turn praises Zeliboba for being so polite. Zeliboba is so pleased to receive the praise that, when Aunt Dasha tries to leave the store, Zeliboba repeatedly opens and closes the door, inadvertently preventing Aunt Dasha from getting past Zeliboba and leaving. The two characters comically exchange various pleasantries each time the door opens and closes, demonstrating to children the numerous ways one can say, "Thank you," "Please," and "You are welcome."

This episode elicits smiles and a sprinkling of laughter at the writer's table, including from Luis. It feels good to laugh. And I know that when this is over, I'll remember this as the breakthrough moment.

For the rest of the day, Luis jumps from one group of writers to another, critiquing scripts with gentle encouragement. Anton does the same, having assumed a more collaborative stance.

Robin's classmates bring freshness, passion, and openness to our writers' group. They also seem more comfortable than their older colleagues at grappling with cross-cultural differences while still creating scripts that are uniquely Russian in tone, content, and essence.

On the fifth and last training day, the writers master "Western-style" physical comedy that smoothly integrates our show's educational goals. Some of the best scripts, like a goofy song rhyming nose (*nos*) with the Russian word for rose, is a highlight for all.

One animation storyboard teaching children about the emotions "happy" and "sad" leaves everyone in the room speechless. The scriptwriter reads: "A little boy and girl walk hand in hand in a park, each holding a balloon, looking happy. Accidentally, the boy lets go of his balloon. The little girl sees him crying and then releases her balloon into the air and smiles. The boy stops crying, and together, they watch their balloons ride high into the endless blue sky."

An American version of this script might have shown the children sharing the remaining balloon rather than leaving them both with no balloon. As an American, this script strikes me as very Russian. The girl not only shows an unwillingness to enjoy her balloon when her friend has lost his, but also demonstrates the comfort of shared experience when she lets her own balloon drift away with his. Although probably not appropriate, and maybe even a little confusing for an American audience, the scene is perfect for Russia, resonating deeply with the painful choices Russians are grappling with today.

When the workshop is over, the writers give Luis a standing ovation, lining up to shake his hand and exchange hugs. They are sorry to see him go.

Later as Luis folds himself into the back of his taxi to the airport, he looks at me and says of the Russians, "At first you want to kill them, and then you never want to leave them." Smiling, he says the experience has changed him forever.

————————

The writers meet weekly through the next month, shuttling between Robin's dorm room and Vika's office at ORT. Fortunately, her floor of the TV station was not occupied during the takeover. The scriptwriters critique each other's work, modeling typical television writer's rooms in America. They select scripts that will move on to the final round to be evaluated by *Ulitsa Sezam*'s producers and researchers in New York and Moscow.

One evening each week or sometimes twice a week, the Moscow team of producers and researchers gathers at Vika's office while the American *Ulitsa Sezam* team congregates around a speaker phone at *Sesame Street* headquarters. For the next few hours, in the morning New York time, and the evening, Moscow time, we evaluate each script and storyboard for its educational efficacy and entertainment value. Sometimes, the scriptwriters or freelance film directors sit in on calls when their work is being discussed.

In the beginning, the Russian team members were reticent to share their views. But after understanding that the Americans genuinely want to hear their opinions, they become even more vocal than the Americans. These group phone calls often have ten people on the line and offer us all insights into cultural differences between our countries.

For example, one time while discussing the translation of a *Sesame Street* clip that is a parody of the classic children's story, "The Three Little Pigs," the Big Bad Wolf Muppet blows down the piggies' houses and then opens his own business, coaching others on how to blow down houses.

Nana, who is sitting in on the call in our Moscow office, shakes her head at the clip, and explains that most Russians neither own homes nor run a private business, and for them, such concepts are incomprehensible. "How in our scripts are we supposed to present people who are entrepreneurial—even if they are puppets—when so many Russians think making money is bad?" she asks.

Even the iconography of the American Muppets encompasses cultural ideas that are indecipherable to many of the writers. For example, Nana insists a character like Oscar the Grouch would never exist in Russia.

"What is he? Is he a hippie, a punk, or a rapper?" She explains that such individualistic behavior was considered unacceptable in communist society. "Oscar the Grouch is a nonconformist, and in Russia he would have been put in prison," Nana jests.

From the scripts rolling in, I can tell that our writers are developing an entirely original writing style for this show, creating a unique approach to humor, motivation, and intonation for post-Soviet society. It looks like the pacing will be slower than the American show, its stories sweeter but not falsely sentimental because the Russians already have enough drama in their real lives.

There are still challenges. Two months after the writer's workshop, Anton is back to his old self, badmouthing *Sesame Street* and the "arrogant Americans" who are always "telling the Russians what's wrong with their scripts." Increasingly, Anton's attitude is damaging team morale. He doesn't bother showing up for our daily morning writers' meetings or the script review meetings by phone with our counterparts in New York. And scripts from his Black Hen writers are rarely accepted while the film school cohort have been prolific and on target with their delivery.

Tensions come to a head one day when I arrive to Vika's office where we are still temporarily working, and I find Anton composing pornographic political limericks on the new computers purchased to replace those seized from our old office. I make a decision with Misha to let Anton go and, within a week, he's gone. The other Black Hen writers stop submitting scripts too.

Misha and I promote two of our strongest scriptwriters, Nana Grinstein and Anna Kalin, to co-head writers in his place—hoping the third time's the charm.

Nana proves exceptional in her new role: sensitive to the other writers' feelings and adept at developing a common language when critiquing scripts. I often see her hunched over scripts and advising her fellow writers who are, for the most part, her peers. Robin proves herself indispensable in mediating cultural and linguistic misunderstandings related to the new scripts and translations of dialogue in the American segments to be dubbed.

The core producing team spends hours alongside the writers in Vika's ORT office; Irina still hasn't yet provided a space for us to work. Robin and the lead Russian producers have been watching and voting on which American *Sesame Street* segments should be included in the Russian series and dubbed into Russian. Fortunately, after working first with Larissa, who had dubbed the initial *Sesame Street* segments, we later found a superb dubbing studio, *Pifagor*—capable of voicing over the colossal number of clips selected from the American library, representing 40 percent of the show's content.

By summer's end, the writers have merged into a close, tight-knit group. It's common to see them at lunch, laughing and smoking while spiritedly discussing scripts.

Two days before I'm supposed to leave Moscow, Irina calls my hotel room. As I race to answer the phone, the scripts, storyboards, and papers on my bed go flying. "Natasha, I've found the perfect person to be *Ulitsa Sezam*'s chief director," she announces. Some time ago, in the interest of bolstering our allies, I had asked Irina if she could recommend a high-profile film or television director who could join our team and possibly quell some of the opposition to Russian *Sesame Street* in the press.

I'd pretty much forgotten about it, but apparently Irina hadn't. While she was attending the Kinotavr Film Festival in Sochi, she was introduced to Vladimir Grammatikov, a cinematic giant of Soviet children's film. Always an enterprising gal, she'd followed up on my request by asking him if he could recommend any children's directors for *Ulitsa Sezam*.

Grammatikov offered to help, proposing Irina give him some time to come up with a few options. Irina starts laughing as she tells the story. "So, when I get back to Moscow, in July Grammatikov shows up at my office and says, 'I found the guy who you should consider to direct the series. It's me.'"

"That's incredible!" I'm thrilled someone so accomplished and famous is interested. I tell Irina that I want to meet him as soon as possible.

The next day, I arrive at Irina's office, and Grammatikov (who goes by "Volodya") is already there, sprawled on the couch, the two of them laughing like lifelong friends. Volodya looks about fifty, thin with a narrow face and a bushy mustache. He strikes me as incredibly self-possessed and has a terrific sense of humor. Irina has shared with me his filmography and, frankly, I feel a bit intimidated. My interviewing this seasoned icon of children's cinema—when I haven't even directed one children's program—is ridiculous. Nervously, I sit next to Volodya on the couch. Irina leaves us to speak alone.

When I ask Volodya about his previous work in children's films, he recounts his experience directing big-budget films, including *Mio in the Land of Faraway* with Christian Bale and Timothy Bottoms, the most expensive film adaptation of Astrid Lindgren's book ever. I gulp back my nerves and try not to appear too overwhelmed as he describes his even more extensive background in film and theater. His position as the former director of Moscow's famed Stanislavsky Dramatic Theater, and his directorial experience at the Obratzsov Puppet Theater, make him an ideal choice for *Ulitsa Sezam*. I can't believe our luck.

However, Volodya isn't sure when he would be available to direct *Ulitsa Sezam* because he's in the middle of casting a Russian version of Frances Hodgson Burnett's *A Little Princess*. This seems odd, considering Warner Brothers has just released a film based on the same novel. When I mention it, Volodya glibly remarks, "But my dear Natasha, my version will portray the emotion and the wonder that the Western movie lacks."

His consummate self-confidence, talent, and dry sense of humor make me desperate to work with him, but he barely hides his disdain for the medium of television. I get the sense he views *Sesame Street* as a low-brow kiddie show compared with the great silver screen. And when I begin speaking about compensation, he acts as though he'd be doing us a huge favor to become the chief director.

Nevertheless, I recognize that we need Volodya for his enormous skill and creativity, and most of all, as our public face. Having successfully advanced throughout the years of communist cultural censorship, he has the political savvy our controversial program needs.

I plead. I flatter. I do everything I can to appeal to both his vanity and the urgency of the times. "There's no better time than now to produce television because TV is becoming the greatest source of information for young people growing up in Russia today. We need your enormous creativity and energy on our team."

Volodya's expression softens. To my delight, he accepts the position and can start in two months, in mid-September. I couldn't be happier.

Before we say goodbye, I ask him if he can recommend a woman director for *Ulitsa Sezam*. I tell him we plan to hire three directors, who will rotate between filming and preparation in the studio as a way to triple our speed.

"Does it have to be a woman?" he asks.

"Yes."

He looks at me with a bemused expression and says he will think about it.

Irina peeks her head into the office to check on us. Seeing that we seem to be getting along, she exaggeratedly tiptoes to her desk so as not to interrupt us, her heels still noisily click-clacking.

After Volodya leaves, she comes over to me. "*Dusha Moya*, guess what?" She beams like a cat delivering a mouse to its master. "We found *Ulitsa Sezam* a new office, and it will be ready in two weeks!" She claims Video Art has already started renovating Moskinap, an old camera factory that's only a five-minute walk across the street from ORT.

I can't believe Irina didn't tell me this as soon as I walked in the door. I quietly congratulate myself on standing up to her during my last trip. This is the best news in months!

Serendipity strikes again. While I am visiting Midhat in his office later that week, the phone rings. It's the director of ORT's Children's Studio, who recommends Tamara Pavliuchenko for the position of studio supervisor and coordinating director of *Ulitsa Sezam*. Word must have gotten out that we are looking for women directors.

Tamara is formidable, a no-nonsense, battle-tested, award-winning film and television director. She comes from an illustrious theater family and is a graduate of the prestigious Leningrad Institute of Theater, Music, and Cinematography. She's also worked in children's television for thirty years. Her husband is also a director, and her adult daughter, Natalya Negoda, is a famous actress, whom even I have heard of. She appeared in the gritty 1988 film *Little Vera*, a smashing success where Natalya performed the first explicit sex scene in a Soviet state-sponsored film.

There's a reason I'm hell-bent on hiring women, and it's not only to redress the harassment and discrimination I experienced in my television career so far. Throughout my time in Russia, I've learned a crucial lesson: hire women. They work hard, show up to work on time, and drink a tenth as much as the men do. There's an old Russian expression, "Russian men aren't satisfied to merely drink themselves under the table; they want to drink themselves six feet into the ground."

I meet Tamara in Midhat's office where we can have some privacy. Tamara is impressive. She asks sharp questions about the production, revealing the depth of her expertise. I hire her on the spot and have no doubt she will be a powerful addition to our team. With Volodya joining us in mid-September and Tamara on board, I expect our already fast-moving production locomotive will become a bullet train.

Now I feel comfortable enough to return to the States and Ken for a little R & R.

18

A RUSTY CAR IN EVERY NEIGHBORHOOD

I spend a month with Ken, first in New York and then briefly in Martha's Vineyard again for a much-needed recharge. I'm back in Moscow by early September 1995—excited to begin brainstorming with artists on *Ulitsa Sezam*'s set, the "neighborhood" where the Muppet characters and human actors will perform together.

Our beehive colony has expanded to more than 250 media professionals who are writing, creating music, and filming throughout Moscow. We've already completed twenty beautiful new live-action films with many celebrating Russian culture including *gzhel*, showing the artistic process of creating traditional white and blue Russian pottery, and *kugikly*, depicting peasant folk music with pan pipes made from reeds. Additional filming is underway in Armenia, Kazakhstan, and Ukraine.

Our biggest challenge lately has been multitasking between the editing of scripts and storyboards and reviewing live-action films from the rough cut to fine cuts and recording music. Fortunately, we've reduced the turnaround time for script revisions to two days from four and reviewing films from a week to four days. This is a huge accomplishment, but we must go faster, and for this we need a place to work.

So I'm on the phone with Irina again, pestering her about the new office when she tells me that, because of construction delays, we can't move into the new office as we had hoped. Nobody's fault. Certainly not *her* fault.

I'm so fed up.

Five minutes after the call with Irina, I gather the members of our team who are working out of Vika's office and tell them, "Stop whatever you're doing, grab a chair, a computer, or a printer, and follow me. We're doing our own office takeover."

Ten minutes later, six of us are marching down the hallway and out the front entrance of the TV station, carrying chairs and one beige desktop computer, and crossing a busy street to the Moskinap camera factory, where we climb six flights of stairs to our new quarters.

The new office smells like fresh paint and wet cement. We hear laughter and someone playing the guitar. As we walk deeper into the space, we find a group of workers sitting in a circle on cement blocks with bottles of vodka and a half-eaten cake on the floor between them. All around them, the cavernous space is in a chaotic state of midconstruction, with planks of wood leaning against the walls, half-open bags of cement spilling onto the floor, and nails everywhere. They are surprised to see us.

"It's Sasha's birthday," one of the workers says, by way of explanation. He's aware that he and his buddies should be working and not celebrating. But his explanation only makes me more annoyed, considering today is Robin's twenty-third birthday and our team has no place to celebrate. If anyone deserves a party, she does.

In a rush to leave at our prompting, the workers forget an unopened bottle of champagne. Misha pops the cork, holds the bottle aloft, and makes a toast to Robin. It's freezing inside the hollow space without heat, but we're all thrilled to finally have a home for *Ulitsa Sezam*. And Robin is delighted when I surprise her with a pink birthday cake from a fancy French bakery. We all sing "Happy Birthday."

As we sit making jokes—mostly at Robin's expense—the thin fall light slowly fades away. By six o'clock, we're in complete darkness. Apparently, Irina hasn't paid for electricity yet. But we are here to stay, electricity or no electricity.

The next day we supplement the sixth-floor office with additional furniture items, equipment, and supplies. After hearing about how we are creating a new television show for the country's children, the neighbors one floor below permit us to hang extension cords out our windows and tap into their electrical lines. They invite us to use their phones lines as well.

When the workers return, they find that we have taken over one of the rooms in the large space, swept up the nails, and have no intention of vacating the place. Ignoring us, for the next five weeks, they continue to hammer and drill alongside our creative team until the renovation is complete—well, except for a toilet seat, which appears impossible to find in all of Russia.

———————

In no time at all, the office is haphazardly more fully outfitted and buzzing with activity. I love that Misha has taken to wearing his favorite coffee-stained Cookie Monster tie every day. I had given him the tie as a gift. Claiming his spot, Misha hangs a sign over one of the largest desks: "TIME IS MONEY. I HAVE NO TIME."

The addition in mid-September of Volodya as our new chief director and Tamara, who joined a month earlier, elevates the status and vitality of our production to a whole new level. And with the new studio crew hired, our merry band has ballooned to three hundred people.

On Volodya's first day at work, he tackles the most urgent problem: the Muppets. We've been debating their design, personality, and color for six months, and nothing seems satisfactory. Borrowing a page from Konstantin Stanislavsky, the famous drama director and actor whose improvisational approach to character development has been adopted worldwide, he gathers the creatives together—writers, directors, and producers—and organizes a game, splitting the group into four teams.

Once the groups have assembled, Volodya suddenly jumps on the table and begins imitating a wild animal. "If your Muppet were an animal—how would he move?" he shouts. "Would he be wild—like this?" He extends his neck and sniffs loudly. "What kind of noises would he make? How would he eat a banana?" He bends his thin, flexible body forward, juts out his head as he grabs an imaginary banana, peels it, and pretends to eat it, noisily snorting. Everyone falls into fits of hysterics.

Volodya's playful ingenuity ignites the group's creativity. The team improvises for two hours and compiles a list of endearing characteristics and physical traits for the three Slavic Muppets.

The first, Zeliboba, the large full-body Muppet formerly known as Domovoi, gradually takes shape as an eight-foot, hound-like animal with a long muzzle, floppy ears, and a keen sense of smell. One young writer yells out, "Zeliboba sticks his big nose into everything and instinctively understands what it is by smelling it. He can even smell the name of a song."

The Russians envision Zeliboba to be a few inches taller than Big Bird. And he will incorporate some of the personality traits decided upon earlier by the producers and writers, such as sweetness, compassion, and embracing a spiritual approach to life. I thank my lucky stars that no one is talking anymore about the Zeliboba-Muppet being an old man or a religious figure. Instead he's a large child-like creature of the forest who lives in a massive treehouse.

Naturally, I'm already wrapping my head around what this could mean regarding the materials needed to build this treehouse. But the producers have their hearts set on an arboreal Muppet, and I will not disappoint them.

I dream of days like these. I'm having so much fun.

We break for lunch and walk in a pack across the street to ORT's cafeteria. To get to the canteen, we must circle through a labyrinth of underground tunnels that were constructed in the 1960s to protect against possible air raid attacks from the West.

The selection at the cafeteria is limited to fried chicken, meat cutlets, or hot dogs, carrots smothered in mayonnaise and topped with sugar, or soup. For a vegetarian there's little to choose from, and I'm always hungry. I ask the server if I can get the carrots without the mayo and sugar.

"*Nyet.*"

I order coffee, which is actually black water faintly tasting of coffee, and I join my colleagues at a table where they are engrossed in a lively conversation about the colors for their Muppets. I stare into Misha's bowl of beef *borscht*. The chunks swimming in a thick top layer of oil are not "meat" but slabs of fat masquerading as meat. Just seeing it makes me want to throw up. He looks at me with sympathy.

Meanwhile, the conversation about the color of the Muppets continues and Volodya fills me in, explaining that "the Russian Moppets cannot be red because the red color causes harmful vibrations that will upset the psyche of young children."

This makes no sense. "But Elmo is red, so how could the color red be bad if millions of kids love Elmo?" I ask.

Volodya gives me an incredulous look. "Have you never read Vasily Kandinsky's philosophical treatise on the theory of colors—about how different colors evoke specific emotions?"

Um . . . no. Not exactly. Or at all.

"I-I-I'm familiar with Kandinsky as a famous, twentieth-century artist," I stammer.

My ignorance is met with wide stares. My coworkers insist the master's hundred-year-old schema is essential in choosing the colors for our Russian *Moppets.*

No one can compete with the Russians' capacity for abstraction and existential debate. I remind myself that this is precisely what I love about working with them.

While the discussion continues, I pull out Ed Christie's initial sketches of Zeliboba from my leather saddlebag. His drawing shows the tree spirit as a giant green furry creature resembling a pile of leaves and mulch.

Passing around the drawings, I tell the group, "In New York, Ed said that fleshing out the design for the Russian tree spirit gave him the most freedom ever—because, unlike Big Bird, no one knows what a tree spirit Muppet would look like."

The group reacts positively, and one producer notes with encouragement that in Kandinsky's monograph, the color green represents "feelings of stillness and passivity."

I hate to be a naysayer, but I must object. "The Russian Muppet can't be green because Oscar the Grouch is green, and we've already dubbed loads of clips with Oscar from *Sesame Street*'s library. We can't have two puppets that are the same color in the show."

Feeling bad, I suggest, "What about yellow? Big Bird won't be in *Ulitsa Sezam*, so one of the Russian Muppets could be yellow. . . ."

I face a sea of shaking heads.

"Kandinsky believes yellow transmits a sensation of madness," Volodya intones, quoting the deceased oracle.

By the time lunch is over, the Russians have reached a consensus. They've chosen blue for Zeliboba—a supposedly peaceful and calming color that arouses feelings of spirituality. This intrigues me because several months earlier, at the writer's workshop, I remember one homophobic scribe had insisted we couldn't choose the color blue because blue is "code" for being gay. Apparently, that doesn't matter now, and we can have a blue puppet! To make the Zeliboba-Muppet look as though he's a spirit from the forest, they expand on Ed Christie's idea and propose sewing tufts of earth-toned fabric, feathers, leaves, and bark into his furry pelt.

We spend the afternoon delineating the physical and personality traits of the other two Muppets. The female hand-puppet will be called Businka, meaning "Little Bead." And following Kandinsky's complex set of visual principles, the group decides she should be pink.

Businka takes shape as an energetic, furry fireball who darts and bounces, exhibiting what Vika dubs *joie de vivre*. Several of the women reiterate themes from earlier discussions—how important it is for Businka to challenge typical stereotypes for girls.

"Instead of always being told to be obedient and submissive, Businka should take risks, be very excitable, and sometimes, disobey orders," one insists.

Volodya picks up on the word "excitable," suggesting that Businka be "hysterical and crying all the time."

This is out of the question. I'm relieved when Robin, who has been quiet until now, says as much. "Having Businka cry all the time would make her incredibly annoying, and as she is the only girl character, this would limit her appeal to audiences and writers as a character modeling positive behavior."

Robin's reasoning wins the day, and we move on to the prickly subject of whether the female Muppet plays sports.

In Russia, women are expected to comport themselves in a "feminine way." Job ads for secretaries in newspapers might even specify, "Physical attractiveness is a requirement of the job." Only recently have attitudes about women playing sports started to change. I tell the group, "You have to decide on this because the scriptwriters will need to know if they should include Businka in scenarios where the Muppets are playing soccer or bouncing a ball together."

The room grows silent. Volodya responds first. "By having the girl puppet play sports, you are putting the girl in the boy's body, and the boy in the girl's body. This is harmful because children, even at age three, have a clear perception of gender stereotypes, and we wouldn't want to contradict this view of the world."

Another "scientific theory." *Ugh*.

Nana stares at Volodya. "Do you want Russian girls growing up today with the same stupid gender stereotypes we had to live with?"

"It would be a much more memorable character, and funnier, if the girl puppet does the exact opposite of what people expect," suggests Vika, making a mischievous face. She proposes that Businka participate in sports and be a dancer who loves performing the Lambada, a Mexican dance popular in Moscow.

The men who had advocated otherwise are shamed into capitulation. Businka is born as a fearless, Lambada-dancing Muppet who loves sports and is open to new experiences.

To serve as a counterweight to Businka's exuberance and Zeliboba's Zen vibe, the team decides the boy hand-Muppet should be based on a quintessential Russian archetype: the bumbling, obstinate ne'er-do-well, a romantic and ambitious dreamer loved by all but damned by his incompetence.

Excited, one writer is laughing so hard, he can barely get out his words. "Yeah, the boy puppet makes even the simplest of problems complex—like inventing a contraption to dry his wet socks, only later to discover a 'clothesline' already exists."

Everyone laughs, recollecting similar hapless characters depicted in Russian novels.

They choose to name the boy Muppet Kubik, which means "Cube," denoting the character's nerdy awkwardness. Several producers lobby for this character to be an entrepreneur who carries a Filofax organizer and is constantly struggling to find success in newly capitalist Russia but somehow always fails.

I ask, "Wouldn't you want Kubik to occasionally be successful, so that children are encouraged to experiment and take risks, even if the result doesn't always work out?"

My teammates take this to heart. The creators settle on Kubik being a sweet, academic sort whose character celebrates individuality and the freedom to make mistakes—novel concepts in Russia.

The live-action director suggests, "The best part of Kubik's personality is that he's a perfect straight man to Zeliboba's hilarious antics."

It's incredibly satisfying seeing the writers and producers collaborating.

Outside, the sky is glowing purple and pink as the sun sets. One of the writers expresses concern that Russian parents might not want their children to act like Businka, with her uncontrollable, often annoying impulsivity, or Kubik with his outsized ambition and obstinance, or Zeliboba with his boundless, irrepressible curiosity and tendency to ignore rules. She notes that these traits elicited reproach in Soviet society.

The team discusses how Soviet children typically are reared to be silent, still, and obedient—the opposite of individualistic risk-takers and energetic pint-sized challengers of authority. Ultimately, however, the producers decide they want the Muppets to embody the traits and values that will help the next generation be successful in New Russia.

The following week, the amended sketches of Zeliboba and the new drawings for the other two Muppets are sent to Ed Christie at the Henson Company in New York by FedEx. Inspired by the team's suggestions, Ed says he will need several weeks to develop more detailed drawings of the new Muppets. During this period, faxes and emails fly between the Russian and American groups, hammering out the final details, including the fabric, wardrobe, type of feathers, and particular leaves sewn onto Zeliboba's coat.

One day at the Moscow office, when Tamara is eyeballing the latest final Henson Company drawings of Zeliboba laid out on a conference table, she suddenly yells, "Instead of *lapti* [traditional straw sandals], Zeliboba should wear enormous white Nike-style sneakers like all the kids in Moscow are wearing!" Everyone loves this idea. Someone else then shouts, "And Zeliboba should wear a wide paisley tie." This idea also receives praise.

With the Muppets taking shape nicely and having completed about one-third of the live-action and animated films, it's time to turn our attention to developing the Russian set for *Ulitsa Sezam*.

The creation of the *Sezam* set, the neighborhood—where Muppets and human actors will perform together—is the most technically complex and expensive component of the production. We have just four months to design and construct the scenery and dress the set before the filming of studio episodes begins in late January 1996.

During the week, Volodya, Tamara, and I review portfolios from over thirty Moscow art directors with scenic design experience in film and theater. We settle on Maria Rybasova ("Masha"), a woman who towers above the rest in professional stature but not height. She walks through the door of our Moskinap office, no taller than four feet one, with large green eyes and chestnut-colored hair woven into a tight long braid falling down her back. She's forty-two but looks at least ten years younger.

As she answers our questions, she nervously brushes her bangs off her forehead. She speaks softly about the sets she created for major Moscow theatrical productions, including Chekhov's *The Seagull* and *The Cherry Orchard*. Her work is breathtaking: imaginative, meticulous, and beautiful.

Masha volunteers that she has no experience designing sets for television, much less sets inhabited by puppets. Multi-episodic entertainment television is so new to Russia that few art directors have experience designing sets as elaborate as the one planned for *Ulitsa Sezam*. But Masha's undeterred by her inexperience. When asked to share her vision for the show, she's hesitant at first, believing the Americans must have their own entrenched concepts. But once she understands that she will have broad artistic license, she unleashes a torrent of exciting ideas.

A few days later, Masha returns to the office with designs.

"I stayed up several nights and conceptualized a set that I think will surpass any previous children's TV show in Russian history," she says with fire in her eyes. Her ambition and self-confidence are remarkable, precisely what we need.

She is aware that each new international *Sesame Street* coproduction includes some design elements from the American show alongside original features. For example, one feature of every international coproduction is a public space where the community gathers. But the design of each country's public space is unique. For example, the Mexican *Sesame Street* production is built around a plaza, while the Norwegian show takes place in a train station; South Africa's set is a marketplace.

Masha's dilemma is that her set must depict a distinctly Russian neighborhood—but which one? Should it evoke the architecture of Tsarist Russia, the recent Soviet period, or an unknown future? Also, what aesthetic and cultural elements from Ukrainian and non-Slavic cultures, such as post-Soviet Central Asian cultures, should be incorporated into her design? This is especially important because *Ulitsa Sezam* is intended for broadcast across the entire former Soviet Union. Her confusion is understandable. Until the 1950s, most city-dwelling Russians lived in cramped, state-owned, concrete communal apartments, with sometimes up to ten families sharing one kitchen and one bathroom. In communist Russia, the construction of any private dwelling exceeding 450 square feet was grounds for imprisonment. This policy led to rows of identical drab apartment buildings stretching as far as the eye can see, marring the landscape of every major Soviet city. And adjacent to these architectural monstrosities remained pockets of magnificent neoclassical, nineteenth-century mansions from Russia's romantic past.

Unfortunately, Masha has little time to consider which epoch to choose because Russia is experiencing massive product shortages: lumber, fabric, hardware, glue, and other materials, and we will need to ship many of these items from America before scenic construction can begin.

Masha likes to work alone, but in the interest of speeding up the drawing process, I encourage her to collaborate with her colleagues from the film and theater community at a brainstorming session. This will also enable us to project an image of inclusiveness. She doesn't like this idea, and neither does Misha Davydov, my co-executive producer, who says firmly, "'Brainstorming' is for birdbrains. Besides, most of these set designers won't even sit in the same room, let alone talk to each other."

Over the next few days, I plead with Masha to reconsider as a personal favor, assuring her that she will have the final say regarding the design. I tell her we need to bolster *Ulitsa Sezam*'s standing in the creative community. She reluctantly agrees, albeit with predictions of doom. Misha insists none of the directors will come unless we pay them.

The following week, in the Moskinap conference room, Misha is surprised to see all the directors we had asked to help seated around the table. None had requested compensation. Dr. Genina joins as well.

Right away, the directors butt heads. Those raised in rural Russia feel strongly that *Ulitsa Sezam*'s set should reflect life beyond Russia's depraved and immoral cities. One director, renowned for his uniquely modern interpretations of Chekhov's plays, bellows, "The heart and soul of Russia are her majestic rippling rivers and birch trees. To be true to Russia, *Ulitsa Sezam*'s set design must be rooted in nature."

An avowed city mouse expresses an alternative point of view. "The only people still living in the countryside are those waiting for death. They are not the ones who will rebuild our country."

The debate continues, with country advocates clinging tenaciously to their romanticized vision of the *selo* (village) and *priroda* (nature)—words evoking a nearly sacred reverence for almost all Russians. These are similar to phrases Americans hold dearly, like "family farm" and "apple pie."

One of the fundamental differences, however, between 1990s America and Russia is that the Russian city mouse is generally far richer than the country mouse. While poverty rates have been rising of late in rural America, most rural villages in post-Soviet Russia are destitute.

As one director points out, "The inequalities between urban and rural populations are huge and rapidly growing in the wake of communism's collapse." Masha insists, "Our challenge is to develop a set design that will appeal to all Russians—rural and urban, as well as our Soviet brothers."

The most famous director in the group then stands up and silently waits for the others to give him their full attention. Stroking his beard as if seized by a vision, he opines in a deep, resonant voice, "Our country is deeply damaged, and our soul is sick. How can we expect to reform or reeducate our children without incorporating nature's beauty and healing powers?" The group seems mesmerized by his poetic lament and he continues, "Our set should have a forest with real trees so our children can rediscover their connection to the motherland."

It's a lovely sentiment, but all I can think is, *Oh no, not the trees again.* Does he mean *live trees*? Trees we'd somehow have to keep alive during our four-month indoor shoot? And I'm terrified that the next director will propose filming the entire TV series in the Siberian taiga.

Listening to them argue, I reach back to a lesson Jon Stone, *Sesame Street*'s original director, had taught me: the most effective *Sesame Street* set is one that imitates reality—where children learn and play in an environment resembling where they live. He was the one who came up with the idea for the American set to resemble a gritty, urban neighborhood of cracked brownstone tenement buildings with Latin and soul music streaming out of the windows.

But at the mere mention of design elements from the American show, I'm attacked.

"Natasha, in your *Sesame Street*, Oscar the Grouch lives inside a filthy garbage can. That's disgusting!" exclaims one director. "We would never put a trash can in our set because it is unsanitary and dangerous. Children might think it's acceptable to crawl inside the trash can."

"Not the trash can again," I mutter under my breath.

In the afternoon, I call on Dr. Genina to speak. Time and again, she's proven a diplomat in the face of such philosophical disagreements, and she commands respect. She's like a schoolmarm who makes her students redo their homework again when they turn in poor assignments. She's invincible and brilliant and I know she'll get the results we need.

Dr. Genina suggests a compromise: a design that combines architectural elements from the city *and* countryside. "For example, our fictional neighborhood could be based on a medium-size town and include recognizable structures from Russia's past and present."

Masha nods enthusiastically. I am pleased the women are getting along so well.

As the group dives into deciding which structures should be included, Masha suggests featuring the *Khrushchobis*—those prefabricated, five-story cement complexes built during Khrushchev's era that dominate every large and medium-sized city. The name is a combination of the Soviet leader Khrushchev and *trushobi*, the Russian word for "slum." For *Ulitsa Sezam*'s set to look realistic, like the American set, Masha says, "These familiar crumbling eyesores must be included in my design."

Dr. Genina points out that a critical feature of the Khrushchev-style apartment complexes is an interior courtyard (*dvor*), with trees and often a playground. "Perhaps *Ulitsa Sezam*'s set could be conceived around a courtyard."

Early Soviet architects conceived the *dvor* as an idealized communal space where people from the surrounding buildings could mingle, regardless of social status or wealth. The *dvor* would serve as a communist cell of sorts where professionals—such as dentists, doctors, and academics—cross paths with working-class laborers—like car mechanics and factory workers—all performing social benefits to their community.

Building on Dr. Genina's idea, Masha proposes, "Yes, we could build a shed where neighbors in the apartment complex come to fix their bicycles." Then, she adds, only half in jest, "But if we want the courtyard to be *realistic*, then it should also have a rusty old car, shards of broken glass, and a rat-infested dumpster with garbage all over the place."

Another director quips, "Yeah, and instead of the neighbor who fixes bicycles, he should be a snitch who reports on his neighbors to the KGB." This gets a good laugh.

Dr. Genina reconsiders her concept, expressing concern that if the television show is set in a *dvor*, some children may think their courtyards are safe places to play when they are not.

Masha takes this in and begins herculean efforts to appease both city and country factions by patiently sketching and resketching options based on their recommendations. At first, no drawing satisfies everyone. But by the end of the evening, a consensus is reached, with the group acknowledging that a modern-day courtyard will best serve as *Ulitsa Sezam*'s public gathering place. Everyone leaves with a more hopeful feeling that perhaps our show can make the *dvor* safe once again.

———————

Masha works away from the office, and two days later returns with intricately detailed sketches of the scenic structures: a twentieth-century Romanesque Revivalist redbrick two-story apartment building with a wrought-iron balcony for our *Ulitsa Sezam* family, a rural wooden dacha for the caretaker of the courtyard, and a giant oak tree seen through a stone archway demarking the entrance to the courtyard, which will be Zeliboba's "tree house." The depiction of the tree, with its variegated bark branches and thin pencil lines for the veins of each leaf, looks like a botanical illustration from a museum. Everyone is astounded by the scale, originality, and realism of the designs.

However, we hit a bump when Masha unfurls a large paper roll depicting her vision of the interior of *Ulitsa Sezam*'s courtyard.

A silver spaceship and a giant pink elephant with multicolored tassels and jeweled *howdah* dominate the *dvor*. Volodya and I pore over the magnificent urban-rural fantasyland as team members circle the drawings laid out on the conference table, complimenting Masha and fawning over the interplanetary vehicle and the beast. Masha's talent is so great that undoubtedly in America she would have a mantel full of Oscars for Best Production Design.

But while Masha's drawing incorporates many features agreed upon in our earlier discussions, I'm struck by how her technicolor fantasy world has absolutely nothing to do with Russia's realistic past or its future. For example, since when are elephants native to Russia? And how does the elephant fit in with teaching Russian children how to resolve real-life problems by relying on themselves rather than on spaceships or exotic animals to carry them away? I hate to object to anything in Masha's designs, mainly because she has labored through the night to create them, but nervously, I question her inspiration for the elephant and space capsule.

She pauses, thinking, and then responds. "Children expect to see fanciful elements in their television programs, and the Muppets do lots of things that children cannot do in real life, such as flying or jumping off buildings."

"But it's the Muppets doing these things, not the children," I say gently.

Not wanting to diminish Masha's enthusiasm after she had worked so hard, I suggest we regroup the next day to continue our discussion.

That night, Leonid and I meet for dinner at a new Armenian restaurant. I need a good meal, and Leonid needs to vent about Irina. She's still refusing to sign the agreement with *Sesame Street*. Even worse, she hasn't paid a cent back to Sesame Workshop for the money loaned to her. As Leonid complains about Video Art, I have trouble finding any space in my brain to absorb what he's saying. I am having too many problems myself.

I tell Leonid about the day's events and Masha's elephant.

He cringes. "You know, many Russians yearn for a world that offers our children a better, happier, and easier life than their own. They want *Ulitsa Sezam* to be the childhood they never got to experience." He tears off a piece of Lavash bread. "But I thought you'd understand this by now, Natasha."

The following day, Masha seems more amenable to adjusting her concept drawings. She sits down at the big conference table with Volodya, Tamara, a few producers, and me, and begins proposing alternative ideas.

Instead of an elephant, she suggests placing hand-carved traditional wooden sculptures in the shapes of bears, rabbits, and foxes so children can play in the courtyard.

One of the producers says, "When I was a child, my mother always sent me out to buy fresh bread from a kiosk." Masha loves this idea. She then goes off and sketches a picnic table with three girls playing tea party and adds a neighboring shed for fixing bicycles in the *dvor* and a bakery. Her colorful drawing of an antique-style bakeshop with the Cyrillic lettering, "Hot Bread," arched over the transom, evoking nostalgia for old Russia, draws ooh's and aah's from the team.

"Our *dvor* will be a place where neighbors talk to each other, share gossip, and help one another." She moves her colored pencil. "My *dvor* will be realistic, but also a safe, friendly, and happy place—taking what's positive about the courtyard from the past and redesigning it within a modern context," she says.

With each new suggestion reflecting Russian life, I feel floods of relief.

At ten o'clock the following day, Masha walks into the office carrying a minia-ture cardboard model—made to scale—of the *Ulitsa Sezam* set. Each cutout is exquisitely hand-drawn, including tiny caramel-colored loaves of bread in the bakery window and wood carvings of boars and birds on the window shutters. To see our future set imagined with such precision and beauty—down to the lamppost with a tiny green "Ulitsa Sezam" signpost—leaves me speechless.

Team members come to the conference room to see the maquette, all mar-veling at Masha's artistic genius. Although a myriad of arcane technical details remains to be resolved before our scenic rendering can come alive, we finally have a design that everyone agrees on—no small achievement. I tell Masha she's exceeding Volodya's expectations and mine. She bows her head slightly, embar-rassed by the attention, and whispers under her breath, "and my expectations for myself." Considering her stratospheric talent, her humility is remarkable. I tell her again how grateful everyone is.

Later that day, I share with Masha that she's going to America to see *Sesame Street*'s studio and meet the head of the show's art department. For the past weeks, I've held back, waiting for her to complete her full set of construction drawings with elevations and color charts.

"I can't believe it." She places her hand over her mouth and just holds it there, as though her tiny hand could contain the delight exploding inside her body.

I thoroughly enjoy playing fairy godmother, even though it's *Sesame Street* paying for her trip and not me. Masha will put the finishing touches on her drawings over the next few weeks, and I cannot wait to introduce her to *Sesame Street*'s art director. Masha is going to dazzle him and his colleagues. But before going to America with Masha, we must begin auditions for the show.

19

SAD SONGS FROM THE MOUTHS OF BABES

After two years of endless drama and uncertainty, it's time to listen to the children singing. Casting the child roles for our TV show is the part I have been looking forward to the most. It's November 1995, and the treacherous weather has started making it difficult to navigate the city's streets, partially immobilized by snow and ice. I arrive late at Gorky Film Studios.

My driver drops me off at the gated entrance to Moscow's most prestigious moviemaking site. Like many prerevolutionary structures in Moscow, the studio looks rundown. I stop at the security kiosk and a guard looks at my passport, then waves me inside the compound.

Hiking up my collar to brace against the cold, I make my way across an expansive yard to the designated building, cautiously stepping over tiny mounds of frozen spit that shine like diamonds on the icy path—the only evidence of human beings in this ghostly place. With the evaporation of state film funding, only a small part of the studio remains open, allowing short-term space rental. Thanks to Volodya's relationship with the studio head, we're granted permission to hold auditions here over the next three days.

I'm counting on Volodya's name and fame to attract children from across Russia. Still, casting is always a gamble, and perhaps no one will show up in this biting cold.

I needn't have worried. I enter the room and find more than 160 children and their parents waiting—far more than we'd anticipated. Many of them came from nearby cities while others traveled hundreds of miles from far-off villages. In addition to her studio directing duties, Tamara is also coordinating the auditions and hastily setting up additional chairs. I take off my coat and help her. I love that Tamara pays no attention to hierarchy. She once told me, "I don't relate to the concept of 'liking' or 'disliking' work—work is work. Whether you like it or not, you should be open to doing anything!"

I see Volodya warmly welcoming parents and children as they remove their heavy wool coats, hats, and scarves. Many children wear miniature fur hats with earflaps and look adorable. Volodya directs the parents and children to sit in the waiting room. Each child takes a seat in one of the straight-backed wooden chairs lined up in a row against the wall, with their mothers nervously hovering nearby. Casting calls appear to be the dominion of mothers, not fathers.

As I survey the waiting room, I'm struck by how different the scene is from the frenetic casting sessions I once visited in New York. It's far quieter; the parents speak in whispers, and there's little interaction among the adults or children. However, from their worried expressions I take it that the stage mothers exhibit the same clawing anxiety as their American counterparts.

The girls and boys auditioning are between the ages of four and eleven. For the most part, the children are not professional actors, but that's no problem—*Sesame Street* favors a more natural acting style. Some mothers have dressed their children in their Sunday best. The stakes, I know, are high; a role comes with a salary that can support a family of four for nearly a year, and whoever is chosen will have their lives changed forever.

The plan is to cast the role of Katya, the daughter in *Ulitsa Sezam*'s nuclear family, and fifteen other children representing a diversity of ethnicities, who will appear as extras in the show and remain in Moscow for four months of filming. Volodya has told me that the casting of child actors is more complicated than casting adults. For this reason, he's choosing to audition the children first.

I stand off to the side in the waiting room, trying to be unobtrusive. Volodya asks me not to let on that I am an American. "Most children and their parents have probably never met a foreigner before. They might feel intimidated."

I don't mind being undercover—it's not the first time I've had to make myself invisible. And it's a joy to witness one of Russia's most incredible children's directors work his casting magic.

Volodya explains that he will invite each child to come into a room away from the other children and sing a song of their choosing, taking turns, one at a time. The director's assistant calls a five-year-old boy with red hair and freckles first. His mother puts her hand on her son's back and pushes him toward the adjoining room while she stays behind. The assistant closes the door.

There's a single chair in the center of the room, with two chairs opposite. A third is against the back wall for me.

Inside the room, the red-headed boy stands rigidly, uncomfortable in brown, starched pants cut too high above his ankles, making him look even younger than he is. This may be intentional—I've heard that children's television directors often want to hire older children who look younger. Volodya chats easily with the boy, telling jokes that make him laugh and put him at ease.

Then, without smiling, the boy announces that he will be singing a song from the film, *Belorusski Vokzal* (Belorussia's Train Station), and he prefers to stand. His voice unnaturally drops several octaves to a booming alto, and he stoically sings the lyrics as though he's a cadet in an army band:

> Birds don't sing here
> Trees don't grow here
> It's only the front
> The planet is burning
> Our motherland is covered in smoke

Volodya pats the boy on the head when he finishes, telling him to wait with the children in the other room. Volodya and Tamara jot down notes. I feel blindsided, thinking how odd it is for a child to sing a song about World War II at tryouts for a comedy show.

Next in line is a four-year-old blonde girl with big blue eyes. Her doting mother insists on staying with her for the audition, and Volodya agrees. The child fidgets while her mother brushes away loose strands of hair from her face. The girl pulls on the lace hem touching her legs, making a face in response to the itchy fabric.

Volodya asks her to begin. The little girl stands straight and still. She sings several verses from "*Katyusha*" (Little Kate), a melancholy Russian folk song about a young woman who bids her lover farewell as he marches off to the front.

> The apple and pear trees were blooming
> The mist floated over the river
> Katyusha was walking out to the shore
> To the tall, steep shore

I watch the girl's mother, who is silently mouthing the words.

> Oh, you, song, the song of the maiden
> You fly along behind the cloudless sun
> And, to the soldier on the far border,
> send regards from Katyusha . . .

Another sad melody. I'd expected this morning to hear boisterous, upbeat Russian equivalents of "Old MacDonald Had a Farm" or "The Itsy-Bitsy Spider."

Instead, incredibly, nearly every child we listen to launches into a sad melody with tragic lyrics—little soprano voices singing of loss, death, and war.

As the first session ends, Volodya thanks the group for auditioning, then dismisses them. Some children look like they're about to cry, while others look ecstatic that the session is over. Tamara apologizes to Volodya and me, explaining that she must leave to attend to another *Ulitsa Sezam* crisis.

Volodya and I trudge through the bitter cold to a nearby canteen for lunch.

The musty-smelling cafeteria with only a few metal tables does not look promising. I take a bowl of soup without really being sure what it is. After the intense morning, Volodya is hungry. He fills up his plate with pickled cabbage, potatoes, and something gray that looks vaguely like beef.

When we sit down, I ask Volodya about the song selections. "They're not imitating each other, because each child is performing in complete isolation. So, why aren't they singing, you know, happy children's songs like 'Riding in My Car?'" I sing a few lines from the famous Woody Guthrie song, spitting out the "brrm brm" sound of the car off-key.

Volodya is amused but seems surprised by my confusion. "These are the songs that bring children comfort. Their grandmothers sing these songs to them," he explains, taking a knife to his beef and continuing. "For us, these melancholy songs are about our past and the people we have lost. Grandparents want to share their melancholy feelings with the people they love."

When I don't look convinced, he continues, "Natasha, you shouldn't think of these ballads as sad. They are lyrical, poetic. Russian children listen to poetry and music from a very early age, and they expect lyricism and sadness in music, as in their lives."

We sit in silence for nearly a minute as I pretend to eat my soup while considering to what degree I sound like an Ugly American. One of our producers had recently told me, "Happy is not a Russian concept." By contrast, Americans smile more than Russians and stereotypically pretend to be happy, often at the expense of their well-being.

"Are there any other more upbeat traditional Russian children's songs that children can sing?" I ask.

Volodya grins mischievously. "Of course, there are! We have revolutionary marching songs that children sing at their Communist Party summer camps."

Then, right there in the lunchroom, he breaks out into a booming, over-the-top rendition of a patriotic ballad.

Lenin is always alive,
He is always with you,
In all the bad times and,
In all the good times,
Lenin is in every spring,
In every happy day,
Lenin is inside you and me.

I laugh. I suspect he's poking fun at me, but I can't be sure. As we walk back to Gorky Studios, Volodya tells me that he's actually been developing a new type of segment—short lyrical moments for Kubik's character. "The American *Sesame Street* broadcast doesn't have anything like these moments, which are purely for the Russian mentality. These segments will intone quiet sorrow."

This sounds like a terrible idea to me. Volodya explains that Kubik would walk around with a little stuffed tiger who always feels lonely. "Children will love Kubik's tiger because they also feel sad."

I don't even know how to respond to this.

By the end of the day, we have auditioned more than forty children. We still have two more days, but Volodya seems to have already made up his mind about who should play the lead child role. He's drawn to Katia Mikhailovskaya, an athletic and cheerful ten-year-old with a short blonde bob and a beautiful singing voice. Her given name is the same as the fictional character's. Volodya likes her carefree and natural, unaffected disposition, which he feels most of the other children lack—at least so far. And he adds, "She follows directions to perfection."

Four days after completing the auditions, I'm still mulling over my conversation with Volodya. It feels a bit tone-deaf on my part to keep insisting my colleagues produce upbeat songs when they have suffered so much, but this is, after all, a kid's comedy show. When Volodya arrives at the office, I ask to show him one of my favorite *Sesame Street* songs from the 1960s, which is still popular today. In it, a bunch of monster Muppets wildly bounce up and down, singing a tune made up of only one word, "Mahna-Mahna" and they repeat this word over and over to a catchy melody.

Five seconds into the video, I see the ends of Volodya's mustache curl up in a smile.

I laugh too. The song is infectious.

"Okay, okay." He struggles to contain his laughter. "We can include some of these American-style songs, but for the show to speak to Russians, we have to include our lyrical melodies as well."

"But we will prioritize comedic musical parodies typical of Sesame Street, right?" I ask hopefully.

Volodya agrees, or I think he does.

A few days later, I learn from Robin that Volodya is going in a completely different direction, making these melancholy, slow-moving segments a leitmotif of the entire series while using up a good portion of our music budget. In fact, he has been commissioning several composers to write somber lullabies based on Russian poetry. I review the newest of these segments; I see why Volodya likes them. The songs are witty, soulful, and touching, but I wonder if they belong in our show.

When Volodya comes to the office, I raise my concerns, and he loses patience with me. "Even Pushkin was raised on sad Russian folk tales read to him by his peasant nanny. All Russian children get in contemplative moods that are just as worthy as happy ones!"

"But we *agreed* to prioritize comedic musical parodies!" I insist. I want to tear my hair out. Obviously, the mutual understanding Volodya and I had come to about these "lyrical" segments was not as mutual as I had thought.

I head out of the office to cool off. I'm convinced we need modern, catchy musical numbers to make our show a hit, but I sense I'm losing the battle.

I seek allies, calling again on Dr. Genina. She's a big fan of the American show's musical diversity. Still, when I ask for her support, she says she's curious to first see how Volodya's lyrical videos will test with our target audience. She tells me that she'll evaluate the segments with a group of seventy-six Russian preschoolers.

Recently, she made a critical change in adapting Sesame Street's research testing methodology to Russia. She explains that she'll be using this modified approach when testing Volodya's segments. While observing testing with American children in New York, she noticed that the children talked, moved around, and even danced while watching Sesame Street videos during the evaluations. The children paid little attention to the adults who were operating video cameras in the room. However, she found this approach did not work in Russia.

"When we filmed Russian children in the presence of adults, they sat stiffly upright and stared at the TV screen like obedient robots and barely reacted to the videos. Then, when we removed the adults from the room, leaving one adult who stayed hidden to run the video camera, the children's behavior sharply changed—they laughed, made faces, pointed at the television screen, and moved about having fun."

After listening to Dr. Genina, I wonder if Volodya's belief that Russian children love somber songs is because he only observes them when adults are present.

———————

A week later, having completed focus group testing of some of Volodya's melancholy segments with children between the ages of three and five, Dr. Genina comes to our office to share her findings. "The research results were more shocking than I had expected," she announces.

She shows me the recorded videotape with Russian children. The child viewers sit in a row on a hardwood bench, waiting excitedly to see the new *Ulitsa Sezam* show that includes both upbeat and melancholy songs. The first video segment shows Businka singing a sad lullaby to a mosquito to help the insect fall asleep. In a funny twist, she sings herself to sleep, and the mosquito stays awake.

Within the first minute of the video, the children get distracted, poking each other and laughing at nothing having to do with the video. One kid leaves his seat to play with toys in the back of the room. Another child picks up a fake pistol and shoots it at the television screen, then points the gun at a sweet little girl with braids sitting next to him, pretending to shoot her. The children are equally distracted in the subsequent two sessions featuring other melancholy songs.

I know I'm a cultural outsider. I know I'm biased toward *Sesame Street's* musical style. But the Russian children in the focus group don't love sad songs. That's evident.

Volodya doesn't buy it. When he arrives at the office and I tell him about the research results, he shakes his head and says, "I'm so convinced the lyrical segments will be successful that I'm not going to even talk about testing."

Luckily, Dr. Genina is not easily dissuaded. She returns to ORT to show Volodya the video where the lyrical segments had tested poorly.

A reasonable man, Volodya takes a deep breath. "Well, I guess that settles that." He agrees to halt further production of any additional "lyrical" segments. However, he is still convinced our show cannot be purely entertaining; there have to be some elements of sadness for it to be truly Russian. In the end, we compromise and include the lyrical segments already shot.

20

ELMO SAYS "GOOD NIGHT" IN RUSSIAN

It was Masha's dream to visit *Sesame Street* in New York. While designing the Russian set, she'd immersed herself in the American show's folklore, and now the day has come for her to visit the studio where it all began in Queens. I'm there too—back home for two weeks.

The moment Masha sets foot on America's most famous street, she stops dead in her tracks, stunned by its enormity and the amount of equipment. Craning her neck toward the ceiling, she stares at the lighting grid—criss-crossing metal tracks running the length of the studio and the elaborate, detailed scenery filling every inch of the studio.

I see her eyes widen, realizing she probably doesn't recognize even a quarter of the technology in the studio. Russian television equipment is eons behind the West.

She notices the painted scenery panels hanging from cables suspended from the ceiling and asks, confused, "Why is the scenery hanging from the ceiling?"

Before I can answer, Lisa Simon, the American director, calls for the actors to return to the set. They resume their positions, standing in front of the suspended scenery panels, which are level with the top of their heads. Each puppeteer raises the arm that supports a Muppet and begins performing. The camera films the action taking place above the puppeteers' heads framed against the scenic panels. Masha watches in awe as the puppeteers move comfortably, manipulating puppets while standing. Masha clasps her hands together as though in prayer.

"This is sheer genius!"

"Yup—the genius of Jim Henson," I respond, taking pleasure in her joy. I whisper to her that working with these heavy foam and fabric Muppets is physically draining, and Jim Henson came up with the suspended scenery panels to allow the puppeteers to preserve their energy and backs.

Masha walks around the studio, ogling the realistic-looking scenery and props. When she sees Big Bird's nest, she lifts her tiny frame over the top rim and peeks inside. Her eyes dart from one detail to another, taking it all in with hungry eyes. She sits on the famous brownstone stoop between live takes and asks me to take her photograph.

The American producers and puppeteers greet Masha like a soldier on leave from the front. For months, they've heard about the trials and tribulations of the Russian production and are all happy to help. Masha gingerly retrieves the *Ulitsa Sezam* set plans from her satchel. Victor DiNapoli, *Sesame Street*'s art director, spends half a day with her, going over her detailed drawings and miniature maquette. He suggests repositioning scenery and props to optimize the set for shooting puppets—creating more hiding places for the puppeteers when they're performing.

Masha is initially quite deferential to Victor, but the two artists quickly find a common language that has nothing to do with my translating. It's gratifying to see.

After a few hours with Victor, we return to the studio and talk with the chief audio engineer, the lighting director, and camera operators who offer valuable insights. Trailing behind, I translate and videotape these conversations for later reference when Masha returns home. Finally, she pauses her interrogation of my *Sesame Street* colleagues, turns to me, and says, "I think we can do this, but we will need a lot of help."

"We are here for you," I reassure her.

The crew sets up another scene. Rosita, *Sesame Street*'s first bilingual Spanish-English-speaking Muppet, performed by Carmen Osbahr-Vertiz, positions herself on a *rollie*, a small rectangular cart on wheels. Crouching down so that the top of her head clears the camera frame, Carmen extends her arm upright in the air to operate Rosita while resting her back on a foam back support. Masha watches how Carmen uses her feet to move the cart, which allows more controlled and smoother movement of the Muppet. The director yells, "Cut."

As the crew is resetting for the next scene, Masha walks over to the cart: a flat, rectangular-shaped piece of wood covered in foam with rubber wheels attached to the bottom. She gently pushes the cart, marveling at how smoothly it rolls over the floor.

I tell her that the cart is indispensable to the puppeteers, who use it to perform even small movements like when the Muppets rock back and forth in laughter. Masha notes there are tremendous shortages in Moscow, and we will need to purchase the rubber casters, hinges, and wood in America to allow for their reproduction in Moscow, as well as hundreds of boxes of nails. By the end of the day, I joke with her that the list of items she needs me to ship to Moscow looks like a wartime requisition list to supply half a million troops. She just nods. We both know that shipping anything to Russia will be a nightmare involving an insane amount of paperwork, not to mention the high customs fees and the likelihood of damage or theft.

While we're talking, I notice that Masha is gasping at the sight of Elmo, performed by Kevin Clash. "Oh, I can't believe it! That's Elmo!" she murmurs, excited as a four-year-old.

"Do you want to meet him?" I ask.

Masha, overcome with emotion, can barely respond. We walk over to Kevin, who is goofing around with his Muppet while waiting for filming to begin again.

In Elmo's three-year-old, high squeaky voice, he says, "Elmo wants to meet you."

Masha bends her head so far down in embarrassment that she nearly disappears around Kevin's knees. Leaning in closer to Masha, the Muppet softly encourages, "Elmo says, don't be afraid."

Masha starts giggling and covers her mouth.

Kevin's called to the set, and after filming a scene, invites Masha to join him in the lounge reserved only for the puppeteers. Not quite believing her good fortune, Masha follows him.

"It is such an honor for everyone at *Sesame Street* to meet you and to be a part of helping Russia," Kevin acknowledges as I translate. He is the perfect ambassador.

Masha nods, deeply touched. "My twelve-year-old daughter, whose name is also Masha, loves Elmo. I watched all the *Sesame Street* videos in English that Natasha gave me with my daughter." Her voice catches at the end.

Kevin, who still has his arm inside Elmo's slumped body, suddenly raises it, making Elmo's head pop up—nearly knocking Masha off her feet in surprise.

"Really? Little Masha loves Elmo too?" Kevin asks in his character's voice. And then, still in Elmo's voice, impulsively offers, "Let's call Masha's daughter, so Elmo can say hello!"

"But it's one o'clock in the morning in Moscow," Masha protests. Kevin waves away her concerns. We spend the next few minutes teaching Kevin how to say in Russian "*Elmo tebya lubit*" ("Elmo loves you") and "*Spokoiny Nochi*" ("Good night").

I use the phone in the lounge and ask the studio's operator to call Moscow. Masha's husband answers and then wakes up their daughter. A minute later, we hear Little Masha's small groggy voice. When she hears Elmo's voice, she shrieks in delight, audible to the entire room.

We are all laughing, and I feel tightness in my throat. This moment is pure magic—watching Elmo's high squeaky voice travel through the phone lines from New York to a little girl in Moscow to say, "Good night."

Kevin hangs up the phone and wraps his skinny furry red arms around Masha's tiny frame. She is so happy, even holding back tears. I've never seen her like this.

The green studio light starts flashing; shooting is about to begin. We return to the set.

Later that afternoon, I see Masha sketching in her notebook. I take a peek as she's drawing ivy crawling on the faux brick apartment building on 123 Sesame Street. In Finders Keepers second-hand shop, Masha picks up a large plastic yellow pig and squeezes it, then runs her fingers over the full-body suit of armor in front of the store to see what it's made of. She looks at me. "It's steel," she says.

Her favorite part of the American set is the arbor around the corner from the street.

"Are these real?" she asks, rubbing a leaf between her thumb and forefinger.

"They're fake," I say.

"We don't have anything like these fake trees," she says, shaking her head in disbelief. I remember that Masha's set design calls for Zeliboba to live inside a tree and her drawings include a fifteen-foot-tall oak, and I get nervous. Are we going to have to ship an entire tree to Russia? Apparently, the answer is yes.

We go back to the art department, and Victor helps Masha look through scenic prop catalogs for the kind of oak leaves she wants. With each turn of the page, Masha shakes her head, "No, no, not that. Russian oak leaves are different from American oak leaves. Russian leaves have only six points and are rounded at the tips, whereas the American leaves have eight points and have pointy ends." New York's largest scenic design company has all the *wrong* leaves for Russia. She sketches the correct leaves from every angle to help us research where to find suitable foliage after she leaves.

I wanted to tell Masha that she should forget about her six-pointed oak leaves, but I can't. "Every horticultural detail must be true to life if the audience is to believe in the show," she says solemnly.

I admire her passion.

———————

Masha returns to Moscow, impatient to revise her concept based on what she's seen. I remain in New York to check on the production status of the Russian Muppets. When I arrive at the Henson Company Mansion, Ed leads me to the area of the workshop where several artists, with varying shades of purple and green hair and pierced body parts, are hunched over a ten-yard piece of mesh netting. They are weaving strips of sky blue, royal blue, aqua, and pink shantung and organza fabrics into the synthetic fur mesh that will become Zeliboba's exterior coat. Unlike Big Bird, made of expensive ostrich feathers imported from China, Zeliboba's design uses boas and marabou feathers.

Ed tells me that Zeliboba will be one of the largest Muppets ever constructed: more than seven feet tall. "His construction design is based on a system of conical spiraling boned supports," Ed explains. The Henson elves will sew fake pieces of bark, moss, twigs, and leaves into Zeliboba's coat, conforming to the Russian producers' wish for Zeliboba to be "at one" with nature.

We move on to Businka, the hand-rod Muppet, whose hairstyle seems to be causing problems. The Russians want to make a modification to the design, requesting by fax that the Muppet's braids extend upward toward the ceiling and shake when she moves, as though an electrical charge struck her and continues to surge through her body and to the ends of her hair. Ed resists telling me that he's already allocated too much time to construction of the girl Muppet, and he still needs to work more on the boy hand-Muppet, Kubik.

But when I send a fax reporting Ed's objections, my Russian colleagues reply that they will only accept Businka for their show if she has electrified braids.

After much pleading, Henson's artisans rise to the occasion, inventing a new kind of hair made of squiggly cloth that can bend into various wild positions, like a scrunchie with wire. Upon seeing photographs of the new coif days later, the Russian team members declare that Businka's bright, fuchsia-colored wiggling locks and rainbow-colored bows will make her a star, especially to girls.

Kubik's furry orange body is similar in size to Businka's. His wispy strands of red hair randomly stick up from his head, giving the Muppet a disheveled look, similar to an absentminded professor, and adds unexpected increased movement to the puppet's head. When the Russian producers see photographs of Kubik, they swiftly fax back: "Kubik does not look Russian."

Reaching the end of his patience, Ed vents to me, "Kubik's a friggin' Monster—what do the Russians think a *Russian Monster Muppet* is supposed to look like?"

Still, we agree that something is amiss with Kubik's face. "It's the eyebrows," I suggest. Grabbing more short black hairs off the worktable, I hold them up to Kubik's brow. "He needs more brow. He has to look more like Brezhnev."

Ed laughs and offers to fill them out. "He will look like a Russian Groucho Marx, only without the mustache."

"My teammates will love it."

21

A FOREST SPRITE TAKES FLIGHT

With the three Slavic Muppets nearly completed, we must find Russian actors with adequate strength, flexibility, and dramatic experience to perform Zeliboba, Kubik, and Businka. As you cannot separate Muppet from performer, it is imperative to hire the right puppeteers. But it turns out that auditioning actors to perform puppet roles is much more complicated than casting for non-puppet roles.

When I arrive back in Moscow after the quick turnaround in the United States, I go directly to our office. To my astonishment, I discover that Volodya and Tamara have made no arrangements to hold auditions to cast adult actors for the roles of *Ulitsa Sezam*'s Muppets. Volodya insists, "Tamara and I know who Moscow's best actors are, and we will choose them without tryouts." Tamara nods in agreement.

"We have to have open auditions." I look at them in disbelief. "Isn't that the essence of *Ulitsa Sezam*? Creating an opportunity for all?"

Tamara looks alarmed. "You know Natasha, all kinds of people could turn up—all kinds of unprofessional people, even mentally ill people who have no business being there."

I don't have time to respond to such a remark before Volodya interrupts, saying, "It would be a complete madhouse and a waste of time."

Their warnings make me believe there might be something unusual about casting in Russia that I must not understand. But my gut tells me that hand-picking actors to perform the Russian Muppets would be a big mistake. I learned this from the American *Sesame Street* puppeteers, who said that the best way to find puppeteers is by throwing a wide net. They told me that the greatest puppeteers come from nontraditional acting backgrounds. Often the most well suited are acrobats, mimes, dancers, and comedians. These performers all have a high level of physicality and affinity for physical comedy. Unlike performing stiff marionettes operated by strings, Henson's soft, hand and body Muppets require enormous strength and agility.

Ultimately, casting of the Russian Muppets is not entirely Volodya and Tamara's decision; Sesame Workshop and the Henson Company have already engaged someone to help with casting puppeteers in Moscow. The two companies traditionally assist with puppeteer casting for all *Sesame Street*'s international coproductions. And anyway, as I tell Volodya and Tamara, our mutual funder, USAID, requires our auditions to be open to all Russians. Their Moscow representative plans to observe *Ulitsa Sezam*'s audition process, "watching democracy in action."

Tamara whispers to Volodya, "We don't need *democracy* when it comes to casting." Reluctantly, the Russian directors acquiesce, but not without a parting shot from Tamara: "I promise you, Natasha, we will not find any useful or fresh faces for our show."

The Henson Company arranges for Nigel Plaskett, a talented British puppeteer, to fly to Moscow to help with the audition process. Nigel is an accomplished actor who was part of the team performing the role of the robot in the remake of *Lost in Space*. He realized from this performing experience that he preferred the anonymity of puppeteering and now uses his considerable skills to create puppet characters for film, television, and stage worldwide.

Before Nigel's arrival, our advertisement appears in Russia's national newspapers: "Calling on actors, performers, comedians, dancers, and acrobats for a new children's television show. Must be able to sing and act. Must be in excellent physical condition and willing to work full time."

We also create posters and send production assistants to post the announcement on bulletin boards at drama schools and on lampposts throughout the city.

We are immediately bombarded with calls from people wanting to audition. At one drama school, we have to replace the poster five times because students keep tearing it down, hoping to limit the competition.

The week auditions are set to begin, Cheryl Henson, Jim Henson's daughter, flies into Moscow from New York with a giant trunk filled with twenty-odd furry Muppets from earlier Henson productions for us to use during the audition process. Cheryl's an experienced American puppet person in her own right, having learned at her father's knee. Additionally, she speaks some Russian from her studies at Yale.

With so much in common, Cheryl and I had become fast friends in New York. We saw each other socially and she was a guest at my wedding. When I first introduced Ken to Cheryl, he was a bit starstruck, noting her tall, slim, good looks and fabulous sense of style. "She is certainly one of the most glamorous people I've ever met," he professed, which was true for me as well. With her experience and knowledge of Muppet folklore, she's a tremendous asset to our production.

On the first day of auditions, Volodya and Tamara are surprised when 260 performers walk into the squat cement building not far from the TV station and Moskinap. The candidates are as diverse as we had hoped: experienced stage actors, circus mimes, acrobats, dancers, and students from Moscow's theatrical schools. Few have any puppeteering experience.

At first, the actors hesitate to handle the Muppets Cheryl brought with her from America. "Each of these must be worth thousands of dollars," says one, fearful of damaging it.

Cheryl gently encourages the thespians, assuring them that nothing bad will happen.

This prompts a mad rush to the grab bag, a giant cloth sack filled with puppets of all shapes and sizes. There's laughter as the actors pull out the Muppets and disappointment as some actors don't get the puppet they want. Many of the performers have never held a puppet in their hands before.

I glance across the crowded room where the auditions are to take place. At six-foot-four, Nigel's easy to spot—the puppet master stands in front of a mirrored wall and calls for the group to gather around.

The training process will reveal the proficiencies of the different performers: their flexibility, physical strength, and imagination. Nigel begins by sliding his arm inside the sleeve of a gray puppet with spiky orange hair and demonstrating how to move the Muppet's head from side to side and up and down while maintaining the correct eye focus for a hypothetical camera filming the Muppet. He tells the large group that the format of the auditions will be a continuous training/evaluation session where he will observe their performances and make cuts accordingly each day, winnowing down the number of candidates. On the fourth day the final four puppeteers will be selected. Those chosen to perform the roles of the Slavic Muppets will travel to New York for further training by the puppet masters at *Sesame Street* two weeks later.

The pressure is on.

Nigel explains that a Muppet's eyes are two black dots against a white background and that the placement of the eyes makes them appear ever so slightly cross-eyed. He points out a triangle on the Muppet's face, sometimes referred to as the "magic triangle" between the eyes and nose. When correct eye focus is achieved, the Muppet appears to be looking right into the camera. Nigel says, "But, of course, the Muppet isn't actually looking directly at an object; it's an illusion, and turning the Muppet even slightly makes it appear as though the Muppet is looking at something else." Nigel invites the first group of actors to try.

The performers crowd in front of the mirror, holding their puppets aloft over their heads while struggling to achieve proper eye focus. Nigel walks among them, touching a shoulder, shifting an arm, helping make the adjustments to achieve the correct eye focus. Next, Nigel and Cheryl show the actors how to use their thumb and forefinger inside the puppet's head to synchronize the opening and closing of the mouth with each syllable of dialogue.

Nigel bounces up to one of the actors and asks, "How do you say in Russian, 'My name is . . . ?"

The actors line up in front of the mirror and recite *Men-ya-zo-vut* ("My name is . . .") while moving their Muppet's mouth, synchronizing movement with each syllable. Many of them do not have the hand-to-eye coordination or strength necessary to hold their arms upright for an extended period. Their muscles strain as they attempt to manipulate the grip inside the puppet's mouth and deliver controlled movement. They drop their arms, moaning and grabbing their shoulders in pain. Others keep at it, improving their eye focus and maneuvering the mouth to achieve synchronized speech.

The tasks get even more complicated. Nigel divides the performers into groups and sends them off to the corners of the room to develop and then perform improvised skits, allowing him to evaluate how readily they inhabit their puppet.

It's a creative assignment I'd never have thought to give. I am out of my depth, and so grateful Cheryl and Nigel are in Moscow. Volodya and Tamara, who also joined the casting session, are speechless as they observe Nigel's process, its multistage complexity and intensity. They say it's unlike anything they've seen before.

I notice how Cheryl's presence injects both gravitas and electricity into our training sessions. The Russian actors relish learning puppeteering alongside the daughter of the famous creator of the Muppets. Despite her illustrious background, Cheryl is unpretentious and a hard worker. Along with everyone, she throws herself into the ten-hour training sessions and demonstrates enormous empathy, knowing exactly how to put actors at ease. And the actors appreciate Nigel's dry sense of humor. Later, they declare him and Cheryl honorary Russians.

Cuts are made at the end of the first day, trimming the number of candidates by almost half—to 150—and on the following day to 20. Nigel, a relentless taskmaster, sends the remaining candidates home with a set of two string-joined Ping-Pong balls with eyes painted on them so that they may continue practicing eye focus using one hand in front of their bathroom mirrors.

———————

After the third day, Nigel announces, "Only one day left before we narrow our selections to the top six candidates, and one day after that to choosing the final four. You need to work hard," he adds, as the poor souls drag themselves out the door.

That night, Nigel, Cheryl, Volodya, Tamara, Robin, and I meet at a new private Italian restaurant so exclusive that it has no exterior sign. It takes an hour to find it. We discuss the day's performances and propose who we think should make it to the next round. Nigel looks exhausted, but after a few glasses of wine, he perks up and tells us stories about his glory days working with Cheryl's father on the film *Labyrinth*.

Tamara and Volodya look at him admiringly. Their respect and deference make me a little jealous, but he deserves it. Tamara, who'd been the most vocal against holding open auditions, now tells Nigel that she never imagined it would be possible to winnow down 260 candidates to 10 in only 3 days. "You are a genius," she gushes.

Volodya concurs, admitting his bias against open auditions was just plain wrong.

Amazingly, by the end of the dinner, we've narrowed the candidates down to a group of six talented performers. The leading top three male actors are Stanislav Klimushkin (called "Stas"), Andrei Kuzichev, and Vladislav Kysov. Nigel is undecided as to which of the three male performers should get the starring Zeliboba role and which should perform the rod-hand Muppet, Kubik; two puppeteers will be needed to operate Kubik's head and right hand.

The conversation shifts to the girl Muppet, Businka. Elena Treschinskaya (Lena), a petite woman with long, flowing reddish-brown hair, clearly stands out as the most talented puppeteer among those who made it to the final round. She has been staging puppet shows throughout Russia, and she alone has puppeteering experience. Everyone agrees that Lena should perform the role of the female monster.

Nigel resolves to watch Stas closely and observe how he performs in comparison to the other male actors. He wants to gauge their capacity for improvisation and what voices and personality traits the performers can come up with for each of the Muppet characters. He believes through this exercise, he will be able to eliminate in a day the two actors in the group whose performances are less compelling.

Although we don't have the actual Slavic Muppets yet because they are still under construction at the Henson workshop in New York, we show the actors detailed color sketches of the proposed Russian puppets and describe their personalities. Nigel asks the candidates to imagine how each of the Russian Muppet characters might move, speak, and behave. Next, each performer gets paired with a puppet similar in style to the Russian Muppet they would perform in *Ulitsa Sezam* if chosen.

As Nigel watches Lena perform, he marvels at the risks she's willing to take to create an irresistible and relatable character. She's also notably compassionate. Rather than lording her substantial expertise over her compatriots, she helps them figure out how to manipulate their own puppets. Lena's a sponge, absorbing every golden tidbit that Nigel bestows.

Meanwhile, some of the actors who are more used to following a theatrical script have trouble expressing themselves without words on a page and grow frustrated. I see Nigel noting this.

I was surprised at first that beautiful Lena would choose to be a puppeteer instead of a film or theater actress. But watching as she slips her arm inside the puppet sleeve and magically transforms bits of cloth and fur into a bouncy and screen-stealing original character, I begin to understand why she chose this path. She seems to express her deepest emotions through her puppetry. Maybe it's a catharsis of sorts.

Still curious, during a break, I ask Lena why she prefers puppetry to traditional stage or film acting where her face is visible.

"Puppeteering is the purest form of acting because your face is hidden, so no ego is involved," she replies. "The performance is all about the puppet and not about the actor's appearance. As a puppeteer you can be freer."

Later that night at my hotel, in the restaurant, we meet again to continue mulling over strengths and weaknesses of the different candidates. Nigel says all the five men in the last round are very talented and could perform the job, but we still must eliminate two and we have to choose which of them will be our Zeliboba.

Nigel tells our group that he still has some reservations about Stas, unsure whether the skinny, relatively unmuscular, chain-smoking young man has the physical stamina to manipulate Zeliboba, the largest and most complicated of *Sezam*'s Muppets.

But he also sees something special in Stas. "While Stas's manipulation of the puppet is not very good, it is likely to improve with training, and he has a great voice and personality for the character," he says.

With some hesitation, Nigel finally chooses Stas.

The next day, when Nigel gives the good news to Stas, the young man looks shocked.

"I was sure that I would be eliminated," Stas exclaims.

As the only actress to make it to the final round, Lena had assumed she'd be hired, and when Nigel tells her she got the part of Businka, her response is priceless. "I had a dream last night where I was talking to Mr. Henson in a studio with puppets hanging from the ceiling," she recalls. "I didn't know if they were his puppets or someone else's, but it was so cool that I was walking with Mr. Henson, surrounded by these puppets, and now I'm performing one of his puppets."

The same day, Nigel chooses Andrei and Vlad as the other two male performers. Andrei will take the lead—performing Kubik's head and voicing the Muppet, while Vlad will operate Kubik's right hand.

Although Andrei had never held a puppet in his hands before, his performance during the training sessions led him to embrace puppetry as if it were his calling. Vlad is younger than the other actors (he's seventeen) but appears to be a gifted puppeteer, and Nigel expects his performance will improve over time.

The four chosen actors continue intensive puppeteer training with Nigel for the next five days. After Nigel has gone, they will be expected to continue doing practice drills three to four hours a day in the Moscow studio at ORT and send videocassettes of their efforts to Nigel in London for feedback. And then, in two weeks, on to New York for them all.

On the last day of training, Nigel announces to the puppeteers that several of *Ulitsa Sezam*'s scriptwriters and producers will come by the studio to meet the new performers.

When they arrive that afternoon, Nigel invites each of the guests to slip on one of the grab bag Muppets and try to operate it themselves while standing facing the wall of mirrors. Some of my coworkers look uneasy.

"You should all be familiar with the difficulty of operating Muppets, so you understand the limitations the puppeteers face in performing what you write in your scripts," Nigel says. I grab a puppet and join in.

Alongside Nigel, Cheryl leads the way, showing *Ulitsa Sezam*'s writers and producers how to hold their Muppets aloft and use their fingers inside the head to move the puppet's mouth to lip-sync to the music. Awkward and clumsy, none of us are very successful at operating the puppets. But everyone is giggling, banging into each other, and having a lot of fun.

Nigel puts a cassette tape in the boom box and plays a Michael Jackson tune, "You Are Not Alone," which he says is good for training non-English speakers to "lip-sync" with their puppets because of the song's repetitive lyrics.

Raising our arms in the air, each holding a puppet, we begin singing. As we get more comfortable with our furry alter egos, our singing gets louder and louder, and the performances more outrageous. The performers playfully butt heads as they jockey for better positions in front of the mirror. Stas, Vlad, Andrei, and Lena stand at the back of the studio, laughing at the spectacle of all of us struggling to operate our puppets.

Cheryl is in her element, placing her Muppet's furry arm on the shoulders of the puppets on either side of her, while the other performers do the same. Everyone starts swaying from side to side, belting out the lyrics to the Michael Jackson song with more passion than Michael himself. As I watch our reflection in the mirror—our furry Merry Muppet ensemble moving in unison from left to right, any sense of being American or Russian dissolves, and we become one united Muppet family, trying to sing in harmony.

22

MOPPETS IN AMERIKA

Except for Lena, none of the puppeteers seem ready for the rigors that filming *Ulitsa Sezam* will require. Every time I visit the puppet training room at the TV station, I find them practicing with the random puppets that Cheryl brought over, or madly doing calisthenics. Stas anxiously repeats, "There's no way I'm going to be ready to film in a month," as though it's his mantra. It's true that the Russian puppeteers have enormous raw talent, but they still need additional training to advance to a level where they can perform in the studio for up to ten hours straight.

In early December 1995, I accompany the puppeteers to New York City for four days of training at *Sesame Street*'s studios. There, I expect they will gain confidence and refine their puppeteering techniques.

Leading the workshop is puppet master Marty Robinson—the puppeteer behind Telly Monster, Mr. Snuffleupagus, and Slimy the Worm. Marty conducts the puppeteer training for many of *Sesame Street*'s international coproductions. He is also a big fan of Russia's rich puppet traditions, and eager to meet the Russian actors.

Marty is six-foot-two, with long, wavy, salt and pepper curls, a wiry body, and a charismatic oversized personality. When the four Russian performers first arrive at *Sesame Street*'s studio in Queens and see the American puppeteers performing, they seem awestruck, if not a bit self-conscious. Stas says they feel like interlopers—too inexperienced to share the same air with these seasoned Muppet performers. By contrast, Lena appears to have found the home she's been looking for all her life.

Marty leads the visitors to a rehearsal room adjacent to the *Sesame Street* sound stage. The puppeteers line up facing a wall of mirrors. I take a seat in the corner and listen to Marty dispensing his puppetry wisdom.

"The building blocks of puppetry are creating movements to express breathing, walking, and falling, while also expressing emotion. In addition, you must learn proper lip-synching and eye focus."

He paces the room, enunciating his words with explosive gestures. "Think of puppetry technique like playing the piano. Your ten fingers are like the eighty-eight keys of the piano. You have to know where every finger goes to make your performance sound like music. Chords are added as the puppeteer expresses more and more complex emotions."

He explains that Muppets are larger than life, so their expressions should be big. "While scratching your head vigorously might be too much for a stage actor, and kind of hokey, it works for a Muppet whose facial muscles have a limited range—you need strong symbols to communicate the puppet's emotion to the audience," he says, then assigns the Russian actors a palate of moves and techniques to work on.

The puppeteers practice in front of the mirror, then view video playbacks of their performances, with Marty providing feedback. He urges them to be bolder—have "bigger" actions and then gradually pull back their performances if needed, rather than giving a lackadaisical performance at the outset for fear of overacting or looking stupid.

The puppeteers work hard for Marty's approval. In their eyes he's a god, and they look to him for what's needed for them to be ready to film in Moscow next month. "You have to be prepared to look like idiots if you want to create the kinds of characters who children will love forever," he jokes. Marty prides himself on looking like an idiot, which he says has led to his delivering some of the most memorable performances on the American show. His wacky humor puts them at ease—most of them anyway. I notice that Stas appears more uncomfortable than the rest. His lack of confidence is hurting his performance of Zeliboba, and his anxiety about performing seems to be growing, rather than diminishing with practice.

This trip to New York is for not only training but costume fitting. The Henson Company team arrives at the studio, carrying large cases containing the new Russian Muppets. Each Muppet must be modified for each performer's body—perhaps adjusting the length of a sleeve or the amount of foam inside the mouth.

It's the puppeteers' first encounter with *Ulitsa Sezam*'s new Muppets—their long-awaited alter egos. The actors swoon at the sight of Zeliboba, Kubik, and Businka. Andrei and Lena gingerly lift their rod-hand Muppets, slipping their arms inside, and Vlad slides his hand into Kubik's right-hand sleeve. Stas, standing tall, steps into Zeliboba's full-body costume, careful not to rip the seams left open so the outfit can be more closely fitted to his body.

Ed and his crafty Muppet minions carefully trim strips of fabric and fur around Zeliboba's mouth, shortening them so the Muppet's mouth movements will be visible on camera. They cut the fur strands around Zeliboba's protruding eyeballs for the same reason. Ed, who is typically reserved, lets his excitement take over as he witnesses the embodiment of his creatures by the Russian performers. Like a proud papa bear, he takes Businka and, sliding his hand inside the Muppet's head, moves the mouth with his fingers, explaining that "The hand has to fit snugly inside. If there's too much space around the performer's fingers, moving the mouth up and down and sideways, then the head will not move to its fullest capacity, which diminishes the range of the performance."

Stas tries to walk in his costume but keeps stepping on the fur train at the back, nearly running over Lena. When he suddenly takes a spill, Marty yells, "That's it! Perfect falling, Stas!" Stas picks himself up, and everyone laughs, including the artisans putting in pins, marking the new hem.

While Stas waits, Marty shows him how to snap off Zeliboba's paws to get cool air onto his arms—during filming, it can get really hot inside the puppet.

Over the following days, Marty sets up each of the puppeteers with a video monitor hooked up to a camera. Holding their Muppet aloft with their hand inside the puppet's head, the puppeteers begin moving their puppets from side to side, struggling to acclimatize to the image on the monitor—the reverse of what the naked eye usually sees. When a puppeteer moves his arm to the right, the arm on the screen moves left. Thus, the puppeteer sees the image that the audience sees. The actors first experienced this during auditions with Nigel, but it continues to be disorienting, as well as physically and mentally exhausting. But the puppeteers become increasingly adept at maneuvering the puppets and maintaining proper eye focus. And they learn to crouch, keeping their heads below the "safe" camera frame so that only the Muppet is in the frame—not the puppeteer.

Marty walks around the studio, tapping the actors' shoulders, pushing their heads to the sides, and sometimes taking a performer's Muppet to demonstrate a technique. He spends a lot of time guiding Andrei and Vlad on coordinating Kubik's body's movement.

"You have to learn how to move together so that you are like one," he tells them. "As there are two of you, you have twice the flexibility of a rod-hand puppet like Businka."

As Andrei and Vlad continue to struggle to move the Muppet in unison, Marty bobs his head knowingly. "Once you solve this problem, the things that you'll be able to do with this Muppet will astound you. You'll even be able to juggle."

They look at Marty in disbelief, as though he has just told them their Muppet has magical powers. He encourages them to find the soul of their puppet's character. "The Muppets are not an imitation of humanity but a distillation of recognizable human character traits translated into a new expression of character."

Lena practices off to the side, seemingly in her own world. Marty watches, smiling with his hand on his chin. He tells her, "That's great. I like your technique. Your position is excellent."

Looking up at Marty, Lena lets go of the wire rod in her hand supporting Businka's furry arms.

"*Oooo,*" she exhales, touching her fingers to her shoulder, indicating the pain from holding her arm vertically and to the side for so long.

When it comes time for her to showcase what she's come up with for Businka, she mesmerizes everyone with her rendition of the Lambada, crossing Businka's furry arms across her chest and swaying her Muppet's skinny pink torso from side to side. Lena debuts a high-pitched, undulating laugh she's developed for Businka, which is remarkably distinct and captivating.

We watch her in awe.

During a brief stop in training, Stas sidles up to her, and I overhear him confiding in her. "I'm still struggling to find Zeliboba's laugh."

Lena wraps Businka's tiny furry arms partway around Zeliboba's wide torso and rests her puppet's head on Zeliboba's chest in a sweet gesture of support. It's such an intimate moment I must look away.

Marty works intensively with Stas, trying to bolster his self-confidence. "Your puppet is much larger and more of an animal-puppet than the others," he says. "Zeliboba is not as bound by reality as the other smaller hand-puppets."

He asks Stas if he can borrow the puppet to demonstrate what he means. Stas steps out of his costume and holds it while Marty steps in. Stas places Zeliboba's head over Marty's extended arm and shoulders and Marty is transformed into Zeliboba. As Zeliboba, Marty races around the room, growling and running at the puppeteers who are all laughing and falling over themselves to escape from him. He folds the puppet in two, bending to the ground and sniffing with his giant nose, demonstrating how Zeliboba uses his acute sense of smell, one of his character traits.

When Stas reclaims his costume, he practices similar movements, lumbering instead of walking, pushing his head forward and growling. Marty teaches him how to whip his body around in a single movement. This startles and delights his fellow puppeteers.

Seeing Stas's progress, I realize that we needn't worry about his capabilities. Before our eyes, he is growing into Zeliboba, developing his own organic and unique performance as a sweet, bumbling, good-natured character who enchants. Throughout the week, *Sesame Street*'s producing staff and the actors from the American show stop by to satisfy their curiosity about the Russians. The warmth between the groups is palpable.

A week later, the Russian puppeteers return to Moscow. Our intense schedule has taken its toll on me. I'm exhausted and have no appetite. At my apartment, I collapse on the couch and fall asleep for eighteen hours. When I finally wake up, still feeling unwell, Ken is sitting by the edge of the couch. He pushes the hair from my face and tells me I need to see a doctor.

"I'm fine," I say, slowly getting up. "Just tired."

As soon as I stand, waves of nausea take over.

Ken insists.

A visit to the doctor three days later confirms that I'm perfectly healthy.

It's just that I'm pregnant.

Six weeks pregnant, to be exact. The news amazes me, and shocks Ken. We hadn't exactly been careful, but I didn't expect to get pregnant so easily. Although Ken is at first nervous about me being pregnant in Moscow, he quickly comes around as he feels increasing joy in the knowledge that he will become a father. I stubbornly convince myself that my pregnancy will change nothing.

At the New York office, Anna Connolly, my stateside associate producer, shows me samples of leaves and bark she's tracked down from Lincoln Scenic, a faux horticulturist's mecca in midtown Manhattan. And after hours and hours of research, she's finally found the correct oak leaves from a manufacturer in China. Next, we have to figure out how to transport four hundred pounds of artificial leaves and bark to Moscow. Anna discovers shipping anything between China and Moscow is too complicated, so the fake flora will have to be flown to New York and then hand-carried to Russia.

I expect activities in Moscow will slow down over the winter holidays. Most Russians regard the Orthodox religious celebrations as more sacred than the politicized national holidays created by the Soviet regime, such as Great October Socialist Revolution Day or Red Army Day. Throughout the country, work comes to a grinding halt from December 31 until mid-January. I'm grateful for the break.

Two nights before our American Christmas, Ken and I stroll down Columbus Avenue. It's bitter cold and I feel like the luckiest girl in the world, with my hand stuffed snugly inside Ken's warm oversize coat pocket. The scent of pine fills the air as we pass Christmas tree stands with strings of twinkling red and green holiday lights suspended above these tiny urban forests. We stop and watch a family with a baby choosing their evergreen and I squeeze Ken's hand, feeling the thrill of the secret under my wool coat.

When it comes time to return to Moscow, I feel as though my body is not my own and I don't want to go anywhere. I want only to curl up in front of the fireplace in our tiny apartment and sleep—that is, when I don't feel like vomiting. Robin and Leonid already know about my pregnancy, but I haven't told any of my American colleagues working in the New York offices and studio.

I confide to Ken that I'm terrified my condition could be used as a pretext for firing me, or worse, canceling the show. He assures me this is entirely irrational. *Sesame Street* is one of the most progressive companies in America, with a generous maternity policy.

Just to be safe, when I go to my office, I wear bulky sweaters to hide my rounding belly. It's not for long; I'll soon be back in Moscow celebrating 1996 with my team.

Vlad Listyev, head of the ORT TV network, hosting his popular television show months before his murder on March 1, 1995. *Courtesy of ITARR-TASS News; photograph by Nikolai Malyshev/TASS*

From left: Russian *Ulitsa Sezam* producers Piotr Sidorenko and Vika Lukina with Dr. Valeria Lovelace, *Sesame Street* director of research, conducting a focus group research session with children at a Harlem preschool. *Author's collection*

Ulitsa Sezam curriculum workshop participants (including Russian educators, Russian research director Dr. Anna Genina, *Sesame Street* senior vice president of global education Dr. Charlotte Cole, and American producers Robin Hessman and Natasha Lance) gather at Danilovsky Monastery. *Author's collection*

Elena Lenskaya, representative of the Russian Ministry of Education (standing), speaking at the *Ulitsa Sezam* curriculum workshop. Seated, from left, are Dr. Charlotte Cole, senior vice president of global education; Dr. Anna Genina, director of *Ulitsa Sezam* research; and producers Piotr Sidorenko and Natasha Lance. *Author's collection*

Luis Santiero, *Sesame Street* writer (right corner), with the Russian team of *Ulitsa Sezam* scriptwriters in Moscow. *Author's collection*

Chief director of *Ulitsa Sezam*, Volodya Grammatikov (standing), instructing live-action filmmakers. *Author's collection*

Ulitsa Sezam producers at Moskinap camera factory before renovation: (from left) Leonid Zagalsky, Misha Davydov, Natasha L. Rogoff, Robin Hessman, and president of Video Art Irina Borisova. *Author's collection*

Ulitsa Sezam's core creative team celebrating the completion of live-action and animation films for the TV series: (top row, from left) Anna Victorova, Anna Connolly, Katya Komalkova, Sergei Novikov, and Volodya Grammatikov; (bottom row, from left) Uliana Savelieva, Tamara Pavliuchenko, Natasha Lance Rogoff, Robin Hessman, Vika Lukina, and Misha Davydov. *Author's collection*

Gravesite of Moscow TV journalist Oleg Slabynko, who was murdered on January 25, 1996. *Photograph by Marina Gordeyeva/Moscow*

Scenic drawing of *Ulitsa Sezam* backdrop for "neighborhood" studio set, designed by the art director, Masha Rybasova. *Drawing courtesy of Masha Rybasova*

First day of shooting *Ulitsa Sezam* in Moscow's ORT TV studio: the executive producer, Natasha Lance Rogoff, with puppeteers Elena Teschinskaya and Andrei Kuzichev with their Muppets Businka and Kubik in the background. *Author's collection*

Ulitsa Sezam technical crew preparing to shoot "neighborhood scenes" in Moscow's ORT TV studio, with cityscape backdrop in view. *Courtesy of Cornelius Fischer*

Taking a break at the ORT studio during a photoshoot in front of Aunt Dasha's cottage: (from left) Businka, Zeliboba, Katya Mikhailovskaya (actress), and Kubik. *Courtesy of Irina Borisova*

Ulitsa Sezam puppeteer performer Andrei Kuzichev, rehearsing his Muppet Kubik in the studio. *Courtesy of Cornelius Fischer*

Businka the Muppet invites Natasha Lance Rogoff and Leonid Zagalsky to a picnic in the *Ulitsa Sezam* studio. *Courtesy of Irina Borisova*

Never too pregnant to direct: Natasha Lance Rogoff on the Moscow ORT TV studio set. *Courtesy of Irina Borisova*

Chief *Ulitsa Sezam* director Volodya Grammatikov horsing around on set while pretending to breastfeed Ernie. *Courtesy of Irina Borisova*

Muppets Kubik and Businka sharing a moment with Katya Mikhailovskaya (actress) and Tiger in the *Ulitsa Sezam* studio neighborhood. *Courtesy of Irina Borisova*

Ulitsa Sezam actors singing on set: (from left) Alexander Lyrchikov (father Sasha), Ekaterina Strizhenova (mother Nina), Muppets Businka and Kubik with Katya Mikhailovskaya (young Katya), and Maria Aronova (Aunt Dasha). *Courtesy of Tatiana Mikhailovskaya*

Stanislav Klimushkin, puppeteer performer of Zeliboba, rehearsing in partial costume at the studio. *Courtesy of Irina Borisova*

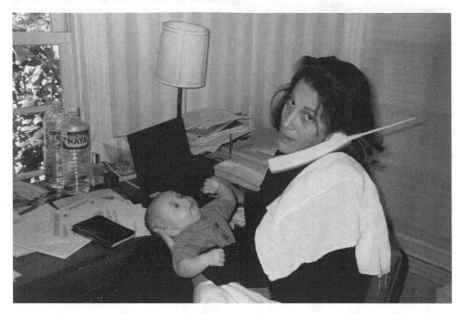

Natasha Lance Rogoff, on maternity leave—juggling a laptop, a phone, and her newborn, Gabriel, while talking to her production team in Moscow. *Author's collection*

Natasha Lance Rogoff
EXEC. PROD., SESAME ST. IN RUSSIA

CBS Evening News reports on *Sesame Street* coming to Russia. *Footage supplied by CBS News*

III

BIRTHING THE BABIES

It's easier to bring drugs into Russia than a full size tree.
—Leonid Zagalsky

23

ULITSA SEZAM'S NEIGHBORHOOD

By the time I return, New Year's celebrations are winding down. Moscow welcomes me with frigid temperatures, darkness by four in the afternoon, and depressing recent electoral results giving the Communist Party a majority in the Russian parliament. Despite all this, our team is laser-focused on designing and building *Ulitsa Sezam*'s set in ORT's largest studio, where we will film the Russian "neighborhood" scenes.

Meanwhile, the electoral swing to the right crystalizes for our team what we are up against. We feel a sense of urgency to speed up production; the recent past has taught us that chaos outside the studio has a way of spilling over. It's been only seven months since the TV station was attacked. Who's to say it won't happen again?

While I was back in the States, Volodya, Tamara, and Masha beefed up our studio construction crew, hiring carpenters, painters, costume designers, set dressers, and additional technical personnel. Our chaotic team has transformed into a cohesive brigade of more than three hundred and our department heads have learned how to delegate responsibilities. Volodya quotes the German Chancellor Otto von Bismarck, who once said, "Russians are slow to get on a horse, but once mounted, they ride fast."

His famous phrase applies here perfectly and Volodya and Tamara also inform me it's time to cast the show's human (non-Muppet) characters.

At the Moskinap office, Volodya insists there is not enough time to hold open auditions for these actors. "I already have a good idea which actors to select, based on the character archetypes developed by our team," he says confidently. "They shouldn't be sophisticated Muscovites or peasants but educated people—but not too educated," he winks.

Over the past month, the writing team came up with personalities and back-stories for our non-puppet characters. Some of the features resemble characters in the American show, but the writers have reinterpreted them for Russian audiences.

There's been some back and forth about the family structure for *Ulitsa Sezam*—choosing a nuclear or a single-parent family and deciding whether the grandmother resides with them, as is common in many Russian households. In the end, the team selects archetypes that we hope will have broad appeal. The mother (Nina), her husband (Sasha), and their eight-year-old child, Katya, will live together in a house on the courtyard. Nina will be a pediatrician, because many Russian doctors are women, while the father's profession, a hardware store owner, will be a new archetype—picked to encourage small business development. The writers give Nina a small garden in front of her home to grow vegetables and herbs that she shares with her neighbors; this creates opportunities for the writers to address the reality of many Russians typically growing food in small family plots. The daughter, Katya, is a typical smart, inquisitive girl who loves animals, reading fairy tales, and listening to music, especially classical music, and she has a bicycle she shares with other children in the courtyard who cannot afford one. The cast also will include a mailman, a traditional character in Russian folklore.

The most popular human role among the writers is the eccentric Aunt Dasha, the caretaker of the courtyard. Some have started calling her "the soul of the *dvor*." All the children on *Ulitsa Sezam* will affectionately call her *Tyotia* (Auntie). She's a quintessential Russian character who lives in a traditional modest cottage and spouts folklore and homespun wisdom. She fosters Russia's cultural past by introducing children in the neighborhood to folk arts like glazing pottery, carving wooden figures by hand, crocheting, sewing dolls, and singing traditional folk songs.

Although Aunt Dasha is a stickler for cleanliness and at times too strict, she's always kind, greeting everyone with affectionate phrases such as "My dears," "My precious ones," and "My doves." Her generosity and warmth were developed with great care—hoping to counter the perception of Soviet-era courtyard caretakers as KGB informers.

In a hastily organized meeting at Moskinap with a few of the writers to flesh out more details for the human actors, one writer expresses her concern that the proposed real-life characters seem unreal because they're "too nice."

Her colleagues push back, insisting, "We must model positive relations between people so children will learn how to trust again, cooperate, and live without fear."

It's great to be back with my team. But sitting at the table with the writers, I start to feel like I'm going to be sick. It's becoming harder to hide my pregnancy from my Russian colleagues who work with me twelve to sixteen hours each day. I've seen Tamara look a bit worried as she notices me running to the bathroom from my desk every half hour.

Later that afternoon, Tamara walks over to my desk, taking me in from head to toe, and tenderly asks, "Natasha, are you pregnant?"

Looking like the cat who ate a canary, I hear myself share my secret. I'm relieved to tell someone other than Robin and Leonid—especially Tamara, who has a grown daughter.

"Congratulations, dear!" She hugs me.

I tell her that I haven't told anyone else from our Moscow production team but plan to later today. Tamara puts her finger to her mouth, making a *shh* sign.

At the end of the workday, with Robin at my side, I assemble the core team. "We are going to have a baby!" I announce as I throw open my oversize cardigan with a theatrical flair, revealing my little bump. There's excitement all around.

Of course, Tamara couldn't keep my secret and had told Misha, who'd proceeded to purchase a bottle of champagne. Now he stands up, pops the cork, and begins pouring a splash into short glass tumblers all around. "We will name the baby 'Broadcaster' because *that* is what we need most: a broadcaster for our show!" He raises his glass and drinks. We celebrate "Broadcaster" long after the champagne bottle is empty. But no drinking for me.

Over the next week, word of my pregnancy spreads to the studio crew, the actors, and the team of freelancers who regularly come by the Moskinap office to drop off film rough cuts and music tapes. The team members who have children ask probing, thoughtful questions that prompt me to imagine life after the baby's born. Questions like "How long do you plan to breastfeed?" and "After the birth, do you plan to bring the baby with you to attend *Ulitsa Sezam*'s premier?" My coworkers have calculated the baby will be six weeks old at the time of the show's anticipated launch in October, *if we get a broadcaster*.

But I have no answers because I haven't given any of this any thought. I've been too busy to read any books about childbirth and beyond. I'm a blind cavefish, oblivious to its surroundings, swimming in darkness and without a vision of what's to come. Their questions make me feel more acutely how my body and professional goals are on diverging trajectories.

And yet I'm touched by how well my Russian teammates take care of me. Everyone comes bearing gifts: cushions to sit on, water to keep me hydrated, and endless amounts of advice and admonishments about pregnancy.

Misha the Bear surprises us all by turning into a superstitious worrywart. He warns, "Natasha, you should stop swearing. It will give the baby a birthmark." Tamara tells me never to sit on cold concrete or the floor because it will "freeze your female organs." And one of the office secretaries says if I cut my hair while pregnant, I'm more likely to have a premature birth.

Most importantly, like the Cosa Nostra, my team is sworn to silence, agreeing not to reveal my secret to my *Sesame Street* colleagues in New York. As irrational as it is, I'm still worried about that.

———————

Leonid shows up at the Moskinap office. I haven't seen him since he's distanced himself from the creative side of the production, focusing exclusively on the broadcast deal. But he has no time to chat. He urgently needs me to accompany him to meet Oleg Slabynko, a high-level executive and producer at RTR, Russia's second largest TV network, airing on Channel Two.

We take Leonid's car to RTR. On the way, he explains RTR may be a viable broadcast alternative to ORT.

Inside the TV station, we walk through the corridors, which look eerily similar to those of ORT. I feel queasy, recalling the time Leonid and I visited Vlad Listyev when we were trying to get a broadcast deal.

Slabynko, a handsome man in his early thirties with voluminous dark wavy hair and a buff physique, comes toward us with an outstretched hand. Not surprisingly, he is familiar with our four-year saga of trying to get *Ulitsa Sezam* on Russian television. He asks if we have support for the project from the Russian government, clearly not wanting to antagonize the current administration. Leonid assures him the Russian ministry of education is behind *Ulitsa Sezam*.

Like Listyev, Slabynko has ambitions to clean up corruption related to advertising at RTR. I breathe in deeply, remembering the moment I learned of Listyev's murder. I hope Slabynko will be okay. My attention wanders to a framed photograph of a cute little girl on his desk.

"It's my daughter," he remarks proudly.

Hoping to seal the deal, we show a video clip of Bert and Ernie dubbed into Russian. In the clip, Bert notices Ernie holding a banana to his ear pretending it's a phone. Bert tries talking to Ernie, but Ernie doesn't respond and says, "I can't hear you because I'm talking on the banana." Bert shows a suffering expression to the camera.

Slabynko bursts out laughing. "I feel like Bert feels every time I talk to the Kremlin." I find him refreshingly relaxed and funny. Unbelievably, he agrees to broadcast *Ulitsa Sezam* on RTR five days a week. He also agrees to give Irina's company the right to sell airtime surrounding the children's program—provided he can convince Reclama Holding (the advertising firm controlling airtime on RTR) to agree to these terms.

Leonid and I exchange glances. Sometimes I think we're like an old married couple, knowing exactly what the other is thinking. We are both sensing a feeling of disquieting déjà vu from our deliberations with Listyev. We aren't even sure if Slabynko has the authority to give Irina commercial air slots on RTR.

But we happily accept his offer.

Before leaving Slabynko's office, I hand the TV executive a present for his daughter: one of the new "Tickle Me Elmo" toys, fresh off the production lines. He hugs me, unusual as we just met, but I like it.

Once we're in the hallway, Leonid lights a cigarette.

"I'm skeptical this deal will happen," he says.

"All we can do is hope," I respond.

After finishing the meeting at RTR, I suggest to Leonid that we go back to ORT and visit the studio where Masha has just begun constructing the set. I want to see how it's coming along. Irina is now finally paying for Moscow production costs, including the astronomical advance fee securing ORT's largest studio where we plan to film *Ulitsa Sezam*'s neighborhood scenes during the next four months. At this point, we can't allow any delays. Even if we were to film twelve hours a day, six days a week, it would take us until the end of April to complete the shooting of all the neighborhood episodes for the fifty-two television shows.

Back at ORT, we take the elevator to the studio. Leonid pushes open the heavy metal door to the 600-square-meter "black box," where fifty men in jumpsuits are frantically sawing, sanding, and hammering out Masha's creative vision. Like Peter the Great's imperial architect overseeing the construction of the Winter Palace, Masha stands in the center of the studio, commandeering the workmen.

Originally built in the 1960s, the studio looks battered, with dented metal walls and a rusty catwalk spiraling upward to a steel lighting grid. The outdated lights, much larger than those used in American television studios, should be in a museum.

Masha directs the crew as they struggle to raise a forty-by-forty-foot backdrop designed to span the length of the back wall. She turns to greet us. Wiping beads of sweat off her forehead, she tells us that crews are working day and night to ensure the scenery and props are assembled in time for filming in two weeks. "In the best of circumstances, this would take six weeks," she says. She looks exhausted, and they've only just begun.

Returning to the task at hand, Masha directs the workmen to grab the rusted cables and pull them harder. The sound of metal scraping on metal fills the studio as the scrim slowly inches upward. It takes several attempts of jimmying the wires up and down to level the top edge of the backdrop.

Once the backdrop is stretched and secured, the crew steps back, silent, mesmerized by its originality and beauty.

I'm usually successful at controlling my emotions but not today. I feel a lump in my throat at the sight of *Ulitsa Sezam*'s first piece of scenery in place.

The wide, vibrantly colored, hand-painted canvas epitomizes Masha's modern Russian city. Like an architectural version of *Where's Waldo*, it's jam-packed with differently sized buildings representing every era of Russian architecture: blue and gold Orthodox churches, quaint burnt-orange and pink rural dachas, austere Stalinesque skyscrapers, ornate prerevolutionary mansions, and the multistory Soviet-era *Khrushchobi* apartment complexes. The jumble of buildings rises from the foreground to the horizon, like flowers in a garden beneath a permanently sunny blue sky dotted with cumulus clouds.

The carpenters continue nailing together beams for every scenic structure. Five hours later, the assembled frames for each building form a semicircle in the courtyard. The crew is especially taken with how the two-story faux-brick apartment building is taking shape, with its elegant second-floor wrought-iron balcony—the largest structure in the courtyard. Masha tells me, "Many of the workers have been unemployed for months and they are grateful to have work and to be creating something beautiful for children."

I don't want to leave but must go to our office at Moskinap to review the newest live-action films.

Later that afternoon when I return to the studio again, I see the bakery, hardware store, and post office exterior walls being put in place. Wood dust is everywhere, and the smell of glue causes me to gag, but none of the Russians are complaining. For everyone in the studio, this is an extraordinary moment.

I practically skip to the television station the next day, excited to see the progress at the studio. As soon as I enter, paint fumes overpower me. I see two workmen on ladders, painting Aunt Dasha's ramshackle dacha, layering multiple coats of blue in various tones to create a muted and aged look. A woman from the art department stands on a wooden crate next to the men, gingerly running a thin brush with white paint over the cottage *nalichniki* (traditional Russian window shutters). Masha tells me the *nalichniki* were hand-carved out of wood by a local artisan who based her designs on drawings of wild animals and geometric shapes used in pagan times. "We want to be authentic," she explains with pride.

Another worker sticks his head through the lattice-framed window of Aunt Dasha's home, and begins theatrically reciting a verse from a Pushkin poem that all Russian children learn by heart in elementary school:

> Children, children, look and see, our fishing nets
> have caught a dead man.

His fellow workers stop, then look up at the carpenter-poet whose verses rhyme in a funny way in Russian. They all start laughing and one worker then recites the next line of the poem.

It's remarkable—the show hasn't even aired, and it's already uplifting people.

But a week before the filming begins, I arrive on set and Tamara is in a panic, trying to supervise activities in the studio.

"We have a problem," she announces grimly. "Shatski, the foreman who manages the tradesmen, has disappeared, along with the original construction plans."

We call Misha at Moskinap, and he frantically tries to find Shatski. Masha arrives on set, shaking and upset. "We cannot afford to lose even one day of construction," she says, frantically urging Tamara to send out a search party to check with his family, his drinking buddies, and anyone who might know where Shatski is. That Masha hasn't made copies of the plans is a mild catastrophe but understandable—the type of xerox machine that can reproduce oversize prints is accessible only to state-run entities.

During the search, one of the crew members suddenly speaks up, "It figures Shatski took off. All these Jews ever care about is money. They just take the money and run."

His words stun me. I'm so disappointed to hear these views from someone on our team. I'm especially sensitive because my grandparents fled Russia because of anti-Semitism and pogroms in the early 1900s. I wait for someone to challenge him, but no one speaks up. The crew also doesn't pay much attention to the remark, returning to their work. I quietly have a word with the worker who insulted my people.

Later that afternoon, Leonid walks into the studio, looking frighteningly pale. He leads me toward the exit, away from the crew. I can't imagine what is going on, but I can tell something terrible has happened.

"There's been another assassination," Leonid whispers, cupping his hand to his mouth. He pulls me into the hallway. "It's Oleg."

"Oleg Vasilev?" I ask, naming a Russian banker we both know.

"No, worse," Leonid whispers, "Slabynko."

"What!" I scream.

Two people pass us, turning their heads.

My breath stops short as I struggle for the right words.

"How is it even possible?" I howl. "Who would want Oleg killed?"

"I don't know." Leonid says.

I think back to the Tickle Me Elmo I gave to him for his daughter, and shudder.

"Oh my God, that child in the photo on his desk has no father now."

Trembling, I remind Leonid not even a year has passed since Listyev was murdered.

"Now it's happening all over again," I say.

Fighting to recover, I ask Leonid, "How can you be so calm?"

Leonid just shakes his head, looks down at the linoleum floor and kicks a loose tile. We shuffle down the hall toward the exit.

I ask, "You remember how Oleg hugged me at the end of our meeting?"

"Yeah, I remember." Leonid sighs. "He was good guy."

We arrive at the exit. Before walking through the glass doors, Leonid looks me in the eye, with a furrowed brow and says, "You do realize this means we have to negotiate the broadcast deal all over again."

I stare at him. "How can you even talk about that right now?"

He shrugs. "Because I have to."

The news spreads through the TV station, though no one knows who killed Slabynko or why. Broadcast news reports revealed that Slabynko was at his apartment with his daughter around six o'clock in the evening when someone knocked on his door. When he answered, a gunman shot him and ran away.

All afternoon, I hear my team debating over how many journalists have been attacked or killed this year alone. It's so depressing. Every television executive fighting to safeguard a free press is targeted. I sit alone in a neighboring office, slowly breathing in and out, trying to calm down. My pregnancy is advancing, and I'm finding it harder to deal with the stress. I feel more vulnerable. I cannot trust my body to react quickly in the event of a crisis. So much has changed.

Later at night when I call Ken, I'm still feeling tormented about Slabynko. He begs me to come home. I consider it briefly. But I can't leave now.

After a twenty-four-hour search, Shatski is found, along with the architectural plans. Apologizing profusely, he explains a family emergency was the cause of his disappearance and was entirely unavoidable.

The construction resumes, but even with the rotating building crews, it is taking longer than Masha had anticipated. On some days, arriving at the studio at eight in the morning, I see the same workers I'd said good night to the night before. Their dedication is astounding, especially considering they're not earning much, at most maybe the equivalent of thirty U.S. dollars a day.

One day, Masha pulls me aside to tell me that she is worried. "I still have to decorate the entire set—all the room interiors—with furniture, lights, pictures on the walls, and bric-a-brac to make the settings look realistic and lived-in."

I tell her to stop and breathe. "Take a moment to appreciate what you and your crew have created. It's remarkable."

"I can't," she moans. "There are too many cooks." Masha is distraught, explaining that every crew member or random visitor dropping by the studio feels entitled to express an opinion and challenge her artistic choices. She gestures to a kindly-looking woman with white hair and a blue apron. "Even Vera, who is supposed to hang the wallpaper I selected for the walls of the family home, is refusing to do so because she feels that it's too modern for a typical Russian home."

Masha has been running on four hours of sleep a night for many weeks. I try to calm her down, reassuring her that *she* and only *she* is in charge. This seems to offer some comfort.

One day later, I witness Masha's dilemma firsthand. I ask one of the production assistants to scatter leaves in the courtyard, to make the gray rubber studio floor look more like the ground on an autumn day. When I come back an hour later, the studio janitor has swept up the leaves. I ask the assistant to put them back again. An hour later when I return, the leaves are gone again.

When I ask the janitor why he keeps removing the floor decoration, he looks at me with a pitying expression and says, "Natasha, do you want people watching *Ulitsa Sezam* to think we are improper—with leaves all over and no caretaker to sweep them up? The courtyard is like your home; it should always be tidy."

Masha rushes over to speak with the janitor and shoos me away.

Even the fire inspector who drops by to give us a citation for a trumped-up code violation has an opinion. One day, while negotiating the "fee" he will exact for a "paint fumes" infraction, he looks over at Aunt Dasha's freshly painted house. "The dacha is all wrong—You should paint it shiny bright yellow instead of that ugly faded blue."

Masha and Tamara are busy, so I try reasoning with him. "Tolya, Russian winters are harsh, and the houses have to look weathered to look real."

"This muted blue just looks worn and dirty," he counters, apparently an art connoisseur. "It has to be a strong imperial yellow—strong like the Tsar's yellow!" Obviously, he's not read Kandinsky.

24

WILL WORK FOR BANANAS!

By the end of January, Volodya can wait no longer. The actors are itchy and impatient. He says he must begin rehearsals with the puppeteers in the studio to give them a sense of the space where they will be performing. Masha agrees and the actors are forced to shout their lines over the din of drilling and hammering as the crew puts finishing touches on the set.

When Tamara announces the start date for filming will have to be delayed by two days due to "a tree malfunction" (Zeliboba's oak tree is not ready), the puppeteers, especially Stas, are grateful for the additional rehearsal time. The Muppet actors have turned their dressing room adjacent to the studio into a gym. Often, when I stop by, they're lifting light weights or doing push-ups and squats, trying to get stronger before shooting begins.

On a Sunday (we work through weekends now), I arrive at the studio and see Masha supervising a crew of about twelve women sitting on the floor, gluing together long pieces of bark in the shape of a tree. Masha and her staff have worked through the night, assembling the tree from hundreds of pieces.

Around noon, Leonid walks in and tells me his harrowing tale transporting three sixty-pound boxes of bark and 125 cartons of oak leaves on a flight one day earlier from New York to Moscow.

With so much going on with the studio set, I couldn't leave Moscow, so four days earlier, I asked Leonid to be our mule, transporting Zeliboba's tree parts from New York. When he arrived back, poor Leonid had to spend ten hours in customs at the Moscow airport.

"The customs agents thought I was carrying contraband, even though I repeatedly told them that the boxes were tree parts." He says with a roll of his eyes. "They insisted on opening every single box." He glares at me for making him our courier.

Tilting his head to one side, Leonid impersonates the languid customs agent he had to deal with: "Well, I don't see in our list of *allowable* imported products any category for 'genuine bark,' so I guess you'll have to pay a big fee on the goods."

Still mocking the customs official, he continues, "*Or* I could classify your cargo as 'unspecified wood products,' and then you'd pay no tax."

Leonid affects the agent's crooked smile while fishing for a bribe and says, "Which would you prefer?"

In response, Leonid says he handed over four cartons of cigarettes as he told the agent, "I would *really* appreciate your kindness in classifying my cargo as 'unspecified wood products.'"

Finally, Leonid was allowed to exit the airport with his train of porters, who loaded the boxes onto two school buses he'd rented ahead of time. They took him directly to ORT, where he dropped off the tree bark and foliage.

Everyone had stopped working to listen to Leonid's harrowing tale and by the end of his story, they're all in stitches. And Leonid forgives me for this moon-struck adventure the minute he sees the fruit of his labor: the ten-by-five-foot-wide tree lying flat on the studio floor with its branches stretched, mid-assembly. As he watches the half-dozen seamstresses, crouched over, sewing leaves onto the branches, I sense his pride over the tree caper.

I press Masha as to when, realistically, she thinks the set will be ready for filming.

She continues to push her needle through the stem of a leaf. Without looking up, she answers, "We will be ready soon. You shouldn't be worried." She seems to be reassuring herself more than me. As I turn away, she whispers under her breath, so only I can hear, "The only thing is, it's possible—once all the leaves are attached—that the tree will be too heavy and will not stay upright."

I assure her that we will find a way to make the tree stand.

At lunchtime, dozens of curious producers from other shows at ORT stop by the studio to wander around the set, gawking at the largest and most ornate scenery ever created for a children's television show in Russia. Ducking in and out of the stage set, I hear their comments about how realistic and cozy everything looks. The most-talked-about feature is Aunt Dasha's house, with its quaint peasant aesthetic and décor of traditional handsewn quilts, crocheted dolls, and a wooden antique chest with hand-painted children's toys. The second most popular is the bakery. Inside, lacquered loaves of black and brown bread rest in bins on the shelves. A group of artists on ladders are busy painting a gypsum-molded straw basket of fresh bread above the signage hanging over the shop's transom. I overhear one person gushing, "I love how the houses face each other so neighbors can pop their heads out of the windows and say hello." As Masha had hoped, like the American show, the set decoration looks real-istic—but *this one* is distinctly Russian.

Amid all this, I notice two production assistants walking past us, carrying a wooden bench. They set it down in the center of the courtyard. "Where did you find this?" I ask, not recalling having seen it on the props list.

A bit chagrined, one PA replies, "We borrowed it." It turns out they'd stolen it from a nearby park. Apparently, this is how we also acquired the telephone box, the picnic table, and a city trash can.

I joke with them, "Communism is over, along with collective ownership."

Masha, however, rushes over, insisting she wants a "real" worn bench for the courtyard. She promises to return it after filming.

The day before shooting is supposed to begin, I arrive on set and see about twenty men cinching ropes around the trunk and thicker branches of Zeliboba's giant oak tree, while other workers holding the other ends of the ropes, fan out three feet apart in a circle. Having secured the knots, Masha yells, "*Raz, dva, tri* (One, two, three)."

With a collective grunt, the workers move backward in unison, keeping the ropes taut. The massive structure rises toward the studio ceiling like a Midwestern barn raising. At full height, the oak tree stands forty feet high, with a gigantic, arched, swinging double door cut into its trunk—the entrance to Zeliboba's lair. A slit at the top of the door serves as his mailbox.

Once the workers secure the tree on its base, they untie the ropes. We wait with trepidation to see if it stands independently.

When it does, the leathery-faced laborers break out in applause, nodding at Masha with respect. The workers slap each other's backs, marveling at the citadel they've erected: a fictional refuge for Russian children. Somehow this tree—made from cork, shipped from China to America, then hand-carried to Moscow and lovingly assembled by a dozen Russian hands—has come to represent everything we hoped to achieve with *Ulitsa Sezam*: the creation of beauty and renewal.

That evening, after working a few hours at Moskinap, I return with Leonid to the studio. Masha is directing the artists completing the final touches on the interior decorations. It's quiet on the set; most of the larger-scale construction has been completed. Only a skeleton crew remains. *Ulitsa Sezam*'s neighborhood is almost ready for its inhabitants.

I say hello to Shatski, who is standing on a ladder at the entrance to the courtyard. Since his disappearance and return, he's redeemed himself by diligently working his crews around the clock. Leonid and I watch as he bangs the final nail into the yellow and green "ULITSA SEZAM" sign, straightening it before slowly descending the ladder. Under my breath, I start humming,

> Sunny days
> Sweeping the clouds away . . .

Leonid joins in.

> On my way to where the air is sweet
> Can you tell me how to get?
> How to get to Sesame Street

At the right moment, we substitute the words *Ulitsa Sezam* for *Sesame Street*, singing the song loudly, paying no attention to the funny looks the tired crew members are giving us.

————————

The happiness I feel on the first day of filming in *Ulitsa Sezam*'s neighborhood cannot be described. Our entire core producing team and all the writers and filmmakers from the Moskinap office file into the courtyard, excitedly pushing up against each other as Tamara and Volodya urge everyone to gather around. One of the writers who had penned many studio scripts asks how long we plan to be filming in the studio. I tell him, "It will take us four months of filming to complete all the neighborhood scenes for *Ulitsa Sezam*'s fifty-two episodes."

As he is wishing the technical crew "good luck" we hear Tamara yelling, "Attention, please!"

Stas, dressed as Zeliboba, steps out from behind the scenery, towering over everyone. In character, the large Muppet speaks. "Dear people, welcome to the start of the first season of *Ulitsa Sezam*."

Team members who had not seen Zeliboba before smile from ear to ear at the sight of this wondrous creature.

Volodya thanks the production and research teams for their immense contributions. He steels the crew for their upcoming marathon, appealing to their passion.

"We all know the atmosphere we will create on this set will transfer to people watching *Ulitsa Sezam* on their TV screens. We want to convey a feeling of delight and joy. Everything is in our hands and depends on us."

Applause erupts, and Volodya then introduces Irina Borisova, who arrives from Video Art to speak in front of our large team for the first time. Throughout the production of *Ulitsa Sezam* she preferred to remain behind the scenes. She begins, "I am insanely happy today, but this road was a long one." Gesturing toward me, she continues. "*Ulitsa Sezam* has turned out to be the baby that took much longer to gestate than that one." She points to my belly. "Now, I very much hope that *our Sezam baby* will finally get birthed, before that one." She laughs.

One of the writers starts making loud, painful groaning noises, pretending to give birth, and everyone cracks up. I only wish Leonid were here to enjoy this moment. He's with Baxter somewhere in Moscow, fighting with broadcasters and advertisers to get our show aired.

Enacting a timeworn superstition, Tamara takes a white porcelain China plate with the blue letters "Ulitsa Sezam" written on the front and smashes it against the leg of a camera tripod. It shatters, and everyone cheers, scrambling to the floor and picking up shards for good luck.

Tamara picks up the largest fragment and hands it to me, shouting with some fanfare, "For Natasha, our Mommy of *Ulitsa Sezam*, as a souvenir." Everyone claps.

The team members, not part of the studio crew, scatter back to the Moskinap office while the studio cast and crew gather around Volodya, who is shouting directions.

The camera operators roll their tripods into position, the grips scamper up the metal catwalk to adjust the ceiling lighting, and the actors disperse to their dressing rooms. An hour later, Volodya calls the actors to the set. I can hardly believe it; at last filming begins.

———————

The initial shooting days are rough. Despite everyone's enormous efforts, the set's construction is not complete, and we're forced to choose filming locations based on where the paint has dried.

At five months pregnant, the heat and swell of people makes me feel slightly faint. Tamara places a stool for me next to the action so I can sit down. The puppeteers struggle under the weight of their puppets, complaining about the paint odor and boiling temperatures beneath the Tungsten studio lamps. Stas, carrying an extra ten pounds of feathers, fur, and silk on his body, pronounces that he's suffocating inside his costume. Every five minutes, he asks to halt filming so the wrangler who assists the puppeteers can help lift Zeliboba's puppet head, allowing Stas to briefly breathe easily. Eventually, we have to remove some of the foam packed into Zeliboba's head to make it lighter.

Volodya overhears one of the crew members calling Stas a "spoiled wimp." Wasting no time, he turns to the speaker. "This is a new experience for Stas. Have some compassion and give him time to adjust."

I wish we had that time, but we don't. Our schedule is tight due to lost days from the tree fiasco. We run fans during rehearsals to cool the set down and eliminate paint fumes, only turning them off when rolling the cameras. Several times this leads to our blowing out the electrical grid, forcing us to lose even more time.

We also discover that Stas's video monitor—an expensive piece of imported equipment strapped to his waist inside his costume—doesn't work properly. Instead of the video screen showing his fellow actors performing beside him on set, Stas sees pixilated white dots where they are standing, like characters on *Star Trek* beaming themselves up to the *Enterprise*.

Performing virtually blind, Stas miscalculates distances between the actors and himself. He keeps bumping into the other actors and one time nearly runs over little Katya.

Fortunately, our Russian technical crew is exceptionally adept at dealing with equipment problems, an essential life skill honed during Soviet times. They quickly figure out how to connect the Western device to the antiquated Soviet equipment. Using aluminum foil and wires, they rig up an apparatus resembling a hat a kid might make if she were trying to communicate with aliens. The system somehow improves the video monitor's transmission, and the white fuzzy dots on Zeliboba's monitor turn into fellow actors.

Zeliboba's performance improves markedly.

I'm constantly impressed by Russian ingenuity. One time the props department needed a sieve to strain seeds for a scene in a script, but none could be found in Moscow's stores. Without missing a beat, one of the grips suggests using pantyhose. When I asked him where he came up with the idea, he said he'd read about it in a popular magazine called *Science and Life*. Winking, he added, "The pantyhose trick is from the section on life, not science."

The biggest challenge for Volodya and Tamara turns out to be shooting episodes using synchronized sound and editing the show in real time from inside a production control room. The control room, one floor above, overlooks the studio floor behind a giant pane of glass. In the control room, a bank of TV monitors plays the video feed from the studio cameras and audio equipment records the actors. They are expected to use an intercom system and microphones to communicate with the actors on set. This is a relatively new approach. Most Russian film and TV directors are more accustomed to directing actors from the studio floor and recording audio that is later synched to picture in postproduction, after the filming is complete.

Volodya says he finds this American approach "cumbersome." The puppeteers are not adequately synching their puppets' mouth movements with the audio track and their inexperience requires him to do multiple takes, which is taking too much time.

While filming continues at a glacial pace of two and a half minutes per day—compared to the American show's average of twenty minutes—it starts sinking in that if we don't improve our directing technique, we won't complete the episodes in time.

I arrange for Lisa Simon, *Sesame Street*'s American veteran director, to spend a week in Moscow, helping the Russian directors increase their filming speed. The workshop's seasoned veterans are doing everything they can to help us succeed. I remind myself to thank them profusely when I get back to New York.

When Lisa arrives at the Sezam studio, she immediately notices the puppeteers getting tired by midmorning and slowing down the pace of filming. She suggests delivering a crate of bananas to the studio every day, so the puppeteers can snack and keep up their energy. More importantly, Lisa spends twelve hours each day at the studio demonstrating techniques to reduce the number of filming takes.

By the end of Lisa's visit, we've miraculously increased filming to ten minutes a day. Volodya says he's indebted to Lisa most of all for reminding him of how necessary it is to take pleasure in his work despite the difficulties. This is her legacy, and a box of bananas delivered every morning, even after Lisa's departure.

As the shooting becomes more sophisticated, Volodya discovers that directing human and puppet actors together creates challenges he hasn't previously faced.

Some of the "human" actors resent their furry thespian counterparts for having all the best and funniest lines, leaving the human actors to play the boring straight parts. To compete, the human actors are overacting and speaking to their puppet counterparts in high-pitched artificial baby voices.

Volodya's patience is godlike, and his humor is essential to keeping the team on track. One morning when Stas shows up late for the first call and is spotted hurriedly stuffing himself into his costume behind Aunt Dasha's house, Volodya jokes loudly to the crew, "Looks like Zeliboba spent the night at Aunt Dasha's"—implying the Muppet had a late-night tryst with the older auntie.

Even though Stas's tardiness stole ten minutes of filming time from everyone, the entire cast is in hysterics. They adore Volodya. Each day he gently nurtures the performers, guiding them to personify their characters more fully, particularly Vlad and Andrei, who struggle to operate Kubik smoothly.

The two actors have an interesting relationship. They've known each other since high school and now for all practical purposes are joined at the hip, manipulating the hand-rod puppet for hours at a time. Still, their performance is awkward, often out of sync. For example, during filming, Vlad, performing Kubik's right hand, has a tendency to wildly wave his arm like a traffic cop and scratch the puppet's head, as though he has lice. Kubik's right arm often gets more attention than the actual Muppet, to the chagrin of Andrei, Kubik's lead puppeteer and voice.

When the situation becomes untenable, Volodya calls for a quick intermission and descends from the control room onto the studio floor, sliding his hand into Kubik's right sleeve to demonstrate to Vlad what he's doing wrong. He whispers something in Andrei's ear. As Andrei tilts the Muppet's head down while saying the line, "I'm feeling a little sad today," Volodya starts swinging his hand maniacally, as if he's leading an orchestra, imitating Vlad's oversized performance.

Andrei and Vlad double over, laughing so hard that they can barely get back to work. Volodya's point is made.

But later that day, I overhear Volodya talking with Vlad. I move closer to listen. "What's up with this wild performance?" Volodya asks.

Vlad confides that he's upset playing the puppet's right hand instead of having a speaking role. Volodya knows just what to say, reassuring Vlad that his right-hand performance is an essential part of Kubik's appeal, and the more lovable Kubik is, the more successful the show and Vlad will be.

Vlad nods, seeming to find this reasonable. Over the next few days, his performance gets much better.

By early April, nearing the end of studio filming, we're shooting an average of fifteen to twenty minutes of material per day; each day feels like a victory. While the studio team churns out episodes at a fast clip, the editing and packaging of the show's other segments has already begun. A team of four different editors is working twenty-four-hour staggered shifts at ORT's postproduction facilities, editing together the hundreds of live-action, animation, studio, and dubbed segments into thirty-minute *Ulitsa Sezam* episodes. Amazingly, more than half of the original live-action and animated films are ready to be packaged. And we're well on our way toward completing the show's dubbed content from *Sesame Street*'s international library.

I'm running on excitement and adrenaline. I split my eighteen-hour workday between our office and the ORT studio. Walking up the six flights of stairs to Moskinap at least twice a day makes my legs feel like a ton of bricks, and I often sit on the steps and rest on my way up.

This jumble of cells growing inside my body shows me that running a TV show pales in comparison to producing a little person. The baby does somersaults, energetically competing for my attention, and the team is constantly palming my belly like a basketball to feel it kicking. In the last months, I've changed. Asking my colleagues for help doesn't make me feel weak or vulnerable. We've learned how to care for one another. And it touches me that the team considers my baby a member of *Ulitsa Sezam*'s family.

Volodya constantly teases me. On one difficult day when I was not feeling well, he stuffed a small pillow under his shirt and walked around the studio, talking in a high-pitched voice, imitating me. He directed several scenes this way, making the entire crew, including me, bawl tears of laughter. Another day, he grabbed a plush Ernie doll and held it to his chest as though he were breast-feeding the Muppet. We all appreciate his nonstop antics.

25

FINISH LINES IN QUICKSAND

Filming the neighborhood scenes at ORT's sound stage is the longest stretch of time I've spent away from Ken. Fortunately, we speak most nights when I get back to the hotel, usually around midnight. I rely on him to calm me down whenever the fires I'm putting out become too much.

Buoyed by our success shooting in the studio throughout the spring, my team and I try to disregard the rising restlessness consuming the nation as the Russian presidential election draws nearer. With only two months to go, Gennady Zyuganov, the Communist Party candidate, is rapidly picking up followers. The buzz is sinister—that he will win and change the country's direction.

During a filming break in the studio, I see Tamara sitting on the bench in the courtyard, reading a newspaper. I slide in beside her. Over her shoulder, I read aloud the headline in *Kommersant*, ZYUGANOV PROMISES TO RESTORE RUSSIA'S SUPERPOWER STATUS. His campaign rhetoric is nationalistic and xenophobic.

Tamara shakes her head, clicking her tongue. "I'm nervous about what the election of Zyuganov would mean for all of us at *Sezam*."

In the last few months, as the Russian-American coproduction has gained greater visibility, articles in the Russian press criticizing our show have become more vitriolic. In *Izvestia*, one journalist wrote, "How is it possible that our government could allow McDonald's to build a franchise on Pushkin Square—the site of the revered monument honoring Alexander Pushkin? We must stop this creeping Americanization of Russian culture, with Pizza Huts, McDonald's, and *Ulitsa Sezam*."

Having seen the bronze statue of this great poet sullied by trash—Ronald McDonald's tinfoil hamburger wrappings and milkshake containers—I have sympathy for the press. I imagine Fyodor Dostoevsky and Ivan Turgenev, who inaugurated the statue in 1880, turning in their graves. Although many Russians enjoy the burgers and "service with a smile," others feel only pain.

Despite media criticism of our show and collective anxiety in the studio about Russia's future, Volodya and Tamara masterfully keep everyone on track. During the last week of filming in an imaginative and risky scene teaching the prepositional concept of "up," Volodya secures the Muppet Businka to the crane jib and attaches an inflated helium balloon to her furry hand. The crane operator hoists the jib, and the pink Muppet appears on the studio monitors as if carried aloft by the balloon she's holding. From the ground, the puppeteer, Lena, voices Businka, yelling, "Up! Up!" The crew members stand with their mouths open, staring like three-year-olds as the puppet rises slowly above the courtyard, almost to the lighting grid. When the scene is over, we erupt in applause.

Volodya praises the crew, "Congratulations, we are now functioning like a single being—just like the American Sezam crew, but they've had twenty-five years to get there and we did it in only one." The quality, creativity, and professionalism of the Russian series is indeed astounding.

And it's not only the shooting that's going well; the research is, too.

During the past few months, Dr. Genina and her team tested *Ulitsa Sezam*'s completed live-action and animated films, as well as the first neighborhood episodes, evaluating their overall appeal and educational effectiveness.

On one occasion, Volodya traveled to Lyubertsy City, a working-class suburb of Moscow, to observe Dr. Genina and her team conducting a focus group session with children. When he returned to the studio, he excitedly told the team how much the three-to-six-year-olds loved the characters. He raved about how the kids learned the educational goal of each episode precisely as intended.

Meanwhile, back at the Moskinap office, we are close to completing the final audio mix on the last of the films shot in Russia. But one is problematic. A live-action director has created a peppy music video teaching the letter M. In the video, a group of girls in red and blue tights with pigtails and ponytails dance about while forming the letter M with their arms and legs. The episode was shot with a single camera, held at a low angle, and to my mind, focuses disconcertingly on the girls' backsides.

In reviewing this rough cut with the Russian research team in Moscow, and the American team in New York, concern is expressed that the video may be construed as sexualizing the dancers. The video's director is sitting in on the call, and I praise him for achieving the educational goal of teaching a letter of the alphabet in a creative way. But I'm still worried about the film. If we hadn't already shot it and didn't have such a tight deadline to finalize all the original content for the show, I'd insist we start again. Instead, I propose asking the women in our Moscow office what they think.

Two days later, I arrange a meeting at Moskinap, setting up a video camera to record the women's reactions. Grateful for a break from our exhausting work schedule, my female coworkers delight in being guinea pigs for our focus group.

When I show the video, the response is surprising. I'd expected some opposition to the clip. Instead, not one of my colleagues mentions anything about the film other than that "the tempo is lively and the girls are adorable."

I point out the concerns raised earlier, and the group looks confused. They take turns dismissing any hint of possible impropriety.

Then, Volodya's assistant Irina raises her hand and says, "Well, there's a moment there, with the underwear and little shorts that's slightly disconcerting and might feel jarring to some adults because of what *we* read into the scene, but children don't think that way." She smiles wryly and suggests, "As adults, we're all somewhat corrupted." After a few giggles, the women decide to include the film in *Ulitsa Sezam*.

On our last day in the studio, while the crew is striking the set, carefully preserving every nut and screw, the mood is bittersweet. We have all become very close during the past four months. With Herculean efforts, *Ulitsa Sezam*'s neighborhood is disassembled in twenty-four hours, the flats, props, and Muppets stored away for Season Two. If the show's a success, and the eventual corporate sponsor of *Ulitsa Sezam*'s Season One decides to re-up for another season of fifty-two episodes two years from now, then we will reuse the set pieces and the Muppets.

I'm so proud of our studio team and will be sad to say goodbye. But we're in good shape. Now I feel comfortable returning to the States to see Ken for two weeks.

When Ken sees me, he looks shocked at how my girth has expanded during the months away. But my kind husband tells me that I look beautiful. Not wanting my American colleagues to notice my baby belly, I don't visit *Sesame Street* headquarters. Instead, I work from our apartment, reviewing the latest edited studio neighborhood segments on VHS cassettes. Two weeks fly by, and it's time for me to return to Moscow.

My closest colleague working on the Russia project in the New York office, Anna, will join me, spending ten days in Moscow, working with Video Art's accountants to substantiate *Ulitsa Sezam*'s total production expenditures and provide a report to the workshop and USAID.

Anna meets me at JFK airport. When we check in at the Delta Airline business-class lounge, the receptionist stops me from leaving my heavy carry-on bag in a cubby at the entrance.

"You can't leave your bags there," she yells. "They have to be with you at all times for security reasons." she lectures. I struggle to pull the large suitcase into the lounge.

After Anna and I sit down, the woman rushes over and starts apologizing, "I am so sorry, I did not realize that you are pregnant. In your condition, you could have left your bags at the entrance."

Anna's eyes widen. She looks at the attendant as though she's crazy, then at me.

I thank the woman and turn to Anna. "Well, I guess I have something to tell you."

"I can't believe you didn't tell me!" Anna yells.

When she learns that I'm five months pregnant, I can see she's hurt that I didn't tell her before. I feel guilty and silly for not having confided in her.

"No one in the New York office knows about it," I assure her, trying to make it clear that she wasn't left out. Although I'd hoped to keep my secret a bit longer, I realize that's just not possible.

Once in Moscow, we split up. Anna goes to Video Art's office, and I head to Moskinap. I climb the six flights, but when I enter the office, only Misha is there, playing a video game on his computer, his favorite pastime since learning how to use the machine.

"Where is everybody?" I ask.

He sighs, seemingly irritated by the interruption. "Oh, hi, Natasha. You're back." Without taking his eyes off the screen, he imparts, "I have some bad news." After a moment, he stops playing and swivels in his chair toward me. "You'll want to sit down," he juts his chin at the chair.

"Natasha, as you know, Video Art has been delinquent on making production payments for quite some time," he begins.

I did know about this. Irina had been holding back some payments because of what she called "cash flow problems," but I did not realize the extent of her delinquency.

Gesturing with a defeated expression toward the bathroom, Misha says, "I can't even afford to buy toilet paper."

Continuing, Misha explains how Irina pays the office rent, and how she covered the studio crew's salaries while we were in production. However, some of the lead producers and many freelancers haven't been paid in months. Apparently, Misha has been performing budgetary acrobatics to keep the office up and running. "I tried to make it work by borrowing money from my friends, but I can't do this anymore." Looking me in the eye, he announces flatly, "We have no choice, Natasha, but to exercise our new right under capitalism and go on strike."

At first, I think he's kidding. He's not.

"So, you mean the entire production team is on strike?" I ask.

"Yes," he continues humorlessly, "in solidarity with the freelancers." The full weight of his words hits me. Without any irony in his expression, he adds, "This isn't a Soviet gulag, and we can't be treated like prisoners, toiling away without getting paid."

I hadn't realized how bad things were. Irina had lied to both Misha and me.

Misha apprises me that Vika spent thirty thousand rubles of her savings to pay *Ulitsa Sezam*'s animators, all freelancers. Misha had promised that he would reimburse her by the end of the month. When Irina did not give him the money to pay Vika, the cartoonists then refused to hand over their completed films—thus bringing the packaging of our shows to a complete halt. It's impossible to edit the TV series episodes without the animated films.

I want to scream. We've come so far, almost reaching the end of production, and yet again everything falls apart. My Russian colleagues have put so much into creating this series—musicians have donated their songs because they believed in the show's purpose; master craftsmen spent weeks lovingly sculpting the courtyard's wooden animals; and many talented filmmakers turned down far more lucrative job offers in favor of *Ulitsa Sezam*. I blame myself for ignoring the telltale signs of financial trouble. I run to the bathroom to throw up—where, sadly, there's no toilet paper.

Later that afternoon, Leonid stops by and is stunned to see the ghostly office. I throw up my hands, "Production has stopped!"

He looks horrified, beats his fists in the air and starts yelling at me. "Natasha, how can you put me in this situation?" He looks scared. "I've made guarantees to some *very powerful* people—potential broadcasters, oligarchs—who are not going to understand if the show is canceled. You were supposed to make sure this fucking didn't happen. This is *your* fucking job!" he screams, wiping sweat off his forehead while showering me with epithets in both English and Russian.

Misha gets up and gently places his bear-like paw on his shoulder. "Come on, Leonid, she's pregnant," he admonishes protectively.

Leonid pushes him aside and stomps from the office.

Misha hands me a glass of water, and I take a sip. We sit side by side, staring out the window. "It's not fair," I moan, feeling my eyes tear up. "Every time we get close, success moves farther away."

"In Russia, finish lines are drawn in quicksand, Natasha," Misha says with resignation.

As the light over the horizon recedes, we discuss various options, unsure what to do, and Misha pats my shoulder, again, repeating, "It will probably be okay, you'll see."

We stay like this for another hour, until Misha says we should head out. He holds my hand as I walk down the six flights of stairs, then drives me to my hotel.

In my room, I crawl into bed and throw my hairbrush at the mirror. It hits a corner, and the whole frame crashes to the floor, glass flying everywhere.

———————

The following morning Leonid arrives at my hotel room with a bouquet of peonies, my favorite flower, and sheepishly apologizes. I tell him I understand and forgive him. This is a low point for him. This entire year, while I've been focused on making the series, Leonid's put all his energy into trying to lock a broadcast deal for *Ulitsa Sezam*, and every time something derails any concrete results. And without a broadcaster, we cannot sell commercial airtime surrounding the show. What's worse is admitting that we have damn bad luck—too many television broadcasters killed, and now, with the added complication of Irina's default, it's not only luck that has abandoned us, but also hope.

I tell Leonid that we have to confront *Madam Dusha Moya*. But Leonid is so angry at Irina that he refuses to meet with her. He drops me off at Video Art, alone.

Irina keeps me waiting for forty minutes. Her nervous secretary offers me cup after cup of tea until Irina's at last ready to see me.

She is sitting on her couch and pats the cushion beside her, inviting me to sit. She takes my hand in hers and holds it as if consoling the bereaved. "*Dusha Moya*, I am *so* sorry to have kept you waiting," she implores with exaggerated earnestness. Batting her eyelashes, she contorts her face into a pained apologetic expression. "We've had a *terr-i-bil*, horrible crisis that I'm trying to deal with," she explains gravely.

For a moment, her sweet, oozing voice immobilizes me. Still holding my hand, she coos, "*Natuyla*, you must understand that none of this is my fault." She smooths down her bangs with her fingers. "It's just a tiny, temporary cash flow problem." We're past flattery, and I'm tired of her diversions, but somehow I can't yell at Irina. She has the same effect on everyone: unreserved submission.

Another reason I can't yell at Irina is the truism I mentioned earlier: in Russia, true friends never disappoint each other. There's a tacit understanding that your *friend* will invariably do everything possible to help you without your even asking. And if a promise goes unfilled—for example, Irina's failure to get us an office—you cannot blame someone for their inability to deliver. It took me quite a while to understand this uniquely Russian interpretation. And yet Irina and I both know that she's put me in a terrible situation.

Focusing her doe-like gaze on me, she promises to meet the payroll within the week, and once again, I'm cowed into believing my friend will do whatever she can to help.

Irina's driver gives me a ride back to Moskinap, where there is still nobody working. Misha is absorbed in a game of online solitaire.

I tell him what Irina has promised. He looks at me bleakly. "I won't ask the production team to return to work until I see the money."

When Misha first met Irina, he idolized her. Now his enchantment is over. He's such a good guy; I feel bad that he got bulldozed, but I also think he shares some blame for covering up Video Art's defaulting on payments.

The week passes, and Video Art's nonpayment of *Ulitsa Sezam*'s expenses persists, despite Irina's promises.

Leonid and I spend the next two days dogging Irina—just missing her every time.

Finally, eight days after Irina gave her word, I corral Leonid to go with me to Irina's apartment building at eleven o'clock at night.

When she opens the door, we're shocked by her disheveled appearance: bloodshot eyes, rumpled clothing, and uncombed hair. She gestures for us to be quiet, leading us on tiptoe past her sleeping daughter's bedroom. The door is ajar, and we see toys pulled out of half-opened cartons and strewn all over the floor.

Her apartment resembles a storage facility. There's almost no furniture and cardboard boxes are stacked in the living room. Irina shuffles to the kitchen in oversized white fluffy slippers, still not uttering a word.

Leonid and I exchange looks. Something is deeply wrong. Irina stands with her back braced against the refrigerator door. She looks as though she is ready to burst into tears—which she does. She then slides down the fridge door and collapses on the floor, cross-legged. I sit beside her.

We are a pathetic sight, the two of us: Irina, with dark mascara running down her cheeks, and me, struggling over my belly to lean closer, trying to dry her tears with a tissue. Recognizing Irina's embarrassment at crying in front of us both, Leonid politely excuses himself and goes out to the corridor for a smoke. Gradually, I calm her down.

When Leonid returns, Irina tells us the truth. "My company is out of cash—no money." Irina wants us to know it isn't her fault. (Is it ever? I want to ask.)

Straightening herself up, she brushes the wet strands of hair out of her red-rimmed eyes. "You know, I don't know what actually happened, but I think, after Listyev's murder and Reclama Holding's reorganization, the selling of advertising turned into something akin to a giant pyramid scheme."

That we're in the middle of this is frightful. God, how I hate Russia right now. It's midnight, and I'm sitting on a frigid kitchen floor, exhausted, and my back hurts, and this is not going to make Baxter happy.

Irina explains how Video Art's arrangement selling advertising for Reclama Holding had worked out for everyone, until now. Although the big gorilla ad agency often delayed payments, only in the past month did they suddenly stop making payments entirely to the independent media companies, including Video Art.

"You know how much is left?" she asks, her lip trembling. "Nothing," she answers, flicking the air with her fingers. "It's like a game of musical chairs. When the music stops, you're the odd man—or woman—out." Staring at the floor, she whispers, "This time, I'm the one who's out. I'm . . . bankrupt."

I hold her until her sobbing slows and she's breathing normally.

"As you can see, we were preparing to move out of here into our new apartment," she gestures at the boxes, "but we had to stop."

Irina shifts focus. "What's worse is that *Sesame Street*'s lawyers are in Moscow now, and they're pressuring me to sign a contract defining how future ad revenues would be shared with *Sesame Street*." Flinging her arms toward the ceiling, she exclaims, "This is absurd; I can't sign a contract guaranteeing to pay out a certain percentage when we don't have the money to finish the show. We don't even have a broadcaster! Besides, I don't even understand the corporate language in the contract; not even my lawyer does."

Leonid is aware of *Sesame Street*'s legal squeeze on Irina. He'd recommended they pressure her because he couldn't negotiate other parts of a broadcast deal with Russian TV executives until *Sesame Street* and Video Art agree on their revenue split.

Irina looks crestfallen. "Now *Sesame Street* says I have to declare my company insolvent if I am not able to pay back the loan they gave me."

Even though I'm upset, I hate seeing her so destroyed. Her spirit is broken. If she'd confided in me earlier, we might have been able to find another solution.

Leonid, who has been quietly listening to this, agrees to speak on her behalf with *Sesame Street*'s lawyer and financial comptroller, who are still in Moscow. "I'm sure we can figure something out." He smiles encouragingly. "We are all on the same team, and we all want *Ulitsa Sezam* to succeed."

I hug Irina, feeling more maternal than I ever have in my life. Must be the hormones.

Leonid and I leave Irina's at 2:00 a.m. In the elevator, I tell Leonid, "I never thought Irina could be rattled."

"Everyone gets rattled in Russia, Natasha. It's only a matter of time."

———————

Crawling into bed at my hotel that night, I call Ken to whine. He's sympathetic, but there's an edge to his voice. I ask what's wrong, and we end up getting into a fight about how he thinks I'm not taking care of my health or the baby enough.

The following day, I call Irina and tell her I'm going back to New York to save the production and deal with some problems at home.

Hearing my shaking voice, she asks, "Is everything okay?"

Her concern for me makes me feel even more emotional.

Holding back tears, I apologize for leaving her to deal with *Sesame Street*'s lawyers and the striking employees who officially work for Video Art.

Her voice suddenly softens. "*Dusha Moya*, I will be fine. You shouldn't worry about anything. These problems here are nothing compared with love."

I pause, surprised. I hadn't said anything about Ken. Somehow Irina knew exactly what to say.

———————

Back home in America, I shuttle between my two loves: reassuring Ken over the weekend that I am prioritizing our little family, and passionately reassuring *Sesame Street*'s corporate executives that I'll do anything to save our show.

On Monday morning, Baxter opens the door to my office a crack and, peeking inside, playfully, says "*Zdravstvuy*" ("Hello" in Russian). Then his eyes go straight to my belly.

I freeze, suddenly remembering he doesn't know I'm pregnant. The last time we saw each other, I wasn't yet showing.

After a moment of staring at each other, he speaks. "Oh. Well, I see congratulations are in order."

I swallow. *That's it?* After months of tearing my hair out over my pregnancy, my boss barely comments. I laughed out loud at how stupid I was. Of course, Baxter is unfazed! He has four children and has been through this all before (or at least *his wife* has).

He shuts my office door and sits down.

I brace myself.

He lets out a deep breath. "Natasha, the workshop is having second thoughts about *Ulitsa Sezam* because of the political situation in Russia."

I nod slowly, pursing my lips.

Baxter explains that the company is understandably concerned about the substantial resources they have already spent bailing out Video Art. Furthermore, Irina's refusal to sign a contract or pay back the money she owes to *Sesame Street* persists.

Baxter clearly doesn't know about the strike or Irina's running out of money again. How could he? It just happened. He notices the stack of videotapes on my desk and smiles. "Are these new *Ulitsa Sezam* episodes?"

"Yes, the final ones."

I tell him, proudly, "Actually, we've completed all except one live-action film, and until recently, we were packaging all the shows. Twenty-five episodes are ready to air, except for adding the show opening, which we were planning to film next week."

Baxter cocks his head to one side while puckering his lips, seeming pleased and distressed at once. "You know, Natasha, the board is concerned that if the

Russian election doesn't go our way and *Ulitsa Sezam* never airs, we could lose all the money we've put into the production so far."

Not wanting to make things even worse, I hesitate to tell him about the production strike and Irina's financial meltdown. But he and the company have a right to know.

"Well, I have some other news that isn't so great . . ."

He turns his head to the side and holds it there. Really, he doesn't want to hear it.

After I tell him, Baxter is silent. Then in a resigned tone, he says, "Natasha, I'm not sure *Sesame Street* can continue working with Video Art any longer."

I want to ask who else he thinks we could work with this late in the game. Instead, I argue, "If we hope to save the production, we need to cover Irina's production costs for at least the next two months—through the presidential elections."

Baxter puts his palm to his head.

"At least she's still paying the rent for our Moscow production office. That's a big chunk of the budget," I add optimistically.

"It's not that simple," Baxter deflects. "There's only so many times I can go to bat for *Ulitsa Sezam* before people accuse me of crying wolf."

"I don't think there's any other option," I say under my breath, aware that the workshop already covered Irina's shortfall three months earlier.

Baxter says he will speak with his colleagues and see what can be done.

After he leaves, I lean back in my desk chair and stare at the ceiling, contemplating how *Sesame Street*'s corporate politics are almost as complicated as Russia's media industry.

During the next two weeks, *Sesame Street*'s top brass waffle between temporarily shutting down the production or terminating the project entirely. A delay of even a few weeks would be catastrophic because of the time bomb gestating within me.

With pressure mounting, Baxter asks for my help presenting the case for *Ulitsa Sezam* to his senior colleagues. This is surprising; until now, Baxter has been a welcome buffer between the C-suite and me.

On the day of the big meeting, I look as though someone punched me. I tried to cover up the dark rings under my eyes with makeup, but nothing could make me look anything other than seven months pregnant and a nervous wreck after many sleepless nights.

Baxter and I walk into the conference room together. The COO, Emily Swenson, and the CFO, an intimidating woman who I've only met once before, are installed around a conference table, and Baxter and I take a seat. I eye the CFO who I know never drank *Ulitsa Sezam*'s elixir, lobbying since the beginning for the workshop to abandon the Russian production entirely.

I'm embarrassed being *this* pregnant and having kept my condition from my colleagues for so long. But it's nice that Emily, who recently gave birth to her second child, warmly congratulates me.

Soon after exchanging pleasantries, the CFO focuses on the crisis at hand, apprising the group that default on the U.S. government contract in Russia could have significant consequences for the workshop. The group talks about how the workshop is in a bind because *Ulitsa Sezam* has become a high-profile project backed by senators and other prominent people.

Baxter looks nervous.

I raise my hand, slowly breathing in and out. It's one thing to be tough in Moscow, but in here with these executives, I don't quite know how to find my footing. Still, I have to speak.

"Please don't let Russia's crazy political situation get in the way of all the work we've done," I plead. Once I start talking, I find more courage. "Our Russian team has taken such incredible personal risks to create this show; how can we not stand by them when we're so near the end?"

The CFO responds coolly that it depends on the level of risk.

I shrink in my chair, silently chastising myself for sounding too confrontational.

Baxter attempts to shift the tone of the conversation to the show's financial upside. "Until now, we've limited ourselves to partnering with state broadcasters. But satellite television is exploding, and there are new opportunities globally to partner with independent broadcasters and finance programming by bartering airtime with private advertisers."

A heated discussion ensues about the pros and cons of allowing advertising of any kind on *Sesame Street*'s international shows and what stake, if any, the American company should take in future advertising surrounding the Russian show. The CFO then also asks me what level of investment is needed to finish the production and what is the likelihood of getting *Ulitsa Sezam* aired in an environment with so much opposition.

To all these questions, I give the same answer I'd given to Baxter months earlier. I emphasize how close we are to completing the series and that making a small investment to see the production through is the best possible decision.

Baxter tag-teams, reporting that he feels encouraged after his recent trips to Moscow. He's watched the cost-per-minute rate for advertising on Russian television shooting up. "Revenues from advertising on *Ulitsa Sezam* can be expected to greatly surpass the investment *Sesame Street* has to make now to complete the show," he argues. He advocates *Sesame Street*'s taking a direct stake in negotiating the sale of advertising at the front and back end of *Ulitsa Sezam*.

He is as passionate and protective about the Russian production as I am. When it's time to deliberate, he gives me a look, indicating I should leave the room. I imagine it will take some time before I hear what will be decided.

That night I keep Ken awake, grumbling about my American colleagues. Pacing our apartment, I mumble, "They don't even care if Russia gets to be free. . . . They don't understand what's at stake. . . . Why did I ever agree to do this in the first place? . . . All I want is to get back to Moscow and help my team survive."

Ken's sympathetic but practical as always. He takes me in his arms. "Sweetie, you have to be blind not to see that most American corporations and their boards would have shut down this production long ago."

"Well, they shouldn't have gone down this path in the first place," I mutter. "How can anything *not* be risky in Russia?" I ask, exasperated.

Ken calmly reminds me again how courageous *Sesame Street* has been in the face of insane obstacles.

We both know he sounds like a broken record, but he's trying to help.

"They're just being responsible leaders, trying to reduce the company's exposure," he says.

Ken's right, but I'd hoped they'd have a higher tolerance for risk.

Despite my continued muttering, Ken falls asleep. I join him a few hours later.

The next day I call Leonid in Moscow and tell him that we'll know the workshop's decision about *Ulitsa Sezam* soon, but I fear the production might be at death's door.

He sighs deeply into the receiver. "You know Natasha, President *Clin-ton* was in Moscow just after you left." At a public event at the Radisson Hotel for Western businessmen, he spoke favorably about Big Bird's efforts in Moscow. "There's no way *Sesame Street* can pull out now. It would be too embarrassing."

I hope he's right.

I have been in New York for two weeks already, an eternity in the life span of a television show. Until the work stoppage, the Moscow team had been doing a fantastic job, editing show segments together, adding graphics, and mixing final audio tracks to package the rest of the fifty-two shows. But we still have weeks of work left, and I'm not sure how long it will be until postproduction will resume.

After the weekend, I go to Baxter's office, still nervous about what's to come. He is sitting with Steve Miller, the Group VP for International TV and Licensing, who is now working on Russia. They tell me a final decision will be made at an internal meeting they'll be attending in two days with the workshop's senior management. I'm not invited to the showdown.

On the day of judgment, I impatiently wait in my office to hear the verdict. All I can think about is *Ulitsa Sezam*: Leonid and his beat-up car, Misha playing solitaire alone in his office, Lena raising her arm in the air as Businka, Masha and her beautiful tree.

Baxter walks into my office. I feel my heart banging against my ribs as I look at him warily.

He gives me a thumbs-up sign, grinning.

I stare at him, incredulous. Miraculously, the company's senior executives have approved bailing out Video Art to keep the *Ulitsa Sezam* production on track. I am speechless, hyperventilating, and ecstatic.

Baxter sits down, telling me how he told his colleagues that "The workshop's so pregnant with Russia that there's no possibility of turning back." His choice of phrase is poignant, considering my state. Thankfully, Baxter also got Steve Miller to join him at the meeting, even though Steve was suffering from vertigo and could barely see straight. Baxter literally had to prop him up as Steve told the group that the Nestlé Corporation is getting close to agreeing to underwrite the entire Russian series.

Baxter slaps his thigh. "This is a huge turning point for the Russian series." He explains that a revised licensing agreement between Video Art, Nestlé, and the broadcasters will be drawn up, with Sesame Workshop sharing in *Ulitsa Sezam*'s advertising revenues. Meanwhile, the workshop will immediately provide completion funds for production and the launch.

Over the next days, my excitement about our good fortune is only tempered by my concern about how we are going to get U.S. dollars into Russia to pay for the last months of the production. Our earlier approach—transferring funds to Video Art's bank account in Russia—is no longer feasible because Irina's bank account has been frozen.

Jokingly, I propose to *Sesame Street*'s lawyers that our only option may be for me and my American colleagues to hand-carry U.S. dollars to Moscow so we can finish the production. "You know," I say, "my double-D size pregnancy bra can hold a lot of cash." *Sesame Street*'s lawyer frowns—probably because America's favorite children's television corporation is not in the business of transporting currency.

But the problem of getting cash to Moscow remains. Credit cards are not yet widely used in Russia and Sesame Workshop as a foreign nonentity is not allowed to open a bank account in Russia. Throughout the production, our American team has sometimes carried the legal amount of cash to Moscow, which is any amount up to $10,000. But the amount of currency needed at this point is too great to hand carry overseas.

On Monday, a sunny Spring morning, I decide to walk the fourteen blocks from my apartment to work. The foul-smelling flowers of the Callery pear trees lining the sidewalks make me hold my nose—pregnancy is intolerable.

At the workshop, I again head to Baxter's office, where he informs me that after some extensive corporate gyrations, *Sesame Street*'s lawyers have figured out how to get funds to Moscow. Grinning widely, he knows he's saved our production. I feel so grateful to my Sesame colleagues for having the courage and faith to proceed.

It will take another two weeks for the money to arrive, so I arrange to take the maximum legal amount of cash with me when I return to Moscow. Even carrying "the maximum" legal amount of cash to Russia is not without its risks. Russian customs are less regulated by the state and corruption is a persistent problem. Russian customs agents may haphazardly levy fees on foreign currency taken into Russia. In some cases, they confiscate U.S. dollars for no given reason. It's often smarter to carry cash directly on your body than in a wallet when entering Russia.

That night, Ken looks at my bra resting on the dresser with eight thousand dollars taped into the cups. "This might be our last night together before you find yourself in a Russian jail," he jokes.

I know this tiny amount won't make a dent in our production budget, but at least I'll be able to pay for a portion of what Vika is owed, and also toilet paper for the office, until the larger funds come.

Joking aside, Ken begs me not to leave, feeling it's getting to be too late in the pregnancy, and that tucking dollars into my brassiere and underwear show I've lost all judgment when it comes to my personal safety.

But I must go. It will be my last trip before the baby comes.

26

BIRTH OF AN ANGEL AND A BROADCASTER

At the end of May, I arrive once more at Moscow Airport. I retrieve my bags and make my way to Russian customs, where I look from one agent to another, assessing which of them seems more pliant. I choose the youngest and take my place in line while nervously touching my large breasts and trying to smooth out the hard corners of the stacks of bills beneath my bra. When my turn comes, the agent looks at my passport, noting the multi-entry visa, and without a hitch, lets me pass.

Like a cross between 007 and one of the Spice Girls, I sprint through the airport to the exit, feeling pleased.

Misha and Robin are waiting for me at the Palace Hotel. After long hugs and kisses, we shuffle into my hotel room. Ever the gentleman, Misha turns his back as I remove hundred-dollar bills from my top. He jokes, "I've depended on women's breasts throughout my life, but never so much as now."

Together, we decide on the most urgent production costs to pay while awaiting more funds from the United States. Misha has already put out the word to the team to end the strike and return to work.

I call Ken to report that I am *not* in a Russian prison and then launch myself into work once more.

Within days of the team's reassembling at Moskinap, our production reaches a feverish pitch, with postproduction in full swing again. According to *Sesame Street*'s contract with USAID, we have a hard deadline—to deliver the first ten episodes of *Ulitsa Sezam*, ready for broadcast, on September 1, 1996. I know we'll make it—I have complete faith in Robin and the team. The last piece to film will be the show opening and this is now being scored by Vladimir Shainsky, Russia's famous children's music composer. Our show's opening will be the first combined mixed-medium live-action and animation in any Russian children's television program.

It's exciting, but we *still* don't have a broadcaster for the series. Leonid and Baxter have had no success in getting Russia's major television networks to agree on the terms for airing *Ulitsa Sezam*. They attribute this failure to uncertainty at the TV station owing in no small part to the upcoming Russian presidential elections, now two weeks away.

Along with most Americans, I'd anticipated the West's victory over communism a *fait accompli*. But now, based on predictions heralding Zyuganov a winner, I can see how Russia could easily slide back to communism.

Desperate to understand more on the situation, Leonid and I arrange to meet Igor Malashenko, whom we have not seen since the beginning of our production. While still in charge of NTV's network, he is also now advising Russia's president on campaign strategy. He's likely to have the inside story.

Leonid and I arrive at the swanky, state-of-the-art NTV building overlooking the Moscow River. Malashenko spots us and crosses the studio to greet us. He looks tired.

He discusses the elections, disclosing that Russia's three top state-run and independent television networks have been coordinating electoral coverage. He candidly justifies the action as the only way for Yeltsin to win the election.

"Even with the firepower of the three networks behind us—NTV, ORT, and RTR—Zyuganov could still win," he sighs.

Although our show's broadcast pales next to Russia's future president, I still must ask Malashenko about airing *Ulitsa Sezam*.

Malashenko smiles, perhaps grateful to talk about anything other than Zyuganov. "It's fortuitous you are coming to me now because NTV has gotten a lot more powerful, and we can afford to broadcast *Ulitsa Sezam*." Moreover, he indicates he can also help arrange a second airing of our show on ORT.

I can't believe what I'm hearing. I stand there, in the studio, my mouth open, hardly believing our good luck. Leonid plays it cool, inquiring about the details.

Malashenko proposes setting up a series of interlocking licensing agreements between the two broadcasters, with revenues from advertising surrounding the show being divided among *Ulitsa Sezam*'s American and Russian coproduction partners. "Even if advertising rates were to decline after the elections, we'd still make something," he adds encouragingly.

Leonid looks ecstatic. This is beyond his wildest hopes: multiple broadcasters simultaneously airing *Ulitsa Sezam* on competing channels.

While I struggle to wrap my head around Malashenko's proposal, I can't help but wonder if this will actually happen. Things change so quickly in Moscow. Still—it's promising.

Leonid has a lot of work ahead to get all the parties to agree on acceptable terms—especially Sesame Workshop. The American company will need to recoup its substantial outlay.

On my last day in Moscow before the baby comes, Misha organizes a goodbye dinner for me. At first, I don't want to go. Attending a dinner feels too final. I don't want to feel sad, and I'd hoped to slip out of the county without fanfare.

Because Misha knew the maître d' at a popular Italian restaurant, he reserved a table for our larger core team of about twenty. When I arrive, my colleagues are all seated along a narrow table filled with variously sized glasses and bottles of Georgian wine, champagne, and vodka. Seeing me waddling toward them, Volodya jumps up to greet me and I sit beside him. Mischievously, he offers a glass of wine. I make a sad little face—as he knows, I cannot drink, now that my body's not my own.

Misha stands up, tapping his spoon on his glass, trying to get the group to quiet down. I look from Volodya to Misha, to Robin and all the others, feeling so lucky to have these people in my life. Misha raises his glass, theatrically pronouncing, "For all your many contributions, Natasha, we thank you. And, most of all, we thank you for your constant motivational swearing—none of us would have accomplished what we did without your constant 'Fok, fok, fok' as you tortured us to move faster." I express my gratitude to everyone, as though this is my final goodbye before embarking on a faraway journey. It's a magnificent evening.

The next day, Leonid drives me to the airport. We're silent for much of the trip. Our lives have been intertwined for so many years; we've depended on each other to get over every obstacle. I can't imagine taking this monumental step in my life without Leonid by my side.

At the airport, he walks me as far as he's allowed, and when I hug him, the tears flow.

Leonid affects a casual air. "Come on Natasha, it's not like your life is about to change—forever!" He laughs and gently pushes me toward security. I turn around one last time and see him lighting a cigarette, watching me through the closing sliding glass doors.

I board the plane, and then watch Russia disappear beneath me. I try not to think of everything I'll miss as I fly West, away from the people who've come to mean more to me than I can put into words.

Back in New York, at my apartment, Ken and I cuddle on the couch and watch the returns from the June 16 Russian presidential elections on television. Every major American TV network is covering the Russian election, predicting tremors throughout the globe if Yeltsin loses. Shockingly, the vote ends in a tie.

My stomach is in knots, waiting for July 3, when we'll hear the final results from a second round of voting. When at last CNN announces that Boris Yeltsin has defeated Zyuganov by a narrow majority of 54 percent, I feel I can finally breathe again.

Leonid calls my apartment from Moscow, ecstatic. "At least with Yeltsin elected, Russia's TV executives will finally broadcast our show." Leonid believes he will now have no trouble getting corporate sponsors for our TV series.

I hope this is true. After laboring nearly four years—weathering the assassinations of partners who'd become our friends, car bombings, financial crises, and life-changing personal events, I'm beginning to feel that our show might actually find a home and be seen by millions of children.

"It will," says Leonid. "Just wait."

And that's what I do: I wait. Staring at the phone in our New York apartment, I will it to ring with news of our deal. Baxter, Leonid, Steve Miller, and *Sesame Street*'s lawyers still have to negotiate the terms of the broadcast agreement and the corresponding split of revenue from the advertising.

In most parts of the world, it's standard for television broadcasters to purchase programming for their network. But Leonid explained to me that in Russia the media executives from all three major networks (ORT, RTR, and NTV) expect too much. According to Leonid, the hardest thing about convincing some of these guys to sign an agreement is assuring them that in the end they will have more money in their own pocket than the other guys.

Laughing, Leonid says, "Someone always has to be the loser in any Russian deal."

Creating a "win-win" for all is obviously not a Russian concept. And yet, Leonid and the Sesame Workshop executives anticipate *Ulitsa Sezam* will air in October 1996.

It's two weeks before my due date and I've done nothing to prepare for the baby's arrival. Ken and I finally do what new parents do: drive to Toys R Us and surrender. At the New Jersey megastore, I push a shopping cart down wide aisles laden with every conceivable infant accessory, feeling like an alien visiting a new planet. What is all this baby paraphernalia? And how could a tiny human possibly need all this stuff?

A kindly store clerk notices Ken and me looking helpless and offers to assist us in selecting "the essentials." I want to hug her.

Back home, the pile of newborn chattel looks strangely out of place on the dining room table, next to the stacks of VHS cassettes, set drawings, animation cells, and our computers. I stuff the baby products into the closet, trying to make myself feel less anxious.

Gradually I realize what's upsetting me: I'm entirely unprepared for motherhood. Even the most unmaternal of women would have given more thought to having a baby than I have. They'd probably have at least understood that during the ninth month, a baby would arrive. To his credit, Ken has tried many times to speak with me about the baby—about how the baby would change the way we live, what our priorities are, and how we spend our time—but I've refused to acknowledge this, continuing my denial that "the baby won't change anything."

Amazingly, until seeing the boxes of baby stuff stacked in our apartment, it hadn't set in: we will be responsible for this child. Nothing will ever be the same.

———————

Although officially I'm already on maternity leave, I continue to review *Ulitsa Sezam*'s final packaged episodes on VHS cassettes, which Robin ships to me via FedEx. Usually, I call Robin at the start of her workday in Moscow (2:00 a.m. New York time) to review my video edit changes. I also talk regularly to Volodya and Leonid, not only about the show, but about the plan for the program's big launch in Moscow.

Everything's coming to a head. The days tick by. I feel like a beached whale and am so tired. I have so much to get done before the baby comes.

My little man is considerate: he's late. Four days, now five, past his due date. He must be waiting until I've finished reviewing the last of the show's episodes. Ken, working from home, wanders, somewhat dazed, into the living room where I am lying on the couch with my stomach in the air, speaking Russian into the phone receiver. He stands there a few seconds, affectionately shakes his head, and leaves, muttering, "Our baby is going to be born with a telephone cord instead of an umbilical cord."

Nine days after my due date, the baby still hasn't come. Robin calls that night to tell me the betting pool the Russians set up wagering on my baby's birthday is growing larger every day.

That night, I feel a stirring inside me. I guess it's contractions, so well-described in books I have barely read. Just before leaving for the hospital, I send

Robin a fax, noting the frequency of my contractions: every fifteen minutes. It's finally happening: the most monumental change in my life. In the fax, I say that I'll be incommunicado for at least a day.

But I list the hospital phone number, just in case.

Thirteen hours later, our beautiful, nine-pound boy pushes his way into this world, ten days late. We name him Gabriel because he's an angel—a miracle of calm born amid utter chaos.

When the doctor hands our son to us, the love I feel dispels any doubts I may have had about the wonders of childbirth or our lack of preparation. I understand for the first time what being a parent means, with all the love, fear, tenderness, and worry that parenting brings.

When we get home from the hospital, I discover Gabriel responds more positively when I speak to him in Russian—unsurprising, given how much Russian he's heard in vitro at high decibels. Less than a day after giving birth, I call Moscow and put the phone receiver next to Gabriel's tiny ear so that he can listen to his Russian family sing "Happy Birthday."

I discover that breastfeeding calms me down. It may be the only thing that calms me down, so I love it.

Within days, more good news arrives in a phone call from Leonid. After expressing his congratulations, he screams into the phone, "We did it, Tasha, I got the broadcaster—and not just one but *two*!"

Incredibly, ORT and NTV, the two most important TV channels in Russia, have agreed to air the first season of *Ulitsa Sezam*—repeating the fifty-two episodes over two years, in prime time air slots—five and three evenings a week, respectively. They will also have an option to air a second season to be produced in two years. And the plan includes Sesame Workshop recouping its investment from advertising revenues.

I scream in delight into the phone, startling Gabriel who is attached to my chest in a Baby Bjorn carrier.

"And it looks like Nestlé, the Swiss-based food company, will sponsor the show," Leonid continues yelling, explaining how he and Baxter and Steve Miller managed to convince Moscow's Nestlé executives to become *Ulitsa Sezam*'s sole corporate sponsor.

After I hang up, I can barely contain my happiness. The only one around to share my excitement is Gabriel. When I stop and look at myself talking to this infant about Russian broadcasters, I realize how much I've already changed.

27

LIGHTING UP SCREENS ACROSS THE FORMER USSR

The premiere gala celebrating the on-air launch of *Ulitsa Sezam*, scheduled for October 22, 1996, creeps up faster than expected. The thought of leaving Gabriel after only six weeks to return to Moscow reduces me to uncontrollable sobs. Ken will take off time from his work to be with the baby, but I'm not really sure I'll be able to leave him. My hormones have taken over, demanding that my breasts and I stay in New Jersey.

"You have to go," Ken says with love and pride when I share my hesitation. "You've worked too hard for this moment."

When the time comes to say goodbye, Gabriel is bawling, and Ken must tear him from my arms. Then, he practically shoves me into a cab to the airport.

At JFK, once again in the Delta lounge, everything feels different—lonelier. I notice a milk stain on my blouse and self-consciously start rubbing it. I catch the woman sitting opposite me staring at my postpartum belly, and I imagine she's judging me. I should be wearing a sign that says, "Kick me. I left my newborn at home."

When I arrive in Moscow, the customs agents discover the enormous industrial-size breast pump in my suitcase. I expect the officers to blush and put it back in my bag. Instead, they pull out the suction cups and tubing, suspiciously examining the device as I look on, mortified. When at last, I place the suction flanges over my breasts, demonstrating how it works, they all turn bright red.

Mission accomplished. They let me pass while averting their eyes.

At the hotel, the doorman, Ivan, recognizes me. He warmly congratulates me on the birth, but the Palace Hotel, my home away from home for close to four years, now feels sterile, strange, and impersonal.

The moment I get to my room, I call Ken, asking, "How much has the baby eaten? Pooped? Is he crying? Does he miss me?" No longer are we engaged in lengthy discussions about *Ulitsa Sezam* and the global economy; it's all about the baby. Ken reassures me that Gabriel is safe and happy with Daddy. If the telephone cord could pull me back to them, I'd attach myself to it.

The show's national premiere will be celebrated at a Moscow theater at 4:30 in the afternoon, allowing Russian and foreign journalists enough time to prepare coverage of the momentous broadcast for their evening news programs on both sides of the ocean.

Two hours before the event, amid last-minute preparations for the extravaganza, all I can think of is Gabriel. I picture him at home with Ken, my little family.

It dawns on me that I must pump some milk soon because I'll be on stage and at the afterparty for many hours. I won't have a chance to do it later.

I haven't used the breast pump before, and when I connect the device to the 110-volt-to-220-volt converter and plug it into the electrical socket on the wall in my hotel room, it produces a giant spark. I jump back, just barely avoiding singeing myself. I try plugging it into another socket, and—nothing happens. It's dead.

I stare down at my breasts. Now what?

I call Ken, as if he can do anything from across the ocean. He answers the phone with a groggy voice. It's six in the morning New York time and I imagine he's been up much of the night taking care of the baby. I frantically ask, "How am I supposed to go in front of the entire international press corps like this?"

My sweet husband, the former global chess champion, puts the phone down so he can read one of our baby books. When he returns to the phone, he calmly suggests putting cold compresses on my breasts and stuffing toilet paper in my bra. The stuffing toilet paper was not in the book. The tables seem to have turned. I'm usually the problem solver, but jet lag and hormonal overload have turned my brain to mush. I do what he suggests, ever so grateful.

Ulitsa Sezam's premier gala is a star-studded affair held at the giant Moscow Penta Hotel. With more than six hundred guests, including representatives from every major foreign news outlet, Russian ministers, U.S. Embassy officers, and many *Sesame Street* colleagues from America, it is beyond glamorous. The interior lobby is decorated with American and Russian flags and banners with *Sesame Street*'s green and yellow trademarked street sign with the words *Ulitsa Sezam* and with the logos of Video Art, ORT, NTV, and Nestlé.

Guests start arriving around four in the afternoon. They file into the lobby and gather around the life-size display of Muppet Byrt (Bert), wearing a black Russian *shapka* (hat) with ear flaps, with his furry arm around Enik (Ernie), who wears a Soviet general's cap with a red star. Nearby, giant posters of Zeliboba, Kubik, and Businka are propped on wooden stands. *Ulitsa Sezam*'s creative team—producers, directors, writers, and researchers—assemble inside the theater. Unused to seeing each other in anything other than jeans and T-shirts for close to a year, we marvel at how spiffy we look, all cleaned up in our sparkly dresses, pressed slacks, and ties and jackets.

Inside, the hotel auditorium crackles with excitement as original songs from *Ulitsa Sezam* blast through loudspeakers. The room is so crowded that children must sit on the floor in front of the stage. Television cameras line the back wall, with crews setting up cables to carry the announcement of our Russian-American coproduction on news programs across the globe.

Lights dim, and the room grows quiet. The curtain opens to Zeliboba, our seven-foot, blue, floppy-eared Muppet, awkwardly careening around the stage in white size-thirty sneakers. Directing his attention to the children squealing in delight at the sight of him, he yells excitedly, "Oy, dear adults, boys, and girls, Welcome to *Ulitsa Sezam*!" He invites the audience to turn their attention to the enormous screen on the stage for the first look at *Ulitsa Sezam*, Russia's own *Sesame Street*.

The theater darkens further and on a large screen, the show's opening musical title sequence begins. Against a multicolored animated background of a purple and white schoolhouse, children skip, run, and ride their bicycles on their way to *Ulitsa Sezam* as animated butterflies and letters with eyeballs dance across the screen.

In the first few frames, Zeliboba pushes open the door to the school, his big furry blue face with its giant orange nose filling the screen. The camera pulls back and Zeliboba jumps on a skateboard, joining the other kids. In a nod to rural parts of the former Soviet Union, Kubik is seen pulling a horse-drawn carriage, carrying a bale of hay with children leaning against the haystack, reading books as they pass a boy fishing in a pond. A hot air balloon attached to a straw basket appears with Kubik inside, and all the children jump into the basket with their skateboards, soccer balls, and roller skates. Kubik cuts the string and the balloon rises into the sky with the children and the Muppets waving happily as *Sesame Street*'s green and yellow title "ULITSA SEZAM" fills the blue sky.

When the video ends, children and adults clap wildly. Cameras flash. And then pandemonium reigns as Zeliboba reappears on stage, and his booming voice asks everyone to "Please, quiet down, quiet down." He invites the audience to remain seated for a short panel with *Ulitsa Sezam*'s partners.

Standing in the wings, I feel Irina grab and squeeze my hand. I'm so nervous. As Zeliboba exits to more applause, Irina and I walk onstage, followed by our male colleagues. We take seats along one side of a long table, facing the audience.

Each of our partners speaks briefly, followed by the Russian Deputy Minister of Education, who says, "When I first heard about *Sesame Street*, I thought it was another attempt to introduce American stuff into Russia, but when I saw *Sesame Street*'s other international shows, I realized they are very sensitive to other countries' cultures and intended to make a show that reflects our culture, which *Ulitsa Sezam* has."

Igor Malashenko, the president of NTV, speaks next, followed by Baxter, who thanks USAID and the Russian people. Volodya and Irina express their gratitude for the opportunity to adapt the program, even though, Irina notes, "The road to Russian *Sesame Street* was a long and bumpy one."

Then it's my turn. I nod toward my American colleagues who had traveled from New York to attend the event and are now lined up along the side wall of the theater so as to leave seats for our Moscow guests. My voice is shaking as I begin in Russian. "I applaud our *Ulitsa Sezam* team for their ingenuity, perseverance, and artistry." I talk about how hard everyone worked to create a program that celebrates all children across the former Soviet Union who are taking their places in freer, more open societies.

As I'm nearing the end of my remarks, I feel a hot liquid on my chest. I look down and see two tiny round milk stains spreading on the front of my purple chiffon dress. I cross my arms over my chest and continue, trying not to think about how my costume malfunction will be broadcast to the millions of Americans and Russians on their evening news programs. The milk feels wet against my skin. And I can feel my face turning beet red. Desperate to sit down and be less visible, I finish and take a seat.

The loud applause makes me feel better.

Aside from that moment on stage, the evening is a huge success, followed by an extravagant reception in the hotel's conference room. High-top tables with white linens have been set up, and champagne and vodka flow generously. The Russians and Americans make toasts to each other and to the show's future success.

I spot Baxter across the room with Midhat and Igor Malashenko, roaring with laughter. I walk up to their table and Baxter says to me, "The one thing I will both curse and thank Russia for is introducing me to vodka." He raises his glass; "*Na Zdorov'ye*," he shouts with a perfect accent.

Everyone is aware of how unprecedented it is that *Ulitsa Sezam* is the first program ever to be simulcast on two competing Russian channels. Tonight, television executives who fiercely wrestle with one another for market share and are almost always at each other's throats embrace like old friends. I love seeing these hardened TV executives basking in their shared delight at bringing joy and laughter to millions of children.

Volodya is with the two Nestlé executives. He gestures to me to come join them and asks with a big smile, "So, Natasha, when do we begin the second season?"

He knows we have no idea when we will be able to begin production again. We barely survived Season One. But it doesn't matter. Tonight, we focus on what we've already accomplished together.

For years I've dreamed of this day, and now it's here.

Irina comes up behind me, playfully grabbing my waist. "Dusha Moya, your figure is coming back already," she teases. She looks smashing in a red silk evening dress. I notice she's wearing the diamond brooch she wore on the first day we met.

I can't hide the tears in my eyes. She puts her arm around my waist. "*Natulya*, what's the matter?" she asks gently. "How can you be sad? Isn't this the best party ever? Maybe even better than your wedding?" She winks.

"I miss Gabriel and Ken." I wipe a tear from my cheek.

"Of course, you miss your little angel." She squeezes me tighter.

Choking out words between sobs, I admit, "I worry about how my life is going to change, now that *Ulitsa Sezam* is over."

Irina turns toward me, holding my face in the palms of her hands. "Natasha, don't worry. You're so young. We'll have another season. And you think you will never have another party? What about your next wedding after your second marriage? That next party will be even better!" she jokes.

We are laughing when Leonid joins our huddle and pokes me. "I need a smoke."

I grab my coat and change into boots, and he pulls me outside. It's a crisp, cold night; the snow is falling lightly. Without a word, Leonid puts his arm around me. We walk toward a residential area with high-rise apartment buildings. He stops to light a cigarette and we stand watching Muscovites returning to their homes for the evening.

As the sky darkens, we notice how the yellow lights in several of the windows begin to change colors in unison—from bright red to green to blue. At another building across the way, we see the same thing—colored lights reflecting in the windows, shifting simultaneously. Suddenly, it dawns on both of us that it's six o'clock. Is it possible that the families have turned on their television sets and are all watching—*Ulitsa Sezam*!

I tell Leonid we shouldn't be surprised because the coverage of our show in the Russian press was extensive and there are not many programs for children on Russian TV right now. But we are mesmerized, observing the many windows change colors.

We turn in a circle, looking from one window to another. Under our feet, the snow crunches, and the sound echoes into the night. I imagine millions of machinists, teachers, butchers, street cleaners, miners, doctors, and waitresses—in apartments, dachas, and homes in Novosibirsk, Talin, Kyiv, and throughout the former USSR—laughing in response to Zeliboba's, Kubik's, and Businka's sweet escapades and sheer goofiness.

All these families tuning in to *our* show.

I know the first episode by heart. It's now 6:05 so they're probably watching *Ulitsa Sezam*'s opening scene—when Zeliboba pushes open the giant door to his treehouse and encounters the mailman in the courtyard. The mailman is new to the neighborhood and must meet the residents of *Ulitsa Sezam*. The writers came up with this ingenious way to introduce our new audience to all the key characters in the show. Zeliboba towers over him.

Freezing, I scoot closer to Leonid and rest my head on his shoulder, happy. Our foolish naive persistence defied what many thought impossible—what I had thought was impossible. I breathe in the cold air. I've never felt so much a part of Russia as now.

I whisper to Leonid, "Do you think my life in Russia is over?"

Leonid laughs. "Nothing in Russia is ever over," he says. "It all just keeps repeating itself, like an infinite circle."

Конец (The End)

EPILOGUE

Ulitsa Sezam became an unprecedented hit, broadcasting on Russia's largest two television networks in prime time, across the former Soviet Union. The series premiered in October 1996; it aired on ORT one day a week and six nights a week on NTV, reaching tens of millions of children and families across eleven time zones. The television show was transmitted to Ukraine, the Baltics, and most former Soviet republics where children were still accustomed to viewing Russian-language programs.

The *Ulitsa Sezam* Muppets Zeliboba, Kubik, and Businka quickly became as recognizable to children throughout the former Soviet empire as Big Bird and Elmo are to American audiences. *Ulitsa Sezam* was nominated multiple times for a Teffy award (Russia's equivalent to an Emmy), but Volodya Grammatikov, the show's chief director, said, "As good as our show is, it's unlikely Russian judges will ever give the award to a television show that originated in America."

Subsequent seasons of *Ulitsa Sezam* continued broadcasting well into the Putin era, with the TV series celebrating its ten-year anniversary in 2006. Many of the producers and directors associated with the original production continued to work on the show for many more years. In 2010, the series aired for the last time, no longer supported by Putin's people at the television networks.

After the birth of my second child in 1998, I left Sesame Workshop and set up a digital media company to promote health equity in the United States. I created KickinNutrition.TV, a musical comedy cooking show to educate children about nutrition and wellness in schools and aftercare programs in more than twenty-five states.

Over the past two decades, I have often thought about the incredible events surrounding *Ulitsa Sezam*'s creation and the repression and persecution of artists and journalists that followed under Putin's rule. During the time of our production, we understood little as to why our Russian broadcast counterparts were murdered one after the other, or the reasons for our production office takeover by Russian military forces. Although today the Moscow State prosecutor claims to have compiled 120 volumes of case files on the murder of Vlad Listyev, who is still remembered as a courageous man who gave his life for press freedom, and his assassination remains an unsolved mystery. One presumes the battles surrounding

Russian television at that time—even those related to creating a puppet show—were a proxy for larger confrontations that also laid the ground for Putin's rise to power and the escalating dissension between Russia and the West today.

As tensions between Russia and America continued to rise in 2014, after Russia's annexation of Crimea, I became more curious about what had happened to my brilliant former *Ulitsa Sezam* colleagues who had risked so much to change their country.

Although I keep in touch with Leonid, who still lives in Moscow, I had lost contact with most of the old crew during the past twenty-five years. I did not meet them even when I visited Moscow in 2016 and filmed *Russian Millennials Speak Openly about America*—a video about Putin and Trump that gained 2.5 million viewers on YouTube. However, writing *Muppets in Moscow* gave me the opportunity to reconnect with my former team members and once again travel back to Moscow.

In January 2020, I managed to wrangle a visa and slipped into the frozen capital, excited to be back. Darkness had already descended, but as my taxi neared the city center, brightly colored Russian Orthodox New Year's decorations lit up the streets. Turning a corner, we came upon a grand prerevolutionary building wrapped in netting with hundreds of tiny yellow twinkling lights, like fireflies caught in a web. The city looked brighter, cleaner, more modern. It also felt more sterile.

I arrived at the Radisson Ukraina, a hotel converted from one of the most famous skyscrapers of the Stalin era. At the reception desk, two stylishly dressed women in their twenties greeted me. I realized they were children during the time *Ulitsa Sezam* first aired. I couldn't help but ask, if by chance, they were familiar with my TV show, *Ulitsa Sezam*.

"I *luv* Zeliboba. He's my favorite!" shrieked the woman checking me in. When I told them I executive produced the series, they fawned over me, making me feel like a celebrity, telling me about how in their generation, everyone watched the show. Listening to these two grown women gushing about the Russian Muppets they knew as children made me feel old, but I didn't mind.

Three days later, I called in every favor I could to get permission to visit ORT, the television station where I had filmed *Ulitsa Sezam*.

———————

The entrance had been moved and a metal detector added, as well as a security guard who studied my passport before waving me toward a row of turnstiles where two public relations escorts waited (probably FSB agents from Russia's Federal Security Service), appearing bemused by my presence.

Their puzzlement at seeing an American didn't surprise me. Nowadays, few foreigners, much less Americans, are allowed access to ORT's high-security compound, where pro-Kremlin propaganda and fake news are produced and disseminated to Russia's 147 million citizens.

My escorts pushed open the heavy metal door to Studio No. 13—our studio. My chest tightened. The space looked exactly the same: dented metal walls, a sticky floor and a rusty catwalk spiraling upward to the lighting grid that I had climbed more times than I can remember. I told my minders that twenty-five years ago, I had spent months in this space and had roamed freely throughout the TV station. They didn't seem interested, or perhaps didn't believe me.

I had expected our old stomping ground would have been updated and converted into a slick, modern, high-tech television studio to disseminate propaganda, but only the scenery had changed. I asked one of the escorts, "Why hasn't the studio been updated in all this time?"

A look of embarrassment flashed across her face. "Because of U.S. sanctions, we don't have the hard currency to update it. We've had to make many sacrifices."

Staring at the studio, I closed my eyes, trying to conjure a memory of Zeliboba lumbering across the rubber floor, tripping over his enormous white sneakers while crew members raced around.

I felt like a time traveler stepping into a familiar, yet unfamiliar world.

I asked to visit the studio control room where I'd often sat during the taping of episodes. When we arrived, one minder suddenly remembered that Andrei, one of the station's audio engineers, had worked on *Ulitsa Sezam*. She called him from an internal phone. "There's an American here from *Ulitsa Sezam* who wants to say hello."

I watched as her mouth dropped at his response. She relayed what Andrei had asked: "Is it by chance Natasha Lance?" She handed the phone to me, and I spoke to Andrei, who was working off-site.

My escorts, who until now had been treating me with barely contained contempt, suddenly changed their demeanor toward me. They even cracked a smile for the first time, perhaps recognizing that I too loved Russia. By the end of my visit, my hosts, now broadly grinning, locked their arms in mine and accompanied me to the station's exit. We exchanged warm goodbyes, which had hardly seemed possible two hours earlier.

In the taxi on the way back to my hotel, I thought about *Ulitsa Sezam*'s former television director, whom I'd met the night before at a restaurant. He had continued to work on subsequent seasons of the television series until 2002. Over dinner, he shared with me that he no longer held any hope for democracy in Russia in our lifetime. He said, "I recently rewatched some of the video clips, and I don't know if today we could achieve the same lightness and affection that we had on the set. We were naive then, and over the years, we've become more rational, more closed. People have changed—society has changed—life has changed. It's a different country now."

We sat in silence. I ached for our lost cause—saving Russia—and I felt for him. He has grown children and grandchildren living in Moscow, and it must be very painful. He told me that most of our former colleagues had chosen to step away from television production rather than yield to the uniformly pro-Kremlin and propagandistic programming on Russian state television.

The next day, Leonid, who had since remarried, accompanied me to meet with Irina. Still a powerhouse, she now distributes foreign films to Russian television. Of course we talked about hair, shoes, and our now grown children. But mainly we reminisced about the exhilarating times we survived together. And how precious, anarchic, and fleeting Russia's brief liberalization was, and what might have been done to steer the country differently in the 1990s.

On my third day in Moscow, my good friend Sasha Sklyar, *Ulitsa Sezam*'s deft composer, came by the hotel. We had a nice conversation like old friends lost in time. But I was surprised that this one-time hero of the underground rock scene had been performing concerts where he sang patriotic songs celebrating the Kremlin's annexation of Crimea.

On the morning of January 14, back at my hotel, I turned on the TV and saw President Putin delivering his annual State of the Nation address. It was a surreal moment. Here I was, briefly visiting Moscow, and right before my eyes, the Russian leader made a grab for more power, proposing historic changes to the constitution that would keep him as Russia's leader long beyond the expiration of his term in 2024. He was essentially declaring himself a de facto tsar. I stared at the screen, trying to comfort myself with the thought that Putin's latest embellishment was a sign not at all of strength, but of weakness. But I feared what this would all mean for the people I love, ordinary Russians, and the world.

The next day, I left Moscow.

Cambridge, Massachusetts
Summer 2021

POSTSCRIPT

As the paperback edition of this book heads to press, I feel despair about Putin's horrific war against Ukraine that has brought death and destruction to the European continent on a scale not seen since World War II. As the war drags on, I continue to stay in touch with many of my former colleagues, artists, writers, producers, and educators who have spent their lifetimes fighting for freedom in Russia. Nearly all express horror at Russia's brutality. They are almost universally ashamed, and those with friends and family living in Ukraine—and there are many—are particularly despondent. My former colleagues in Kyiv and L'viv tell me of the incredible challenges they face in day-to-day life, and how they will fight to death to preserve not just their national freedom, but their creative freedom as well.

When the war broke out, many of the people who had worked on *Ulitsa Sezam* protested on Moscow's streets and on social media. But Putin quickly instigated new laws cracking down on anyone publicly opposing the war and several of my former crew had to flee their country or face imprisonment.

Over the past year, while crisscrossing the United States and Europe, speaking about Russia, the Muppets, *Sesame Street*, and the challenges we faced, I have encountered many Russian, Ukrainian, Georgian, and Armenian refugees who speak emotionally about how they grew up on *Ulitsa Sezam* and fell in love with the show's Muppets—Zeliboba, Businka, and Kubik. They shared their stories of how much the show meant to them and their children who saw reruns after the show had been cancelled under Putin. Waxing nostalgia, they thanked me and *Sesame Street* for creating a program that modeled a vision of a joyful, open-minded, and free Russia.

These conversations have given me solace in knowing these champions of justice—Russians and Ukrainians and many other former Soviet nationalities— all grew up on *Ulitsa Sezam*. They are the "*Ulitsa Sezam* generation."

At this moment, I don't know when another chance will come to encourage democracy, inclusiveness, and freedom in Russia, and bring peace to Ukraine, but I continue to feel hopeful, perhaps because I share the sentiment expressed by one of my former colleagues, *Ulitsa Sezam*'s chief film director who said, "I have only one hope: that the generations of children who grew up on *Ulitsa*

Sezam will find a way to create harmony in our country again and end this madness."

Cambridge, Massachusetts
December 2023

ABOUT THE AUTHOR

Natasha Lance Rogoff is an award-winning American television producer and filmmaker of broadcast news and documentaries. She has filmed in Europe and throughout the Soviet Union, from Moscow to Siberia, and in Ukraine, Armenia, and the Baltics. Lance Rogoff executive produced *Ulitsa Sezam*, the Russian adaptation of *Sesame Street*, between 1993 and 1997. She also produced *Plaza Sesamo* in Mexico, which aired throughout Latin America and in the United States. In addition to her television work, Lance Rogoff has reported as a journalist on Soviet underground culture for major international media outlets. She published an early expose of gay life behind the Iron Curtain in the *San Francisco Chronicle* in 1983. And in 1985, ABC's *20/20* aired Lance Rogoff's film, *Rock Around the Kremlin*, featuring banned Soviet rock 'n' roll artists who, ten years later, she recruited to compose original music for *Ulitsa Sezam*. Between 2011 and 2020, Lance Rogoff served as the CEO and founder of an ed-tech firm that produced KickinNutrition.TV, a musical comedy cooking show whose mission is to promote nutrition learning and health equity in urban and rural low-income communities. Lance Rogoff is an associate fellow at Harvard University's Art, Film, and Visual Studies department and lives in Cambridge, Massachusetts, and New York City with her husband Ken Rogoff. They have two children, Gabriel and Juliana.